Management Principles

Compiled by
Dr. Hawela and Ms. Edwards
Greenwich School of Management

PEARSON

Harlow, England • London • New York • Boston • San Francisco • Toronto • Sydney • Auckland • Singapore • Hong Kong
Tokyo • Seoul • Taipei • New Delhi • Cape Town • Sao Paulo • Mexico City • Madrid • Amsterdam • Munich • Paris • Milan

Pearson Education Limited
Edinburgh Gate
Harlow
Essex CM20 2JE

And associated companies throughout the world

Visit us on the World Wide Web at:
www.pearson.com/uk

ISBN 978-1-783-99326-0

Printed and bound in Great Britain.

Contents

Contents

MANAGING IN ORGANISATIONS

Learning outcomes

When you have read this chapter you should be able to:

1 Explain that the role of management is to add value to resources in diverse settings
2 Give examples of management as a universal human activity and as a distinct role
3 Compare the roles of general, functional, line, staff and project managers, and of entrepreneurs
4 Compare how managers influence others to add value
5 Use ideas from the chapter to comment on the management issues in the Ryanair case study

Activity 1.1

Before reading this chapter, write some notes on what you understand 'management' to mean.

Choose the organisation or people who may be able to help you learn about the topic. You may find it helpful to discuss the topic with a manager you know, or reflect on an activity you have managed.

- Identify a situation in which someone has been 'managing' an activity, and describe it briefly.
- How did they go about achieving the task?
- Can they identify the types of activities they worked on?
- What clues does that give you about what 'management' may mean in the organisation?
- Keep these notes as you will be able to use them later.

1.1   Introduction

Ryanair (the Chapter case study) illustrates several aspects of management. A group of entrepreneurs saw an opportunity in the market for air travel, and created an organisation to take advantage of it. They bring resources together and transform them into a service which they sell to customers. They differ from their competitors by using different resources (e.g. secondary airports) and different ways to transform these into outputs (e.g. short turnrounds). They have been innovative in the way they run the business, such as in identifying what some customers valued in a flight – cost rather than luxury – and carried a record 74 million passengers in the year to April 2011.

Entrepreneurs like Michael O'Leary of Ryanair are always looking for ways to innovate to create new products, services and ways of working, to make the most of new opportunities. Other managers face a different challenge – more demand with fewer resources. Those managing the United Nations World Food Programme struggle to raise funds from donor countries – aid is falling while hunger is increasing. In almost every public health-care organisation managers face a growing demand for treatment, but fewer resources with which to provide it.

Organisations of all kinds – from rapidly growing operations like Facebook to established businesses like Shell UK or Marks & Spencer – depend on people at all levels who can run the things efficiently now, and make changes to prepare for the future. This book is about the knowledge and skills that enable people to meet these expectations, and so build a satisfying and rewarding management career.

Figure 1.1 illustrates the themes of this chapter. It represents the fact that people in organisations bring resources from the external environment and transform them into outputs that they hope are of greater value. They pass these back to the environment, and the value they obtain in return (money, reputation, goodwill etc.) enables them to attract new resources to continue in business (shown by the feedback arrow from output to input). If the outputs do not attract sufficient resources, the enterprise will fail.

The chapter begins by examining the significance of managed organisations in our world. It then outlines what management means and introduces theories about the nature of managerial work.

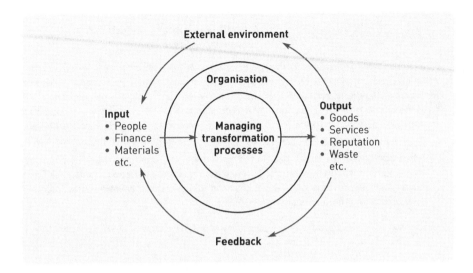

Figure 1.1
Managing
organisation
and environment

1.2 Managing to add value to resources

An **organisation** is a social arrangement for achieving controlled performance towards goals that create value.

We live in a world of managed **organisations**. We experience many every day – domestic arrangements (family or flatmates), large public organisations (the postal service), small businesses (the newsagent), well-known private companies (the jar of coffee) or a voluntary group (the club we attend). They affect us and we judge their performance. Did the transaction work smoothly or was it chaotic? Was the service good, reasonable or poor? Will you go there again?

As human societies become more specialised, we depend more on others to satisfy our needs. We meet some of these by acting individually or within family and social groups: organisations provide the rest. Good managers make things work – so that aid is delivered, roads are safe, shops have stock, hospitals function and all the rest. They don't do the work themselves, but build an organisation with the resources *and* competences to deliver what people need. **Tangible resources** are physical assets such as plant, people and finance – things you can see and touch. **Intangible resources** are non-physical assets such as information, reputation and knowledge.

Tangible resources are the physical assets of an organisation such as plant, people and finance.

Intangible resources are non-physical assets such as information, reputation and knowledge.

To transform these resources into valuable goods and services people need to work together. They need to know what to do, understand their customers, deal with enquiries properly and generally make the transaction work well. Beyond that they look for opportunities to improve, be innovative and learn from experience. Good managers bring out the best in their staff so that they willingly 'go the extra mile': together they develop effective ways of working that become second nature. These 'ways of working' are **competences** – skills, procedures or systems which enable people to use resources productively. A manager's role is to secure and retain resources and competences so that the organisation adds **value** – it is producing an output that is more valuable than the resources it has used.

Competences are the skills and abilities by which resources are deployed effectively – systems, procedures and ways of working.

Value is added to resources when they are transformed into goods or services that are worth more than their original cost plus the cost of transformation.

Well-managed organisations create value in many ways. If you buy a ticket from Ryanair, you can easily measure the tangible value of a cheap flight. In other purchases the value is intangible, as people judge a product by its appearance, what it feels or smells like, how trendy it is, or whether it fits their image. Others value good service, or a clear set of instructions. Good managers understand what customers value and build an organisation to satisfy them.

| Management in practice | Creating value at DavyMarkham
www.davymarkham.com | FT |

Kevin Parkin is Managing Director (and part-owner) of DavyMarkham, a small engineering company. Although the company has a long history, by the mid-1990s it was making regular losses, and its survival was in doubt. Since Mr Parkin joined the company he has returned it to profit, and in 2009 was predicting a 10 per cent increase in sales the following year. He has concentrated on identifying what the company is good at, and then using tough management and financial discipline to make sure staff follow the recipe for success. Mr Parkin has removed poor managers, walks the shop floor twice a day to check on progress, and engages with the workforce.

> It has been essential to tell people the truth about the business, whether it's good or bad, and giving them the enthusiasm they require to make them want to succeed . . . I also ask [my 'mentors' – people I have known in previous jobs] about key strategic decisions, people issues, market penetration, capital spending and general business solutions.

Source: Adapted from Turnaround ace shows his metal (Peter Marsh and Andrew Bounds), *Financial Times*, 27 May 2009.

Commercial organisations of all kinds (business start-ups, small and medium-sized enterprises, on-line firms and international enterprises) aim to add value and create wealth. So do voluntary and not-for-profit organisations – by educating people, counselling the troubled or caring for the sick.

There are over 160,000 charities in England and Wales, with annual incoming resources of over £52 billion (equal to about 3 per cent of Gross Domestic Product), and employing over 660,000 staff (Charities Commission Annual Report for 2009–10, at **www.charitycommission.gov.uk**). Managing a large charity is at least as demanding a job as managing a commercial business, facing similar challenges of adding value to limited resources. Donors and recipients expect them to manage resources well so that they add value to them.

Theatres, orchestras, museums and art galleries create value by offering inspiration, new perspectives or unexpected insights – and often do so in situations of great complexity (imagine the complexity in staging an opera, concert or major exhibition). Others add value by creating businesses or challenging projects through which people develop new skills or insights, and build long-term friendships.

While organisations aim to add value, many do not do so. If people work inefficiently they will use more resources than customers will pay for. They may create pollution and waste, and so destroy wealth. Motorway builders create value for drivers, residents of by-passed villages and shareholders – but destroy value for some people if the route damages an ancient woodland rich in history and wildlife. The idea of creating value is subjective and relative.

Managers face some issues that are unique to the setting in which they operate (charities need to maintain the support of donors) and others which arise in most organisations (business planning or ensuring quality). Table 1.1 illustrates some of these diverse settings, and their (relatively) unique management challenges – which are in addition to challenges that are common to all.

Whatever its nature, the value an organisation creates depends on how well those who work there obtain resources and develop their competences.

1.3 Meanings of management

Management as a universal human activity

Management is both a **universal human activity** and a distinct occupation. In the first sense, people manage an infinite range of activities:

> When human beings 'manage' their work, they take responsibility for its purpose, progress and outcome by exercising the quintessentially human capacity to stand back

Management as a universal human activity occurs whenever people take responsibility for an activity and consciously try to shape its progress and outcome.

Table 1.1 Where people manage

Setting – industry or type	Examples in this book	'Unique' challenges
Business start-ups	Inamo Restaurant – see Chapter 6, **p. 116** and Chapter 7, **p. 130**	Securing funding to launch, creating good internal systems, selling enough to bring in enough cash to continue.
Small and medium-sized enterprises (SMEs)	DavyMarkham – MIP feature above	Generating enough funds to survive, innovate and enter new markets.
Professional business services	Iris (advertising) – MIP feature in Chapter 7, **p. 130**	Managing highly qualified staff delivering customised, innovative services.
Voluntary, not-for-profit organisations and charities	Eden Project – Chapter 13 case study, **pp. 274–5**	Providing visitors with visit to encourage return visit, raising funds for educational work, fulfilling mission.
Public sector organisations	Crossrail – Chapter 6 case study, **pp. 124–5**	Managing high-profile political and commercial interests.
	A Foundation Hospital – Chapter 17 case study, **pp. 351–2**	Establishing suitable control systems to ensure quality.
Large private businesses	Ryanair – Chapter 1 case study, **pp. 23–4**	Responding to changing economic and political environments, managing diverse activities.
High-tech businesses	Google – Chapter 11 case study, **pp. 229–30** Apple – Chapter 12 case study, **pp. 252–3**	Maintaining constant innovation in rapidly changing markets.
International businesses	Starbucks – Chapter 4 case study, **pp. 87–8** Zara – Chapter 16 case study, **pp. 334–5**	Managing diverse activities across many cultures; balancing central control and local initiative.

Note: MIP = management in practice

from experience and to regard it prospectively, in terms of what will happen; reflectively, in terms of what is happening; and retrospectively, in terms of what has happened. Thus management is an expression of human agency, the capacity actively to shape and direct the world, rather than simply react to it. (Hales, 2001, p. 2)

A **manager** is someone who gets things done with the aid of people and other resources.

Management is the activity of getting things done with the aid of people and other resources.

Rosemary Stewart (1967) expressed this idea when she described a **manager** as someone who gets things done with the aid of people and other resources, so defining **management** as the activity of getting things done with the aid of people and other resources. So described, it is a universal human activity – domestic, social and political – as well as in formally established organisations.

In pre-industrial societies people typically work alone or in family units, controlling their time and resources. They decide what to make, how to make it and where to sell it, combining work and management to create value. Self-employed craftworkers, professionals in small practices and those in a one-person business do this every day.

As individuals we run our lives and careers: in this respect we are managing. Family members manage children, elderly dependants and household tasks. We do it in voluntary or charity activities where we do the work (planting trees or selling raffle tickets) and the management activities (planning the winter programme).

Management as a distinct role

Human action can separate the 'management' element of a task from the 'work' element, thus creating 'managers' who are in some degree apart from those doing the work. **Management as a distinct role** emerges when external parties, usually private or public owners of capital, gain control of a work process that people used to complete themselves. The owners are likely to specify what to make, how to make it and where to sell it – controlling the time, behaviour and skills of their employees. The latter now sell their labour, not their products.

Management as a distinct role develops when activities previously embedded in the work itself become the responsibility not of the employee, but of owners or their agents.

This happens when someone starts an enterprise, initially performing the *technical* aspects of the work itself – writing software, designing clothes – and also more *conceptual* tasks such as planning which markets to serve, or deciding how to raise money. If the business grows and the entrepreneur engages staff, they will need to spend time on *interpersonal* tasks such as training and supervising their work. The founder progressively takes on more management roles – a **role** being the expectations that others have of someone occupying a position. It expresses the specific responsibilities and requirements of the job, and what someone holding it should do (or not do).

A **role** is the sum of the expectations that other people have of a person occupying a position.

This separation of management and non-management work is not inevitable or permanent. People deliberately separate the roles, and can also bring them together. As Henri Fayol (1949) (of whom you will read more in Chapter 2) observed:

> Management . . . is neither an exclusive privilege nor a particular responsibility of the head or senior members of a business; it is an activity spread, like all other activities, between head and members of the body corporate. (p. 6)

Someone in charge of part of, say, a production department will usually be treated as a manager, and referred to as one. The people who operate the machines will be called something else. In a growing business like Ryanair, the boundary between 'managers' and 'non-managers' is likely to be very fluid, with all being ready to perform a range of tasks, irrespective of their title. Hales' (2006) research shows how first-line managers now hold some responsibilities traditionally associated with middle managers. They are still responsible for supervising subordinates, but often also have to deal with costs and customer satisfaction – previously a middle manager's job.

1.4 Specialisation between areas of management

As an organisation grows, senior managers usually create separate functions and a hierarchy, so that management itself becomes divided.

Functional specialisation

General managers typically head a complete unit of the organisation, such as a division or subsidiary, within which there will be several functions. The general manager is responsible for the unit's performance, and relies on the managers in charge of each function. A small organisation will have just one or two general managers, who will also manage the functions.

General managers are responsible for the performance of a distinct unit of the organisation.

Functional managers are responsible for the performance of an area of technical or professional work.

Line managers are responsible for the performance of activities that directly meet customers' needs.

Functional managers are responsible for an area of work – either as line managers or staff managers. **Line managers** are in charge of a function that creates value directly by supplying products or services to customers: they could be in charge of a retail store, a group of nurses, a social work department or a manufacturing area. Their performance significantly affects business performance and image, as they and their staff are in direct contact with customers or clients. At Shell, Mike Hogg was (in 2011) the General Manager of Shell Gas Direct, while Melanie Lane was General Manager, UK Retail.

Management in practice   The store manager – fundamental to success

A manager with extensive experience of retailing commented:

The store manager's job is far more complex that it may at first appear. Staff management is an important element and financial skills are required to manage a budget and the costs involved in running a store. Managers must understand what is going on behind the scenes – in terms of logistics and the supply chain – as well as what is happening on the shop floor. They must also be good with customers and increasingly they need outward-looking skills as they are encouraged to take high-profile roles in the community.

Source: Private communication from the manager.

Staff managers are responsible for the performance of activities that support line managers.

Staff managers are in charge of activities like finance, personnel, purchasing or legal affairs which support the line managers, who are their customers. Staff in support departments are not usually in direct contact with external customers, and so do not earn income directly for the organisation. Managers of staff departments operate as line managers within their unit. At Shell, Bob Henderson was Head of Legal and Kate Smith was Head of UK Government Relations.

Project managers are responsible for managing a project, usually intended to change some element of an organisation or its context.

Project managers are responsible for a temporary team created to plan and implement a change, such as a new product or system. Mike Buckingham, an engineer, managed a project to implement a new manufacturing system in a van plant. He still had line responsibilities for aspects of manufacturing, but worked for most of the time on the project, helped by a team of technical specialists. When the change was complete he returned to full-time work on his line job.

Entrepreneurs are people who see opportunities in a market, and quickly mobilise the resources to deliver the product or service profitably.

Entrepreneurs are people who are able to see opportunities in a market which others have overlooked. They quickly secure the resources they need, and use them to build a profitable business. John Scott (Managing Director of Scott Timber, now the UK's largest manufacturer of wooden pallets – **www.scott-timber.co.uk**) recalls the early days:

I went from not really knowing what I wanted to do . . . to getting thrown into having to make a plant work, employ men, lead by example. We didn't have an office – it was in my mum's house, and she did the invoicing. The house was at the top of the yard, and the saw mill was at the bottom. (*Financial Times*, 11 July 2007, p. 18)

Management hierarchies

As organisations grow, senior managers usually create a hierarchy of positions. The amount of 'management' and 'non-management' work within these positions varies, and the boundaries between them are fluid.

Performing direct operations

People who perform direct operations do the manual and mental work to make and deliver products or services. These range from low paid cleaners or shop workers to highly paid pilots

7

or lawyers. The activity is likely to contain some aspects of management work, though in lower-level jobs this will be limited. People running a small business combine management work with direct work to meet customer requirements.

Supervising staff on direct operations

Supervisors (sometimes called first-line managers) typically direct and control the daily work of a group or process. They ensure that front-line staff perform the essential, basic activities correctly – by paying attention to their job, noticing detail, keeping things moving efficiently and courteously to provide the quality of goods or services the customer expects. Supervisors are responsible for monitoring and reporting on work performance in an area, and working to improve it. They allocate and co-ordinate work, monitor the pace and help with problems. Sometimes they work with middle managers to making operational decisions on staff or work methods. Examples include the supervisor of a production team, the head chef in a hotel, or a nurse in charge of a hospital ward. They may continue to perform some direct operations, but will spend less time on them than subordinates.

Managing supervisors and first-line managers

Usually referred to as middle managers, they – such as an engineering manager at Ryanair – are expected to ensure that first-line managers work in line with company policies. They translate strategy into operational tasks, mediating between senior management vision and operational reality. They may help to develop strategy by presenting information about customer expectations, or suggesting alternative strategies to senior managers (Currie and Proctor, 2005). They provide a communication link – telling first-line managers what they expect, and briefing senior managers about current issues – one of the reasons banks got into difficulty in 2008 was because senior managers had no idea of the risks being taken by their traders and loan officers: good middle managers ensure that their bosses know what is going on.

Others face the challenge of managing volunteers. Charities depend on their time and effort, yet commonly face problems when they don't turn up, or work ineffectively – but cannot draw on the systems commonly used to reward and retain paid staff.

Managing the managers

The most senior employee is usually called the 'managing director' or 'chief executive'. Their main responsibility is to ensure that the middle managers work in ways that add value to their resources. In smaller organisations they will deal directly with middle managers, but in larger ones they will work through a team of senior executives in charge of functional areas like marketing or manufacturing. Chief executives influence performance largely by deciding who to appoint to executive positions, and by how they manage this top team. They report to the board of directors about developments in the business, and about issues which require board approval.

Managing the business

Managing the business is the work of a small group, usually called the board of directors. They establish policy and have a particular responsibility for managing relations with people and institutions in the world outside, such as shareholders, national media or government ministers. They need to know broadly about internal matters, but spend most of their time looking to the future or dealing with external affairs. Depending on local company law, the board usually includes non-executive directors – senior managers from other companies who should bring a wider, independent view to discussions. Such non-executive directors can enhance the effectiveness of the board, and give investors confidence that the board is acting in their interests. The board will not consider operational issues.

| 1.5 | Influencing through the process of managing |

Stakeholders are individuals, groups or organisations with an interest in, or who are affected by, what the organisation does.

Whatever their role, people add value to resources by influencing others, including internal and external **stakeholders** – who affect, or who are affected by, an organisation's actions and policies. Some stakeholders have different priorities from the managers, so the latter need to influence them to act in ways they believe will add value.

They do this directly and indirectly. Direct methods are the interpersonal skills (see Chapter 12) which managers use – persuading a boss to support a proposal, a subordinate to do more work, or a customer to change a delivery date. Managers also influence others indirectly through:

- the process of managing;
- the tasks of managing (Section 1.6); and
- shaping the context (Section 1.7).

Rosemary Stewart (1967) was one of the first to study the process of management – how managers work. She asked 160 senior and middle managers to keep a diary for four weeks, which showed that they typically worked in a fragmented, interrupted way – with very little time for thinking and working on their own. More recently, Henry Mintzberg found that within that fragmented pattern of work, managers focus on one or more distinct roles.

Henry Mintzberg – ten management roles

Mintzberg (1973) observed how (five) chief executives spent their time, and used this data to identify ten management roles, in three categories – informational, interpersonal and decisional. Managers use one or more of these roles as they try to influence other people. Table 1.2 describes them, and illustrates each with a contemporary example provided by the manager of a school nutrition project.

Informational roles

Managing depends on obtaining information about external and internal events, and passing it to others. The *monitor role* involves seeking out, receiving and screening information to understand the organisation and its context. It comes from websites and reports, and especially from chance conversations – such as with customers or new contacts at conferences and exhibitions. Much of this information is oral (gossip as well as formal meetings), building on personal contacts. In the *disseminator role* the manager shares information by forwarding reports, passing on rumours or briefing staff. As a *spokesperson* the manager transmits information to people outside the organisation – speaking at a conference, briefing the media or giving the department's view at a company meeting. Michael O'Leary at Ryanair is renowned for flamboyant statements to the media about competitors or officials in the European Commission when he disagrees with their policies.

Interpersonal roles

Interpersonal roles arise directly from a manager's formal authority and status, and shape relationships with people within and beyond the organisation. In the *figurehead role* the manager is a symbol, representing the unit in legal and ceremonial duties such as greeting a visitor, signing legal documents, presenting retirement gifts or receiving a quality award. The *leader role* defines the manager's relationship with other people (not just subordinates), including motivating, communicating and developing their skills and confidence – as one commented:

> I am conscious that I am unable to spend as much time interacting with staff members as I would like. I try to overcome this by leaving my door open whenever I am alone as an invitation to staff to come in and interrupt me, and encourage them to discuss any problems. (private communication)

Table 1.2 Mintzberg's ten management roles

Category	Role	Activity	Examples from a school nutrition project
Informational	Monitor	Seek and receive information, scan reports, maintain interpersonal contacts	Collect and review funding applications; set up database to monitor application process
	Disseminator	Forward information to others, send memos, make phone calls	Share content of applications with team members by email
	Spokesperson	Represent the unit to outsiders in speeches and reports	Present application process at internal and external events
Interpersonal	Figurehead	Perform ceremonial and symbolic duties, receive visitors	Sign letters of award to successful applicants
	Leader	Direct and motivate subordinates, train, advise and influence	Design and co-ordinate process with team and other managers
	Liaison	Maintain information links in and beyond the organisation	Become link person for government bodies to contact for progress reports
Decisional	Entrepreneur	Initiate new projects, spot opportunities, identify areas of business development	Use initiative to revise application process and to introduce electronic communication
	Disturbance handler	Take corrective action during crises, resolve conflicts amongst staff, adapt to changes	Holding face-to-face meetings with applicants when the outcome was negative; handling staff grievances
	Resource allocator	Decide who gets resources, schedule, budget, set priorities	Ensure fair distribution of grants nationally
	Negotiator	Represent unit during negotiations with unions, suppliers, and generally defend interests	Working with sponsors and government to ensure consensus during decision-making

Source: Based on Mintzberg (1973), and private communication from the project manager.

The *liaison role* focuses on contacts with people outside the immediate unit. Managers maintain a network in which they trade information and favours for mutual benefit with clients, government officials, customers and suppliers. Some managers, such as chief executives and sales managers, spend a high proportion of their time and energy on the liaison role.

Decisional roles

In the *entrepreneurial role* managers demonstrate **creativity** and initiate change. They see opportunities and create projects to deal with them. The three friends who created Innocent Drinks in 1998 have faced many such choices – such as whether to widen the range of products beyond the original 'smoothie' drinks (and if so, which products), and/or whether to expand into continental Europe (and if so, into which countries). Managers play the *disturbance-handler role* when they deal with problems and changes that are unexpected.

Creativity is the ability to combine ideas in a unique way or to make unusual associations between ideas.

The *resource-allocator role* involves choosing among competing demands for money, equipment, personnel and other resources. In early 2011 Marks and Spencer (**www. marksandspencer.com**) announced a new strategy, which reflected decisions by the chief executive (and the board) on where to invest funds available for capital projects (such as how much to spend on refurbishing the physical stores, and how much to spend on upgrading the website). In another business a manager has to decide whether to pay overtime to staff to replace an absent team member, or let service quality decline until a new shift starts. This is close to the *negotiator role*, in which managers seek agreement with other parties on whom they depend. Managers at Ryanair regularly negotiate with airport owners to agree on services and fees for a subsequent period.

Mintzberg proposed that every manager's job combines these roles, with their relative importance depending on the manager's level and type of business. Managers usually combine several of these roles as they try to influence others.

They sometimes note two omissions from Mintzberg's list – manager as subordinate and manager as worker. Most managers have subordinates but, except for those at the very top, they are subordinates themselves. Part of their role is to advise, assist and influence their boss – over whom they have no formal authority. Managers often need to persuade people higher up the organisation of a proposal's value or urgency. A project manager:

> This is the second time we have been back to the management team, to propose how we wish to move forward, and to try and get the resources that are required. It is worth taking the time up front to get all members fully supportive of what we are trying to do. Although it takes a bit longer we should, by pressure and by other individuals demonstrating the benefits of what we are proposing, eventually move the [top team] forward. (private communication)

Many managers spend time doing the work of the organisation. A director of a small property company helps with sales visits, or an engineering director helps with difficult technical problems. A lawyer running a small practice performs both professional and managerial roles.

Managers as networkers

Does the focus of a manager's influencing activities affect performance? Mintzberg's study gave no evidence on this point, but work by Luthans (1988) showed that the relative amount of time spent on specific roles did affect outcomes. The team observed 292 managers in four organisations for two weeks, recording their behaviours in four categories – communicating, 'traditional management', networking and human resource management. They also distinguished between levels of 'success' (relatively rapid promotion) and 'effectiveness' (work-unit performance and subordinates' satisfaction). They concluded that *successful* managers spent much more time networking (socialising, politicking, interacting with outsiders) than the less successful. *Effective* managers spent most time on communication and human resource management.

Wolff and Moser (2009) confirmed the link between **networking** and career success, showing building, maintaining and using internal and external contacts was associated with current salary, and with salary growth. Effective networkers seek out useful connections and contacts, and use the information and ideas they gather to create something valuable.

Networking refers to behaviours that aim to build, maintain and use informal relationships (internal and external) that may help work-related activities.

1.6 Influencing through the tasks of managing

A second way in which managers influence others is when they manage the transformation of resources into more valuable outputs. Building on Figure 1.1, this involves the **management tasks** of planning, organising, leading and controlling the transformation of resources. The amount of each varies with the job and the person, and they do not perform them in sequence: they do them simultaneously, switching as the situation requires.

Figure 1.2 illustrates the definition. It expands the central 'transforming' circle of Figure 1.1 by showing that people draw inputs (resources) from the environment and transform them into outputs by planning, organising, leading and controlling. They pass the resulting outputs back into the environment – the feedback loop indicates that this is the source of future resources.

Management tasks are those of planning, organising, leading and controlling the use of resources to add value to them.

External environment

Organisations depend on the external environment for the tangible and intangible resources they need, so they also depend on people in that environment being willing to buy or otherwise value their outputs. Commercial firms sell goods and services and use the revenue to buy resources. Public bodies depend on their sponsors being sufficiently satisfied with their

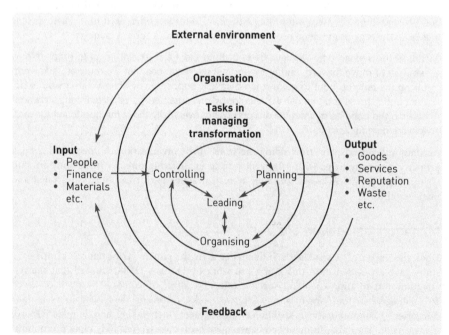

Figure 1.2
The tasks of managing

performance to provide their budget. Most managers are now facing the challenge of how they manage their organisations to ensure that they use natural resources not just efficiently, but sustainably. Part 2 of the book deals with the external environment.

Planning

Planning sets out the overall direction of the work to be done. It includes forecasting future trends, assessing resources and developing performance objectives. It means deciding on the scope and direction of the business, the areas of work in which to engage and how to use resources. Managers invest time and effort in developing a sense of direction for the organisation, or their part of it, and express this in a set of objectives. Part 3 deals with planning.

Management in practice **Planning major rail projects** www.networkrail.co.uk

More than most civil engineering projects, rail projects depend on extensive and detailed advance planning. In 2010 the UK government announced the preferred route for the first stage of a high-speed West Coast railway line. The first stage will run from London to Birmingham, but construction is not expected to begin unto 2015 at the earliest, with completion about four years later. The Crossrail project in London (see Chapter 6 case study, **p. 124**) also illustrates the scale and complexity of the planning required to build a large railway through (and below) the centre of London.

Source: Company website.

Organising

This is the task of moving abstract plans closer to reality by deciding how to allocate time and effort. It includes creating a structure for the enterprise, developing policies for finance and people, deciding what equipment people need and how to implement change. Part 4 deals with organising.

Leading

Leading is the task of generating effort and commitment – influencing people of all kinds, generating commitment and motivation, and communicating – whether with individuals or in teams. These activities focus on all of the other tasks – planning, organising and controlling – so appear in the middle of Figure 1.2. Part 5 deals with this topic.

Controlling

Control is the task of checking progress, comparing it with a plan, and acting accordingly. Managers set a budget for a housing department, an outpatients' clinic or for business travel. They then ensure that there is a system to collect information regularly on expenditure or performance – to check they are keeping to budget. If not, they need to decide how to bring actual costs back into line with budgeted costs. Are the outcomes consistent with the objectives? If so, they can leave things alone. But if by Wednesday it is clear that staff will not meet the week's production target, then managers need to act. They may deal with the deviation by a short-term response – such as authorising overtime. Control is equally important in creative organisations. Ed Catmull, cofounder of Pixar comments:

> Because we're a creative organization, people [think that what we do can't be measured]. That's wrong. Most of our processes involve activities and deliverables that can

be quantified. We keep track of the rates at which things happen, how often something had to be reworked, whether a piece of work was completely finished or not when it was sent to another department . . . Data can show things in a neutral way, which can stimulate discussion. (Catmull, 2008, p. 72)

That discussion to which Catmull refers is the way to learn from experience – an essential contributor to performance – so good managers create and use opportunities to learn from what they are doing. Part 6 deals with control.

The tasks in practice

Managers typically switch between tasks many times each day. They deal with them intermittently and in parallel, touching on many different parts of the job, as this manager in a not-for-profit housing association explains:

My role involves each of these functions. Planning is an important element as I am part of a team with a budget of £8 million to spend on promoting particular forms of housing. So planning where we will spend the money is very important. Organising and leading are important too, as staff have to be clear on which projects to take forward, clear on objectives and deadlines. Controlling is also there – I have to compare the actual money spent with the planned budget and take corrective action as necessary. (private communication from the manager)

And a manager in a professional services firm:

As a manager in a professional firm, each assignment involves all the elements to ensure we carry it out properly. For example, I have to set clear objectives for the assignment, organise the necessary staff and information to perform the work, supervise staff and counsel them if necessary, and evaluate the results. All the roles interrelate and there are no clear stages for each one. (private communication from the manager)

1.7   Influencing through shaping the context

A third way in which managers influence others is through changing aspects of the context in which they work. Changing an office layout, a person's reporting relationships, or the rewards they obtain, alter their context and perhaps their actions. The context is both an influence on the manager and a tool with which to influence others:

It is impossible to understand human intentions by ignoring the settings in which they make sense. Such settings may be institutions, sets of practices, or some other contexts created by humans – contexts which have a history, within which both particular deeds and whole histories of individual actors can and have to be situated in order to be intelligible. (Czarniawska, 2004, p. 4)

Managers aim to create contexts to influence others to act in ways that meet their objectives.

Dimensions of context

Internal context

Figures 1.1 and 1.2 showed the links between managers, their organisation and the external context. Figure 1.3 enlarges the 'organisation' circle to show more fully the elements that make up the internal context (or environment) – the immediate context within which people

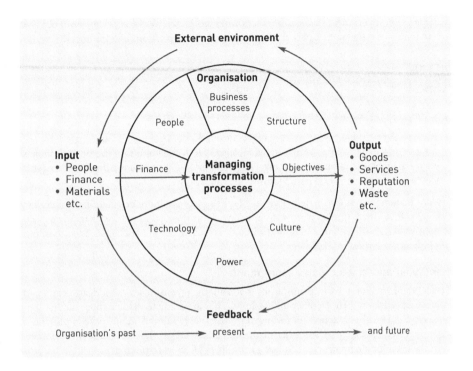

Figure 1.3
The internal and external contexts of management

work. As Mark Zuckerberg built Facebook into the world's largest social networking site, he and his team would have dealt with all of the elements shown in the figure:

- **Culture** (Chapter 3) – distinctive norms, beliefs and underlying values;
- **Objectives** (Chapters 6 and 8) – a desired future state of a business or unit;
- **Structure** (Chapter 9) – how to divide and co-ordinate tasks to meet objectives;
- **Technology** (Chapter 10) – facilities and equipment to turn inputs into outputs;
- **Power** (Chapter 12) – the amount and distribution of power with which to influence others;
- **People** (Chapter 13) – their knowledge, skills, attitudes and goals;
- **Business processes** – activities to transform materials and information; and
- **Finance** – financial resources available and how best to use them.

Figure 1.3 also implies that managers work within constraints – some of the elements will help, while others will hinder them. Effective managers do not accept their context passively – they try to change these elements so that they support their objectives (Chapter 11).

Historical context

Managing takes place within the flow of history as what people do now reflects past events and future uncertainties. Managers typically focus on current issues, ensuring that things run properly and that the organisation works. At the same time, history influences them through the structure and culture within which they work, and by affecting how people respond to proposals.

Effective managers also look to the future, questioning present systems and observing external changes. The arrow at the foot of the figure represents the historical context.

External context

Chapter 3 shows that the external context includes an immediate competitive (micro) environment and a general (or macro) environment. These affect performance and part of the manager's work is to identify, and adapt to, external changes. Managers in the public sector are expected to deliver improved services with fewer resources, so they seek to influence people to change the internal context (such as how staff work) to meet external expectations. They also seek to influence those in the external context about both expectations and resources.

1.8   Critical thinking

Brookfield (1987) stresses the benefits of thinking critically, in that it:

> involves our recognizing the assumptions underlying our beliefs and behaviors. It means we can give justifications for our ideas and actions. Most important, perhaps, it means we try to judge the rationality of these justifications . . . by comparing them to a range of varying interpretations and perspectives. (p. 13)

Critical thinking is positive activity that enables people to see more possibilities, rather than a single path. Critical thinkers 'are self-confident about their potential for changing aspects of their worlds, both as individuals and through collective action' (p. 5). He identifies four components of critical thinking.

Critical thinking identifies the assumptions behind ideas, relates them to their context, imagines alternatives and recognises limitations.

Identifying and challenging assumptions

Critical thinkers look for the assumptions that underlie taken-for-granted ideas, beliefs and values, and question their accuracy and validity. They are ready to discard those that no longer seem valid guides to action, in favour of more suitable ones. A manager who presents a well-supported challenge to a strategy that seems unsuitable to their business, or who questions the need for a new structure, is using this aspect of critical thinking.

Recognising the importance of context

Critical thinkers are aware that context influences thought and action. Thinking uncritically means assuming that ideas and methods that work in one context will work equally well in others. What we regard as an appropriate way to deal with staff reflects a specific culture: people in another culture – working in another place or at a different time – will have other expectations. Critical thinkers look for such approaches suitable for the relevant context.

Imagining and exploring alternatives

Critical thinkers develop the skill of imagining and exploring alternative ways of managing. They ask how others have dealt with a situation, and seek evidence about the effectiveness of different approaches. This makes them aware of realistic alternatives, and so increases the range of ideas which they can adapt and use.

Seeing limitations

Critical thinking alerts people to the limitations of knowledge and proposals. They recognise that because a practice works well in one situation does not ensure it will work in another. They are sceptical about research whose claims seem over-sold, asking about the sample or the analysis. They are open to new ideas, but only when supported by convincing evidence and reasoning.

Thinking critically will deepen your understanding of management. It does *not* imply a 'do-nothing' cynicism, 'treating everything and everyone with suspicion and doubt' (Thomas, 2003, p. 7). Critical thinking lays the foundation for a successful career, as it helps to ensure that proposals are supported by convincing evidence and reasoning.

Managing your studies

Studying management is itself a task to manage. Each chapter specifies learning outcomes. The text, the case study and the 'before and after' activities should help you to achieve these, and you can check your progress with the review questions at the end of each chapter. Working on these will help develop your confidence to think critically in your studies and in your career.

Activity 1.2   Understanding management

Recall the organisation you used in Activity 1.1.

Having read the chapter, make brief notes summarising what you now think 'managing' involves in this company:

- Describe what resources it uses and how it adds value to them. (Refer to Section 1.2.)
- List examples of some of the specialist roles of management (such as a functional or a line manager) and describe what they do in this company. (Refer to Section 1.4.)
- Can you identify examples of managers performing one or more of Mintzberg's roles? (Refer to Section 1.5.)
- What have you been able to find out about how they perform ONE of the management tasks (planning, organising, leading, controlling)? (Refer to Section 1.6.)

Compare what you have found with other students on your course.

Summary

1 **Explain that the role of management is to add value to resources in diverse settings**

- Managers create value by transforming inputs into outputs of greater value: they do this by developing competences within the organisation which, by constantly adding value (however measured) to resources is able to survive and prosper. The concept of creating value is subjective and open to different interpretations. Managers work in an infinite variety of settings, and Table 1.1 suggested how each setting raises relatively unique challenges.

2 **Give examples of management as a universal human activity and as a distinct role**

- Management is an activity that everyone undertakes as they manage their daily lives. In another sense management is an activity which many people conduct, not just those called 'managers'. People create the distinct role when they separate the management of work from the work itself and allocate the tasks. The distinction between management and non-management work is fluid and the result of human action.

3 **Compare the roles of general, functional, line, staff and project managers and of entrepreneurs**

- General managers are responsible for a complete business or a unit within it. They depend on functional managers who can be either in charge of line departments meeting customer needs, such as manufacturing and sales, or in staff departments such as finance which provide advice or services to line managers. Project managers are in charge of temporary activities usually directed at implementing change. Entrepreneurs are those who create new businesses to exploit opportunities.

4 **Explain how managers influence others to add value to resources through**

- The processes of managing. Henry Mintzberg identified ten management roles in three groups which he labelled informational, interpersonal and decisional. Luthans and, more recently, Wolff and Moser observed that successful managers were likely to be those who networked with people inside and outside the organisation.

- The tasks of managing. Planning develops the broad direction of an organisation's work, to meet customer expectations, taking into account internal capabilities. Organising sets out how to deploy resources to meet plans, while leading seeks to ensure that people work with commitment to achieve plans. Control checks activity and results against plans, so that people can adjust either if required.
- The contexts of managing. The internal (organisational) context consists of eight elements which help or hinder the manager's work – objectives, technology, business processes, finance, structure, culture, power and people. The historical context also influences events, as does the external context, which consists of competitive and general environments.

Review questions

1. How do non-commercial organisations add value to resources?
2. What is the difference between management as a general human activity and management as a specialised occupation? How has this division happened?
3. Describe, with examples, the differences between general, functional, line, staff and project managers.
4. How does Mintzberg's theory of management roles complement that which identifies the tasks of management?
5. Give examples from your experience or observation of each of the four tasks of management.
6. What is the significance to someone starting a career in management of Luthans' theory about roles and performance?
7. How can thinking critically help managers do their job more effectively?
8. Review and revise the definition of management that you gave in Activity 1.1.

Further reading

Birkinshaw, J. (2010), *Reinventing Management: Smarter choices for getting work done*, Jossey-Bass, San Fancisco, CA.

A small book by a leading management academic gives a short account of the work of general management.

Handy, C. (1988), *Understanding Voluntary Organisations*, Penguin, Harmondsworth.

A valuable perspective on management in the voluntary sector.

Drucker, P. (1999), *Management Challenges for the 21st Century*, Butterworth/Heinemann, London.

Valuable observations from the enquiring mind of this great management theorist.

Scott, D. M. and Halligan, B. (2010), *Marketing Lessons from the Grateful Dead: What every business can learn from the most iconic band in history*, Wiley, Hoboken, NJ.

Practical insights into management generally from two authors with deep insights into how the legendary band achieved its success.

Weblinks

These websites have appeared in, or are relevant to, the chapter:

www.davymarkham.com
www.charitycommission.gov.uk
www.scott-timber.co.uk
www.bt.com
www.marksandspencer.com
www.networkrail.co.uk
www.facebook.com/facebook
www.ryanair.com

Visit two of the business sites in the list above, or those of other organisations in which you are interested, and navigate to the pages dealing with recent news, press or investor relations.

- What are the main issues which the organisation appears to be facing?
- Compare and contrast the issues you identify on the two sites.
- What challenges may they imply for those working in, and managing, these organisations?

 Annotated weblinks, multiple choice questions and other useful resources can be found on **www.pearsoned.co.uk/boddy**

Case study   Ryanair   www.ryanair.com

In 2011 Ryanair, based in Dublin, was Europe's largest low fare airline, and despite the recession, it had carried over 74 million passengers in the 12 months to the end of April, a record for that period. In 1985, the company began offering services between Dublin and London, in competition with the established national carrier, Aer Lingus. In the early years the airline changed its business several times – initially a conventional competitor for Aer Lingus, then a charter company, at times offering a cargo service. The Gulf War in 1990 discouraged air travel and deepened the company's financial problems. In 1991, senior managers decided to focus the airline as a 'no-frills' operator, in which many traditional features of air travel (free food, drink, newspapers and allocated seats) were no longer available. It aimed to serve a group of flyers who wanted a functional and efficient service, not luxury.

In 1997 changes in European Union regulations enabled new airlines to enter markets previously dominated by established national carriers such as Air France and British Airways. Ryanair quickly took advantage of this, opening new routes between Dublin and continental Europe. Although based in Ireland, 80 per cent of its routes are between airports in other countries – in contrast to established carriers which depend heavily for passengers travelling to and from the airline's home country (Barrett, 2009, p. 80).

Managers were quick to spot the potential of the internet, and in 2000 opened **Ryanair.com**, a booking site. Within a year it sold 75 per cent of seats online and now sells almost all seats this way. It also made a long-term deal with Boeing to purchase 150 new aircraft over the next eight years.

Several factors enable Ryanair to offer low fares:

- Simple fleet – using a single aircraft type (Boeing 737 – most of which are quite new) simplifies maintenance, training and crew scheduling.
- Secondary airports – using airports away from major cities keeps landing charges low, sometimes as little as £1 per passenger against £10 at a major airport; it also avoids the delays and costs caused by congestion at major airports.
- Fast turnarounds – staff typically turn an aircraft round between flights in 25 minutes, compared to an hour for older airlines. This enables aircraft to spend more time in the air, earning revenue (11 hours compared to 7 at British Airways).

© Thierry Tronnel/Sygma/Corbis.

- Simplified operations – not assigning seats at check-in simplifies ticketing and administrative processes, and also ensures that passengers arrive early to get their preferred seat.
- Flying directly between cities avoids transferring passengers and baggage between flights, where mistakes and delays are common.
- Cabin staff collect rubbish before and after landing, saving the cost of cleaning crews which established carriers choose to use.

The company has continued to grow rapidly, regularly opening new routes to destinations it thinks will be popular. It now refers to itself as 'the world's largest international scheduled airline', and continues to seek new bases from which to operate its network.

The airline's success depends on balancing low costs, fare levels and load factors. Airline seats are what is known as a perishable good – they have no value if they are not used on the flight, so companies aim to maximise the proportion of seats sold on a flight. Ryanair use a technique known as dynamic pricing, which means that prices change with circumstances. Typically fares rise the nearer the passenger is to the departure date, though if a flight is under-booked, the company encourages sales by lowering fares.

They also earn a growing proportion of revenue from charges and services such as refreshments, and in 2009 sharply increased the cost of checked in bags: it prefers customers to carry hand baggage into the cabin. Each time a passenger rents a car or books a hotel room on the Ryanair website, it earns a commission. It sells scratch cards on board, offers in-flight gambling and on-line gaming over its website: the chief executive thinks that gambling could double Ryanair's profits over the next decade. The company expects revenue from ancillary activities will continue to grow more rapidly than passenger revenue.

Sources: *The Economist*, 10 July 2004; *Independent*, 7 October 2006; *Financial Times*, 7 June 2006; Barrett (2009); Kumar (2006); O'Connell and Williams (2005); Doganis (2006); and company website.

Questions

1 Identify examples of the resources that Ryanair uses, and of the competences that have enabled managers to add value to them. (Refer to Section 1.2.)

2 Refer to Section 1.4 and note what those occupying the specialist roles are likely to be doing in Ryanair.

3 Refer to Section 1.5 and write down which of Mintzberg's management roles can you identify in the Ryanair case? Support your answer with specific examples.

4 Which aspects of the external general environment have affected the company? (Refer to Section 1.6.)

5 Go to the Ryanair website and look for evidence of the work that managers have been doing to help the company continue to grow.

THEORIES OF MANAGEMENT

Learning outcomes

When you have read this chapter you should be able to:

1 Explain why understanding a good theory helps people to make better choices

2 State the structure of the competing values framework, which relates theories to each other

3 Summarise the:
- rational goal
- internal process
- human relations and
- open systems perspectives

4 Use ideas from the chapter to comment on the management issues in the Robert Owen case study

Activity 2.1   What are 'theories of management'?

Before reading this chapter, write some notes on what you understand by the term 'theories of management'.

Choose the organisation or people who may be able to help you learn about the topic. You may find it helpful to discuss the topic with a manager you know, or reflect on an activity you have managed.

- Identify a situation in which someone had to make a decision or deal with a problem, and describe it briefly.
- What ideas seem to have guided the way they dealt with the task?
- Did they think consciously about why they did it that way?
- Keep these notes, as you will be able to use them later.

2.1   Introduction

Robert Owen was an entrepreneur. His attempts to change worker behaviour were innovative, and he was equally creative in devising management systems and new ways of working. The story of his time at New Lanark illustrates three aspects of management. First, he devised systems to help manage the people he employed and to improve mill performance. Second, Owen engaged with the wider social context, such as when he tried to influence Parliament to prohibit employers from using children in their mills and factories. Third, he was managing at a time of transition from an agricultural to an industrial economy, and many of his innovations tried to resolve the tensions between those systems – as we now face tensions between industrial and post-industrial systems.

Managers today cope with similar issues. HMV need to recruit willing and capable people to work in their stores, and ensure that they add value. Co-operative Financial Services (CFS) try (like Owen) to follow ethical principles throughout their business and still earn profits. Managers know that working conditions affect family life – and try to balance the two by subsidising childcare and offering flexible hours to those with family responsibilities. They also operate in a world experiencing changes equal to those facing Owen. The internet is enabling people to organise economic activity in new ways, sustainability is now on the agendas of most management teams, as is the move to a more connected international economy.

Facing such changes, managers continue to search for new ways to manage their business so that they add value to their resources. They make assumptions about the best way to do things – and through trial and error develop methods of working which seem to work reasonably well, and which they tend to repeat. Although they probably do not use the term, they gradually develop their theory of management – their ideas about the relationship between cause and effect, how a change in (say) working methods will affect (say) staff commitment. The more accurate their theory (the better the evidence and experience they use), the more likely they are to obtain the results they want. A manager using inaccurate theory to guide their actions is likely to have less success.

The next section introduces the idea of theories of management, and why they are useful. Section 2.3 presents the 'competing values' framework, which is a convenient way of seeing the relationship between theories, which the following sections outline.

2.2   Why study management theory?

A **theory (or model)** represents a complex phenomenon by identifying the major elements and relationships

A **theory (or model)** represents a more complex reality. Focusing on the essential elements and their relationship helps to understand that complexity, and how change may affect it. Most management problems can only be understood by examining them from several points of view, so no theory offers a complete solution. The management task is to choose those most likely to work, and combine them into an acceptable solution.

Theories support purpose and values

Managers have different views about the purpose of their role in society, and this affects the theories they use. A feature of many societies is that they have established a balance of power between governments, companies and the 'social sector' – co-operatives, social entrepreneurs, voluntary organisations. Each reflects a different set of challenges, and has encouraged the development of theories about how best to manage in those circumstances.

The theory (or mental model) which a person uses reflects their view of the purpose of their particular job – ranging from serving shareholder interests at one extreme to serving society at the other (Chapter 5, Section 5.4). Their personal values also influence this – some see their job as a technical or financial task, whereas others see that being a manager brings wider responsibilities, including those of dealing fairly and ethically with other people.

Theories identify variables

Whichever broad model of management a person is using, they will use (implicitly) one or more theories, as these help to identify the main variables in a situation, and the relationships between them. The more accurately they do so, the more useful they are. Since every situation is unique, many experienced managers doubt the value of theory. Magretta's answer is that:

> without a theory of some sort it's hard to make sense of what's happening in the world around you. If you want to know whether you work for a well-managed organization – as opposed to whether you like your boss – you need a working theory of management. (Magretta, 2002, p. 10)

We all use theory, acting on (perhaps implicit) assumptions about the relationships between cause and effect. Good theories help to identify variables and relationships, providing a mental toolkit to deal consciously with a situation. The perspective we take reflects the assumptions we use to interpret, organise and make sense of events. As managers influence others to add value they use their mental model (theory) of the situation to decide where to focus effort. The Management in Practice feature below contrasts two managers' mental models.

Management in practice   Practice reflects theory   FT

These examples illustrate contrasting theories about managing staff.

Motivating managers: Tim O'Toole, who became chief executive of London Underground in 2003, put in a new management structure, appointing a general manager for each line to improve accountability.

> Now there's a human being who is judged on how that line is performing and I want them to feel that kind of intense anxiety in the stomach that comes when there's a stalled train and they realise that it's their stalled train.

Source: From an article by Simon London, *Financial Times*, 20 February 2004.

Supporting staff: John Timpson, chairman of the shoe repair and key cutting chain, believes the most important people in the company are those who cut customers' keys and re-heel their shoes:

> You come back for the service you get from the people in the shops. They are the stars . . . we need to do everything to help them to look after you as well as possible. [A bonus based on shop takings] is fundamental to the service culture I want. It creates the adrenalin. That is the reason why people are keen to serve you if you go into one of our shops. And why they don't take long lunch breaks.

Source: Adapted from Secrets of the maverick cobbler, *Financial Times*, 3 August 2006.

Models reflect their context

People look for models to deal with the most pressing issues they face. In the nineteenth century, skilled labour was scarce and unskilled labour plentiful: managers were hiring workers unfamiliar with factories to meet growing demand, so wanted ideas on how to produce more efficiently. They looked for ways to simplify tasks so that they could use less-skilled employees, and early management theories gave priority to these issues. This focus on efficiency reflects a manufacturing mindset, which is still highly relevant in many situations. In other situations, the main challenge facing a manager is how to meet changing customer needs quickly and cheaply – so they seek theories about how to create a system that produces frequent innovations and that can change quickly. As business becomes international, they seek theories about managing across the world.

An even bigger contextual challenge to managers is presented by the world's growing population, rising temperatures and sea levels, and probable shortages in many parts of the world of land, water and energy to cope with this. Most countries face a conflict between the rising cost of health care for an ageing population, and their ability to provide it. Theories about how to manage in societies facing these challenges are in short supply.

Critical thinking helps improve our mental models

The ideas on critical thinking in Chapter 1 suggest that working effectively depends on being able and willing to test the validity of any theory, and to revise it in the light of experience by:

- identifying and challenging assumptions;
- recognising the importance of context;
- imagining and exploring alternatives; and
- seeing limitations.

As you work through this chapter, look for opportunities to practise these components of critical thinking.

2.3 The competing values framework

Quinn *et al.* (2003) believe that successive theories of management (which they group according to four underlying philosophies – 'rational goal', 'internal process', 'human relations' and 'open systems') complement, rather than contradict, each other. They are all:

> symptoms of a larger problem – the need to achieve organizational effectiveness in a highly dynamic environment. In such a complex and fast-changing world, simple solutions become suspect . . . Sometimes we needed stability, sometimes we needed change. Often we needed both at the same time. (p. 11)

While each adds to our knowledge, none is sufficient. The 'competing values' framework integrates them by highlighting their underlying values – see Figure 2.1.

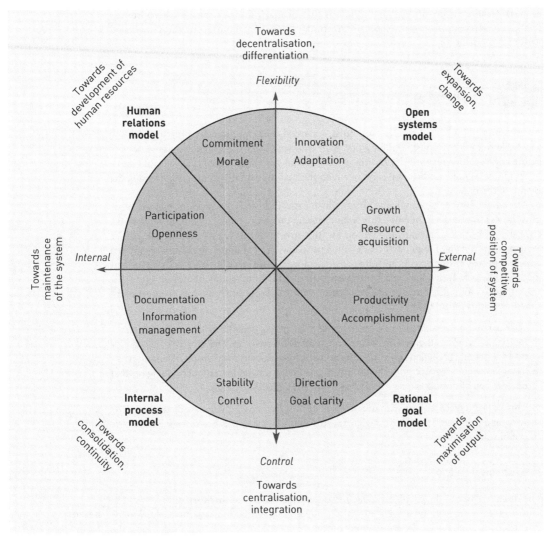

Figure 2.1 Competing values framework

Source: Quinn *et al.* (2003), p. 13.

The vertical axis represents the tension between flexibility and control. Managers seek flexibility to cope with rapid change. Others try to increase control – apparently the opposite of flexibility. The horizontal axis distinguishes an internal focus from an external one. Some managers focus on internal issues, while others focus on the world outside. Successive models of management relate to the four segments.

The labels within the circle indicate the criteria of effectiveness which are the focus of models in that segment, shown around the outside. The human relations model, upper left in the figure, stresses the human criteria of commitment, participation and openness. The open systems model (upper right) stresses criteria of innovation, adaptation and growth. The rational goal model in the lower right focuses on productivity, direction and goal clarity. The internal process model stresses stability, documentation and control, within a hierarchical structure. Finally, the outer ring indicates the values associated with each model – the dominant value in the rational goal model is that of maximising output, while in human relations it is developing people. Successive sections of this chapter outline theories associated with each segment.

2.4 Rational goal models

Adam Smith (1776), the Scottish economist, recorded how pin manufacturers in Glasgow had broken a job previously done by one man into small steps. A single worker now performed one of these repetitively, and this specialisation greatly increased their output. Smith believed this was one of the main ways in which the new industrial system was increasing the wealth of the nation.

The availability of powered machinery during the Industrial Revolution enabled business owners to transform manufacturing and mining processes. These technical innovations encouraged, but were not the only reason for, the growth of the factory system. The earlier 'putting-out' system of manufacture, in which people worked at home on materials supplied and collected by entrepreneurs and their agents, allowed great freedom over hours, pace and methods of work; agents had little control over the quantity and quality of output. Capitalist entrepreneurs found that they could secure more control if they brought workers together in a factory, as this meant that:

> coercive authority could be more easily applied, including systems of fines, supervision . . . the paraphernalia of bells and clocks, and incentive payments. The employer could dictate the general conditions of work, time and space; including the division of labour, overall organisational layout and design, rules governing movement, shouting, singing and other forms of disobedience. (Thompson and McHugh 2002, p. 22)

This still left entrepreneurs with the problem of how to manage these new factories profitably. Although domestic and export demand for manufactured goods was high, so was the risk of business failure.

Frederick Taylor

The fullest answer to the problems of factory organisation came in the work of Frederick W. Taylor (1856–1915), always associated with the ideas of **scientific management**. An American mechanical engineer, Taylor focused on the relationship between the worker and the machine-based production systems that were in widespread use:

Scientific management The school of management called 'scientific' attempted to create a science of factory production.

> the principal object of management should be to secure the maximum prosperity for the employer, coupled with the maximum prosperity for each employee. The words 'maximum prosperity' . . . mean the development of every branch of the business to its highest state of excellence, so that the prosperity may be permanent. (Taylor, 1917, p. 9)

He believed the way to achieve this was to ensure that each worker reached their state of maximum efficiency, so that each was doing 'the highest grade of work for which his natural abilities fit him' (p. 9). This would follow from detailed control of the process, which would become the managers' primary responsibility: they should concentrate on understanding the production systems, and use this to specify every aspect of the operation. Taylor advocated five principles:

- use scientific methods to determine the one best way of doing a task, rather than rely on the older 'rule of thumb' methods;
- select the best person to do the job so defined, ensuring that their physical and mental qualities were appropriate for the task;
- train, teach and develop the worker to follow the defined procedures precisely;

- provide financial incentives to ensure people work to the prescribed method; and
- move responsibility for planning and organising from the worker to the manager.

Taylor's underlying philosophy was that scientific analysis and fact, not guesswork, should inform management. Like Smith and Babbage before him, he believed that efficiency rose if tasks were routine and predictable. He advocated techniques such as time and motion study, standardised tools and individual incentives. Breaking work into small, specific tasks would increase control. Specialist staff would design these tasks and organise the workers:

> The work of every workman is fully planned out by the management at least one day in advance, and each man receives in most cases complete written instructions, describing in detail the task which he is to accomplish, as well as the means to be used in doing the work . . . This task specifies not only what is to be done but how it is to be done and the exact time allowed for doing it. (Taylor, 1917, p. 39)

Taylor also influenced the development of administrative systems such as record keeping and stock control to support manufacturing.

Management in practice   Using work study in the 1990s

Oswald Jones recalls his experience as a work study engineer in the 1990s, where he and his colleagues were deeply committed to the principles of scientific management:

> Jobs were designed to be done in a mechanical fashion by removing opportunities for worker discretion. This had dual benefits: very simple jobs could be measured accurately (so causing less disputes) and meant that operators were much more interchangeable which was an important feature in improving overall efficiency levels.

Source: Jones (2000, p. 647).

Managers in industrialised economies adopted Taylor's ideas widely: Henry Ford was an enthusiastic advocate. When he introduced the assembly line in 1914, the time taken to assemble a car fell from over 700 hours to 93 minutes. Ford also developed systems of materials flow and plant layout, a significant contribution to scientific management.

Increased productivity often came at human cost (Thompson and McHugh, 2002). Trade unions believed Taylor's methods increased unemployment, and vigorously opposed them. Many people find work on an assembly line is boring and alienating, devoid of much meaning. In extreme cases, the time taken to complete an operation is less than a minute and uses few human abilities.

Frank and Lillian Gilbreth

Frank and Lillian Gilbreth (1868–1924 and 1878–1972) worked together to encourage employers to use scientific management principles. Frank Gilbreth had been a bricklayer, and knew why work was slow and output unpredictable. He filmed men laying bricks and used this to set out the most economical movements for each task. He specified exactly what the employer should provide, such as trestles at the right height and materials at the right time. Supplies of mortar and bricks (arranged the right way up) should arrive at a time which did not interrupt work. An influential book (Gilbreth, 1911) gave precise guidance on how to reduce unnecessary actions (from 18 to 5), and hence fatigue. The rules and charts would help apprentices:

> (They) will enable the apprentice to earn large wages immediately, because he has . . . a series of instructions that show each and every motion in the proper sequence. They eliminate the 'wrong' way [and] all experimenting. (Quoted in Spriegel and Myers, 1953, p. 57)

Lillian Gilbreth focused on the psychological aspects of management, and on the welfare of workers. In *The Psychology of Management* (1914) she proposed, like Taylor, that scientific management would enable individuals to reach their full potential. Careful development of suitable working processes, careful selection, planned training and proper equipment, would help them to build their self-respect. If they did something well, and that was made public, they would develop pride in their work and in themselves. She believed workers had enquiring minds, and that management should explain the reasons for work processes:

> Unless the man knows why he is doing the thing, his judgment will never reinforce his work . . . His work will not enlist his zeal unless he knows exactly why he is made to work in the particular manner prescribed. (Quoted in Spriegel and Myers, 1953, p. 431)

Operational research

Another practice within the rational goal model is **operational research** (OR). This originated in the early 1940s, when the UK War Department faced severe management problems – such as the most effective distribution of radar-linked anti-aircraft gun emplacements, or the safest speed at which convoys of merchant ships should cross the Atlantic. To solve these it formed operational research teams, which pooled the expertise of scientific disciplines such as mathematics and physics and produced significant results. Kirby (2003) notes that while at the start of the London Blitz 20,000 rounds of ammunition were fired for each enemy aircraft destroyed:

Operational research is a scientific method of providing managers with a quantitative basis for decisions regarding the operations under their control.

> by the summer of 1941 the number had fallen . . . to 4,000 as a result of the operational research (teams) improving the accuracy of radar-based gun-laying. (Kirby 2003, p. 94)

In the late 1940s managers in industry and government saw that OR techniques could help managers running civil organisations. The scale and complexity of business was increasing, and required new techniques to analyse the many interrelated variables: developments in computing supported increasingly sophisticated mathematical models. In the 1950s the steel industry needed to cut the cost of transporting iron ore: staff used OR techniques to analyse the most efficient procedures for shipping, unloading and transferring it to steelworks.

The method is widely used in both business and public sectors, where it helps planning in areas as diverse as maintenance, cash flow, inventory, staff scheduling in call centres and allocating students to seminar groups.

OR cannot take into account human and social uncertainties, and the assumptions built into the models may be invalid, especially if they involve political interests. The technique clearly contributes to the analysis of management problems, but is only part of the solution.

Current status

Table 2.1 summarises principles common to rational goal models and their modern application.

Table 2.1 Modern applications of the rational goal model

Principles of the rational goal model	Current applications
Systematic work methods	Work study and process engineering departments develop precise specifications for processes
Detailed division of labour	Where staff focus on one type of work or customer in manufacturing or service operations
Centralised planning and control	Modern information systems increase the scope for central control of worldwide operations
Low-involvement employment relationship	Using temporary staff as required, rather than permanent employees

Examples of rational goal approaches are common in manufacturing and services – but a company will often use just one of the principles that suits their business. The Management in Practice feature below gives an example from a successful service business with committed and involved employees. It aims to give customers the same high-quality experience wherever they are, and uses the principle of systematic work methods to achieve this.

Management in practice   **Making a sandwich at Pret A Manger**   www.pret.com

It is very important to make sure the same standards are adhered to in every single shop, whether you're in Crown Passage in London, Sauchiehall Street in Glasgow or in New York. The way we do that is very, very detailed training. So, for example, how to make an egg mayonnaise sandwich is all written down on a card that has to be followed, and that is absolutely non-negotiable.

When somebody joins Pret they have a ten-day training plan, and on every single day there is a list of things that they have to be shown, from how to spread the filling of a sandwich right to the edges (that is key to us), how to cut a sandwich from corner to corner, how to make sure that the sandwiches look great in the box and on the shelves. So every single detail is covered on a ten-day training plan. At the end of that ten days the new team member has to pass a quiz, it's called the big scary quiz, it is quite big and it is quite scary, and they have to achieve 90 per cent on that in order to progress.

Source: Interview with a senior manager at the company.

The methods are also widely used in the mass production industries of newly industrialised economies such as China and Malaysia. Gamble *et al.* (2004) found that in such plants:

> Work organization tended to be fragmented (on Taylorist lines) and routinised, with considerable surveillance and control over production volumes and quality. (p. 403)

Human resource management policies were consistent with this approach – the recruitment of operators in Chinese electronics plants was:

> often of young workers, generally female and from rural areas. One firm said its operators had to be '. . . young farmers within cycling distance of the factory, with good eyesight. Education is not important.' (p. 404)

2.5   Internal process models

Max Weber

Max Weber (1864–1920) was a German social historian who drew attention to the significance of large organisations, noting that as societies became more complex, they concentrated responsibility for core activities in large, specialised units. These government departments and large industrial or transport businesses were hard to manage, a difficulty which those in charge overcame by creating rules and regulations, hierarchy, precise division of labour and detailed procedures. Weber observed that **bureaucracy** brought routine to office operations just as machines had to production.

Bureaucratic management has these characteristics:

* **Rules and regulations**   The formal guidelines that define and control the behaviour of employees. Following these ensures uniform procedures and operations, regardless of an individual's wishes. They enable top managers to co-ordinate middle managers

Bureaucracy is a system in which people are expected to follow precisely defined rules and procedures rather than to use personal judgement.

and, through them, first-line managers and employees. Managers leave, so rules bring stability.

- **Impersonality**   Rules lead to impersonality, which protects employees from the whims of managers. Although the term has negative connotations, Weber believed it ensured fairness, by evaluating subordinates objectively on performance rather than subjectively on personal considerations. It limits favouritism.
- **Division of labour**   Managers and employees work on specialised tasks, with the benefits originally noted by Adam Smith – such as that jobs are relatively easy to learn and control.
- **Hierarchical structure**   Weber advocated a clear hierarchy in which jobs were arranged by the amount of authority to make decisions. Each lower position is under the control of a higher position.
- **Authority structure**   A system of rules, impersonality, division of labour and hierarchy forms an authority structure – the right to make decisions of varying importance at different levels within the organisation.
- **Rationality**   This refers to using the most efficient means to achieve objectives. Managers should run their organisations logically and 'scientifically' so that all decisions help to achieve the objectives.

Weber was aware that, as well as creating bureaucratic structures, managers were using scientific management techniques to control production and impose discipline on factory work. The two systems complemented each other. Formal structures of management centralise power, and hierarchical organisation aids functional specialisation. Fragmenting tasks, imposing close discipline on employees and minimising their discretion ensures that staff within a function perform in a controlled and predictable way (Thompson and McHugh, 2002).

Weber stressed the importance of a career structure clearly linked to a person's position. This allowed them to move up the hierarchy in a predictable and open way, which would increase their commitment to the organisation. Rules about selection and promotion brought fairness at a time when favouritism was common. He also believed that officials should work within a framework of rules. The right to give instructions was based on a person's position in the hierarchy, and a rational analysis of how staff should work. This worked well in large public and private organisations, such as government departments and banks.

Henri Fayol

Managers were also able to draw on the ideas of **administrative management** developed by Henri Fayol (1841–1925). While Taylor focused on production systems, Fayol devised management principles that would apply to the whole organisation. Like Taylor, Fayol was an engineer who, in 1860, joined a coal mining and iron foundry company combine: he became managing director in 1888. When he retired in 1918 it was one of the success stories of French industry. Throughout his career he kept detailed diaries and notes, which, in retirement, he used to stimulate debate about management in both private and public sectors. His book *Administration, industrielle et générale* became available in English in 1949 (Fayol, 1949).

Administrative management is the use of institutions and order rather than relying on personal qualities to get things done.

Fayol credited his success to the methods he used, not to his personal qualities. He believed that managers should use certain principles in their work – see below. The term 'principles' did not imply they were rigid or absolute:

> It is all a question of proportion . . . allowance must be made for different changing circumstances . . . the principles are flexible and capable of adaptation to every need; it is a matter of knowing how to make use of them, which is a difficult art requiring intelligence, experience, decision and proportion. (Fayol, 1949, p. 14)

Fayol's principles were:

- **Division of work**   If people specialise, they improve their skill and accuracy, which increases output. However, 'it has its limits which experience teaches us may not be exceeded'. (p. 20)
- **Authority and responsibility**   The right to give orders derived from a manager's official authority or their personal authority. '[Wherever] authority is exercised, responsibility arises.' (p. 21)
- **Discipline**   'Essential for the smooth running of business . . . without discipline no enterprise could prosper.' (p. 22)
- **Unity of command**   'For any action whatsoever, an employee should receive orders from one superior only' (p. 24) – to avoid conflicting instructions and resulting confusion.
- **Unity of direction**   'One head and one plan for a group of activities having the same objective . . . essential to unity of action, co-ordination of strength and focusing of effort.' (p. 25)
- **Subordination of individual interest to general interest**   'The interests of one employee or group of employees should not prevail over that of the concern.' (p. 26)
- **Remuneration of personnel**   'Should be fair and, as far as possible, afford satisfaction both to personnel and firm.' (p. 26)
- **Centralisation**   'The question of centralisation or decentralisation is a simple question of proportion . . . [the] share of initiative to be left to [subordinates] depends on the character of the manager, the reliability of the subordinates and the condition of the business. The degree of centralisation must vary according to different cases.' (p. 33)
- **Scalar chain**   'The chain of superiors from the ultimate authority to the lowest ranks . . . is at times disastrously lengthy in large concerns, especially governmental ones.' If a speedy decision was needed it was appropriate for people at the same level of the chain to communicate directly. 'It provides for the usual exercise of some measure of initiative at all levels of authority.' (pp. 34–5)
- **Order**   Materials should be in the right place to avoid loss, and the posts essential for the smooth running of the business filled by capable people.
- **Equity**   Managers should be both friendly and fair to their subordinates – 'equity requires much good sense, experience and good nature'. (p. 38)
- **Stability of tenure of personnel**   A high employee turnover is not efficient – 'Instability of tenure is at one and the same time cause and effect of bad running.' (p. 39)
- **Initiative**   'The initiative of all represents a great source of strength for businesses . . . and . . . it is essential to encourage and develop this capacity to the full. The manager must be able to sacrifice some personal vanity in order to grant this satisfaction to subordinates . . . a manager able to do so is infinitely superior to one who cannot.' (pp. 39–40)
- **Esprit de corps**   'Harmony, union among the personnel of a concern is a great strength in that concern. Effort, then, should be made to establish it.' (p. 40) Fayol suggested doing so by avoiding sowing dissension amongst subordinates, and using verbal rather than written communication when appropriate.

Current status

Table 2.2 summarises some principles common to the internal process models of management and indicates their modern application.

'Bureaucracy' has many critics, who believe that it stifles creativity, fosters dissatisfaction and lowers motivation. Others believe it brings fairness and certainty to the workplace, where it clarifies roles and responsibilities, makes work effective – and raises motivation.

Bureaucratic methods are widely used especially in the public sector, and in commercial businesses with geographically dispersed outlets – such as hotels, stores and banks. Customers expect a predictable service wherever they are, so management design centrally controlled procedures and manuals – how to recruit and train staff, what the premises must look like and how to treat customers. If managers work in situations that require a degree of change and innovation, they need other theories of management.

Table 2.2 Modern applications of the internal process model

Some principles of the internal process model	Current applications
Rules and regulations	All organisations have these, covering areas such as expenditure, safety, recruitment and confidentiality
Impersonality	Appraisal processes based on objective criteria or team assessments, not personal preference
Division of labour	Setting narrow limits to employees' areas of responsibility – found in many organisations
Hierarchical structure	Most company organisation charts show managers in a hierarchy – with subordinates below them
Authority structure	Holders of a particular post have authority over matters relating to that post, but not over other matters
Centralisation	Organisations balance central control of (say) finance or online services with local control of (say) pricing or recruitment
Initiative	Current practice in many firms to increase the responsibility of operating staff
Rationality	Managers are expected to assess issues on the basis of evidence, not personal preference

2.6 Human relations models

In the early twentieth century, several writers such as Follett and Mayo recognised the limitations of scientific management and suggested new methods.

Mary Parker Follett

Mary Parker Follett (1868–1933) graduated with distinction from Radcliffe College (now part of Harvard University) in 1898, having studied economics, law and philosophy. She became a social worker and quickly acquired a reputation as an imaginative and effective professional. She realised the creativity of the group process, and the potential it offered for truly democratic government – which people themselves would have to create.

She advocated replacing bureaucratic institutions with networks in which people themselves analysed their problems and implemented their solutions. True democracy depended on tapping the potential of all members of society by enabling individuals to take part in groups organised to solve particular problems and accepting personal responsibility for the result. Such ideas are still relevant – as shown by some flourishing community-trading groups, and by tenants' groups helping to manage social housing.

In the 1920s, business managers invited her to investigate some industrial problems. She again advocated the self-governing principle that would facilitate the growth of individuals and the groups to which they belonged. Since people bring valuable differences of view to a problem, conflict is inevitable, which the group must resolve – and in doing so they would create what she called an 'integrative unity' among the members.

She acknowledged that organisations had to optimise production, but did not accept that the strict division of labour was the right way to achieve this (Follett, 1920), as it devalued human creativity. The human side should not be separated from the mechanical side, as the two are bound together. She believed that people, whether managers or workers, behave as they do because of the reciprocal responses in their relationship. If managers tell people to behave as if they are extensions of a machine, they will do so. She believed that group working had the power to release human potential:

> The potentialities of the individual remain potentialities until they are released by group life. (Follett, 1920, p. 6.)

Elton Mayo

Elton Mayo (1880–1949) was an Australian who taught logic, psychology and ethics at the University of Queensland. In 1922 he moved to the United States, and in 1926 became Professor of Industrial Research at Harvard Business School, applying psychological methods to industrial conflict.

In 1924, managers of the Western Electric Company began some experiments at their Hawthorne plant in Chicago to discover the effect on output of changing aspects of the physical environment. The first experiments studied the effect of lighting. The researchers established a control and an experimental group, varied the level of illumination and measured the output. As light rose, so did output. More surprisingly, as light fell, output continued to rise: it also rose in the control group, where conditions had not changed. The team concluded that physical conditions had little effect, so they set up a more comprehensive experiment to identify other factors.

They assembled a small number of workers in a separate room and altered variables in turn, including working hours, length of breaks and providing refreshments. The experienced workers were assembling small components to make telephone equipment. A supervisor was in charge and there was also an observer to record how workers reacted. They took care to prevent external factors disrupting the effects of the variables under investigation. The researchers also explained what was happening and ensured that the workers understood what they were expected to do. They also listened to employees' views of working conditions. The researchers varied conditions every two or three weeks, while the supervisor measured output regularly. This showed a gradual, if erratic, increase – even when the researchers returned conditions to those prevailing at an earlier stage – see Figure 2.2.

In 1928, senior managers invited Mayo to present the research to a wider audience (Mayo, 1949). They concluded from the relay assembly test room experiments that the increase in

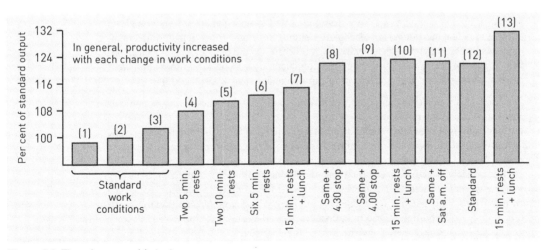

Figure 2.2 The relay assembly test room

Source: After Baron and Greenberg, 1997, p. 13. Reprinted by permission of Pearson Education, Inc., Upper Saddle River, NJ.

output was not related to the physical changes, but to the change in the social situation of the group:

> the major experimental change was introduced when those in charge sought to hold the situation humanly steady (in the interests of critical changes to be introduced) by getting the co-operation of the workers. What actually happened was that 6 individuals became a team and the team gave itself wholeheartedly and spontaneously to co-operation in the environment. (Mayo, 1949, p. 64)

The group felt special: managers asked for their views, were involved with them, paid attention to them and they had the chance to influence some aspects of the work.

The research team also observed another part of the factory, the bank wiring room, which revealed a different aspect of group working. Workers here were paid according to a piece-rate system, in which management pays workers a set amount for each item, or piece, that they produce. Such schemes reflect the assumption that financial incentives will encourage staff to work. The researchers observed that employees regularly produced less than they could have done. They had developed a sense of a normal rate of output, and ensured that all adhered to this rate, believing that if they produced, and earned, too much, management would reduce the piece-rate. Group members exercised informal sanctions against colleagues who worked too hard (or too slowly), until they came into line. Members who did too much were known as 'rate-busters' while those who did too little were 'chisellers'. Anyone who told the supervisor about this was a 'squealer'. Sanctions included being 'binged' – tapped on the shoulder to let them know that what they were doing was wrong. Managers had little or no control over these groups.

Finally, the research team conducted an extensive interview programme. They began by asking employees about the working environment and how they felt about their job, and then some questions about their life in general. The responses showed that there were often close links between work and domestic life. Work affected people's wider life more than the researchers had expected, and domestic circumstances affected their feelings about work. This implied that supervisors needed to think of a subordinate as a complete person, not just as a worker.

Mayo's reflections on the Hawthorne studies drew attention to aspects of human behaviour that practitioners of scientific management had neglected. He introduced the idea of 'social man', in contrast to the 'economic man' who was at the centre of earlier theories. While financial rewards would influence the latter, group relationships and loyalties would influence the former, and may outweigh management pressure.

On financial incentives, Mayo wrote:

> Man's desire to be continuously associated in work with his fellows is a strong, if not the strongest, human characteristic. Any disregard of it by management or any ill-advised attempt to defeat this human impulse leads instantly to some form of defeat for management itself. In [a study] the efficiency experts had assumed the primacy of financial incentive; in this they were wrong; not until the conditions of working group formation were satisfied did the financial incentives come into operation. (Mayo, 1949, p. 99)

People had social needs that they sought to satisfy – and how they did so may support or oppose management interests.

Further analysis of the experimental data has suggested that the team underestimated the influence of financial incentives. Becoming a member of the experimental group in itself increased the worker's income.

Despite possibly inaccurate interpretations, the findings stimulated interest in social factors in the workplace. Scientific management stressed the technical aspects of work. The Hawthorne studies implied that management should pay at least as much attention to human factors, leading to the **human relations approach**. This advocates that employees will work more effectively if management shows interest in their welfare, for instance, through more humane supervision.

Peters and Waterman (1982) published an influential book in which they tried to explain the success of what they regarded as 43 excellently managed US companies. One conclusion

Human relations approach is a school of management which emphasises the importance of social processes at work.

36

was that they had a distinctive set of philosophies about human nature and the way people interact in organisations. They did not see people as rational beings, motivated by fear and willing to accept a low-involvement employment relationship. Instead, excellent companies regarded people as emotional, intuitive and creative social beings who like to celebrate victories and value self-control – but who also need the security and meaning of achieving goals through organisations. From this, Peters and Waterman deduced some general rules for treating workers with dignity and respect, to ensure that people produced quality work in an increasingly uncertain environment.

Peters and Waterman had a significant influence on management thinking: they believed that management had previously relied too much on analytical techniques of the rational goal models, at the expense of more intuitive and human perspectives. They developed the ideas associated with the human relations models and introduced the idea of company culture – discussed in the next chapter.

Current status

The Hawthorne studies showed that the factors influencing performance were certainly more complex than earlier commentators had assumed. Other writers have followed and developed Mayo's emphasis on human factors. McGregor (1960), Maslow (1970) and Alderfer (1972) (see Chapter 13) have suggested ways of integrating human needs with those of the organisation as expressed by management.

An example of a manager who puts this into practice is the chief executive of SAS, a global software company which *Fortune* magazine named in 2010 as the best place to work in America. He says:

> People who are extremely concerned about problems at home tend not to be very productive at work. So our goal is to try to remove as much stress from their lives as we possibly can . . . all these things (medical care, childcare, massage, food, hairdressers and a 35-hour week) tend to make a person's life just a little bit easier. (*Financial Times*, 1 February 2010)

Another example is employee share ownership, as practised by the John Lewis Partnership (**www.johnlewispartnership.co.uk**) (retailing) and Tullis-Russell (**www.tullis-russell.com**) (papermaking). These (still uncommon) methods reflect their managers' theories about how best to encourage staff commitment and motivation.

As the external environments of organisations become less predictable than they were at the time of the Hawthorne experiments, managers and scholars have sought new theories to cope with these conditions, particularly in the idea of open systems models.

2.7 Open systems models

The open systems approach builds on earlier work in general systems theory, and has been widely used to help understand management and organisational issues. The basic idea is to think of the organisation not as a **system**, but as an **open system**.

The open systems approach draws attention to the links between the internal parts of a system, and to the links between the whole system and the outside world. The system is separated from its environment by the **system boundary**. An open system imports resources such as energy and materials, which enter it from the environment across this boundary, undergo some transformation process within the system and leave the system as goods and services. The central theme of the open systems view of management is that organisations depend on the wider environment for inputs if they are to survive and prosper. Figure 2.3 (based on Figure 1.1) is a simple model of the organisation as an open system.

A **system** is a set of interrelated parts designed to achieve a purpose.

An **open system** is one that interacts with its environment.

A **system boundary** separates the system from its environment.

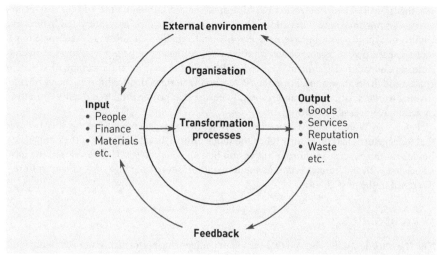

Figure 2.3
The systems model

The figure shows input and output processes, conversion processes and feedback loops. The organisation must satisfy those in the wider environment well enough to ensure that they continue to provide resources. The management task is to sustain those links if the organisation is to thrive. **Feedback** (in systems theory) refers to information about the performance of the system. It may be deliberate, through customer surveys, or unplanned, such as the loss of business to a competitor. Feedback enables those managing the system to take remedial action.

> **Feedback** (in systems theory) refers to the provision of information about the effects of an activity.

Another idea is that of **subsystems**. A course is a subsystem within a department or faculty, the faculty is a subsystem of a university, the university is a subsystem of the higher education system. This in turn is part of the whole education system. A course itself will consist of several systems – one for quality assurance, one for enrolling students, one for teaching, another for assessment and so on.

> **Subsystems** are the separate but related parts that make up the total system.

These subsystems interact with each other, and how well people manage these links affects the functioning of the whole system: when a university significantly increases the number of students admitted to a popular course, this affects many parts of the system – such as accommodation (*technology*), teaching resources (*people*) and examinations (*business processes*).

A systems approach emphasises the links between systems, and reminds managers that a change in one will have consequences for others. For example, Danny Potter, Managing Director of Inamo (**www.inamo-restaurant.com**) a London restaurant where customers place their order directly to the kitchen from an interactive ordering system on their table explains:

> I think the greatest challenge that we faced is communicating our ideas down through the business about what we're trying to achieve. There is a big overlap between essentially the computer software side and the actual restaurant side, to unite those in a way that people [new staff, suppliers etc.] understand has proven rather tricky.

Socio-technical systems

An important variant of systems theory is the idea of the **socio-technical system**. The approach developed from the work of Eric Trist and Ken Bamforth (1951) at the Tavistock Institute in London. Their most prominent study was of an attempt in the coal industry to mechanise the mining system. Introducing what were in essence assembly line technologies and methods at the coalface had severe consequences for the social system that the older pattern of working had encouraged. The technological system destroyed the social system, and the solution lay in reconciling the needs of both.

> A **socio-technical system** is one in which outcomes depend on the interaction of both the technical and social subsystems.

This and similar studies showed the benefits of seeing a work system as a combination of a material technology (tools, machinery, techniques) and a social organisation (people, relationships, constitutional arrangements). A socio-technical analysis aims to integrate the social and technical components: optimising one while ignoring the other is likely to be unproductive.

Contingency management

A further development of the open systems view is the contingency approach (Chapter 9). This arose from the work of Woodward (1965) and Burns and Stalker (1961) in the United Kingdom, and of Lawrence and Lorsch (1967) in the United States. The main theme is that to perform well managers must adapt the structure of the organisation to match external conditions.

Contingency approaches to organisational structure propose that the performance of an organisation depends on having a structure that is appropriate to its environment.

Contingency approaches look for those conditions – which aspects of the environment should managers take into account in shaping their organisation.

As the environment becomes more complex, managers can use contingency perspectives to examine what structure best meets the needs of the business. Contingency theorists emphasise creating organisations that can cope with uncertainty and change, using the values of the open systems model: they also recognise that some functions need work in a stable and predictable way, using the values of the internal process model.

Managers increasingly have to cope with change and innovation (see Chapter 11). An example would be when senior managers in high-tech firms like Apple (**www.apple.com**) or Microsoft (**www.microsoft.com**) create teams to work with a high degree of autonomy (to encourage creativity) on discrete parts of a larger project. The team members will work creatively within a network of informal contacts and exchanges relevant to their part of the task. These human interactions lead to stable or unstable behaviour, and the skill is to balance these extremes. If an organisation is too stable it will stifle innovation, but if it is too unstable it will disintegrate:

> Successful organisations work between these two conditions. [In changing environments], rather than seeking to control their organisations to maintain equilibrium . . . [managers] need to embrace more flexible and adaptive models of change and innovation. (McMillan and Carlisle, 2007, p. 577)

This way of thinking about organisations sometimes uses the terms 'linear' and 'non-linear' systems. 'Linear' describes a system in which an action leads to a predictable reaction. If you light a fire in a room, the thermostat will turn the central heating down. Non-linear systems are those in which outcomes are less predictable. If managers reduce prices they will be surprised if sales match the forecast – they cannot predict the reactions of competitors, changes in taste or new products. Circumstances in the outside world change in ways that management cannot anticipate, so while short-term consequences of an act are clear, long-run ones are not.

Current status

Although theories of management develop at particular times in response to current problems, this does not mean that newer is better. While new concerns bring out new theories, old concerns usually remain. While recently developed ideas seek to encourage flexibility and change, some businesses, and some parts of highly flexible businesses still require control. Rather than thinking of theoretical development as a linear process, see it as circular or iterative, in which familiar themes recur as new concerns arise. The competing values approach captures the main theoretical developments in one framework and shows the relationships between them – see Table 2.3.

The emerging management challenges come from many sources. One is the widely accepted need to develop a more sustainable economic system. Another is the need to balance innovation and creativity with closer governance and control, especially in financial services. Deregulation of many areas of activity is allowing new competitors to enter previously protected markets

Table 2.3 Summary of the models within the competing values framework

Features/model	Rational goal	Internal process	Human relations	Open systems
Main exponents	Taylor	Fayol	Mayo	Trist and Bamforth
	Frank and Lillian Gilbreth	Weber	Follett	Woodward
			Barnard	Burns and Stalker
			Peters and Waterman	Lawrence and Lorsch
Criteria of effectiveness	Productivity, profit	Stability, continuity	Commitment, morale, cohesion	Adaptability, external support
Means/ends theory	Clear direction leads to productive outcomes	Routinisation leads to stability	Involvement leads to commitment	Continual innovation secures external support
Emphasis	Rational analysis, measurement	Defining responsibility, documentation	Participation, consensus building	Creative problem solving, innovation
Role of manager	Director and planner	Monitor and co-ordinator	Mentor and facilitator	Innovator and broker

(airlines, financial services). Still another is the closer integration between many previously separate areas of business (telecommunications, consumer electronics and entertainment). There is also the growing internationalisation of business. Managers today look for radical solutions – just as Robert Owen did in the early days of the Industrial Revolution.

Activity 2.2   What are 'theories of management'?

Recall the organisation you used in Activity 2.1.

Having read the chapter, make brief notes summarising how 'theory' (even if implicitly) has shaped management decisions:

- Which of the quadrants in Figure 2.1 most closely reflects the way the organisation works?
- What examples of rational goal practices have you found? (Refer to Section 2.4.)
- What examples of internal process practices have you found? (Refer to Section 2.5.)
- What examples of human relations practices have you found? (Refer to Section 2.6.)
- What examples of open systems practices have you found? (Refer to Section 2.7.)

Compare what you have found with other students on your course.

Summary

1 Explain the value of models of management, and compare unitary, pluralist and critical perspectives

- Models represent more complex realities, help to understand complexity and offer a range of perspectives on the topic. Their predictive effect is limited by the fact that people interpret information subjectively in deciding how to act.

- A unitary perspective emphasises the common purpose of organisational members, while the pluralist draws attention to competing interest groups. Those who take a critical perspective believe that organisations reflect deep divisions in society, and that attempts to integrate different interests through negotiation ignore persistent differences in the distribution of power.

2 **State the structure of the competing values framework and evaluate its contribution to our understanding of management**
   - A way of integrating the otherwise confusing range of theories of management. Organisations experience tensions between control and flexibility and between an external and an internal focus. Placing these on two axes allows theories to be allocated to one of four types – rational goal, internal process, human relations and open systems.

3 **Summarise the rational goal, internal process, human relations and open systems models and evaluate what each can contribute to a manager's understanding of their role**
   - Rational goal (Taylor, the Gilbreths and operational research):
     - clear direction leads to productive outcomes, with an emphasis on rational analysis and measurement.
   - Internal process (Weber, Fayol):
     - routinisation leads to stability, so an emphasis on defining responsibility and on comprehensive documentation and administrative processes.
   - Human relations (Follett, Mayo):
     - people are motivated by social needs, and managers who recognise these will secure commitment. Practices include considerate supervision, participation and seeking consensus.
   - Open systems (socio-technical and contingency):
     - Continual innovation secures external support, achieved by creative problem solving.

   These theories have contributed to the management agendas in these ways:
   - Rational goal – through techniques like time and motion study, work measurement and a variety of techniques for planning operations; also the narrow specification of duties, and the separation of management and non-management work.
   - Internal process – clear targets and measurement systems, and the creation of clear management and reporting structures. Making decisions objectively on the basis of rules and procedures, rather than on favouritism or family connections.
   - Human relations – considerate supervision, consultation and participation in decisions affecting people.
   - Open systems – understanding external factors and being able and willing to respond to them through individual and organisational flexibility especially in uncertain, complex conditions characterised by the idea of non-linear systems. While a linear system is one in which a relatively stable environment makes some planning feasible, a non-linear system is strongly influenced by other systems. This means that actions lead to unexpected consequences.

Review questions

1 Name three ways in which theoretical models help the study of management.
2 What are the different assumptions of the unitary, pluralist and critical perspectives on organisations?
3 Draw the two axes of the competing values framework, and then place the theories outlined in this chapter in the most appropriate sector.

4　List Taylor's five principles of scientific management and evaluate their use in examples of your choice.

5　What was the particular contribution that Lillian Gilbreth made concerning how workers' mental capacities should be treated?

6　What did Follett consider to be the value of groups in community as well as business?

7　Compare Taylor's assumptions about people with those of Mayo. Evaluate the accuracy of these views by reference to an organisation of your choice.

8　Compare the conclusions reached by the Hawthorne experimenters in the relay assembly test room with those in the bank wiring room.

9　Why is an open system likely to be harder to manage than a closed system?

Further reading

Birkinshaw, J. (2010), *Reinventing Management: Smarter choices for getting work done*, Jossey-Bass, San Fancisco, CA.

> A small book by a leading management academic gives a short account of the work of general management.

Taylor, F. W. (1917), *The Principles of Scientific Management*, Harper, New York.

Fayol, H. (1949), *General and Industrial Management*, Pitman, London.

> The original works of these writers are short and lucid. Taylor (1917) contains illuminating detail that brings the ideas to life, and Fayol's (1949) surviving ideas came from only two short chapters, which are worth reading in the original.

Weblinks

These websites have appeared in, or are relevant to, the chapter:

> www.pret.com
> www.johnlewispartnership.co.uk
> www.tullis-russell.com
> www.inamo-restaurant.com
> www.apple.com
> www.microsoft.com
> www.newlanark.org.uk

Visit two of the business sites in the list above, or those of other organisations in which you are interested, and navigate to the pages dealing with recent news, press or investor relations.

- What are the main issues which the organisation appears to be facing?
- Compare and contrast the issues you identify on the two sites.
- What challenges may they imply for those working in, and managing, these organisations?

 Annotated weblinks, multiple choice questions and other useful resources can be found on **www.pearsoned.co.uk/boddy**

Case study   Robert Owen – an early management innovator   www.newlanark.org.uk

Robert Owen (1771–1856) was a successful manufacturer of textiles, who ran mills in England and at New Lanark, about 24 miles from Glasgow, in Scotland. David Dale built the cotton-spinning mills at New Lanark in 1785 – which were then the largest in Scotland. Since they depended on water power, Dale had built them below the Falls of Clyde – a well-known tourist attraction throughout the 18th century. Many people continued to visit both the Falls and New Lanark, which combined both manufacturing and social innovations.

Creating such a large industrial enterprise in the countryside meant that Dale (and Owen after him) had to attract and retain labour – which involved building not just the mill but also houses, shops, schools and churches for the workers. By 1793, the mill employed about 1200 people, of whom almost 800 were children, aged from 6 to 17: 200 were under 10 (McLaren, 1990). Dale provided the children with food, education and clothing in return for working 12 hours each day: visitors were impressed by these facilities.

One visitor was Robert Owen, who shared Dale's views on the benefits to both labour and owner of good working conditions. By 1801 Dale wanted to sell New Lanark to someone who shared his principles and concluded that Owen (who had married his daughter) was such a man. Owen had built a reputation for management skills while running mills in England, and did not approve of employing children in them.

Having bought the very large business of New Lanark, Owen quickly introduced new management and production control techniques. These included daily and weekly measurements of stocks, output and productivity; a system of labour costing; and measures of work-in-progress. He used a novel control technique: a small, four-sided piece of wood, with a different colour on each side, hung beside every worker. The colour set to the front indicated the previous day's standard of work – black indicating bad. Everyone could see this measure of the worker's performance, which overseers recorded to identify any trends in a person's work:

> Every process in the factory was closely watched, checked and recorded to increase labour productivity and to keep costs down. (Royle, 1998, p. 13)

Reproduced with kind permission of New Lanark Trust www.newlanark.org.

At this stage of the Industrial Revolution, most adult employees had no experience of factory work, or of living in a large community such as New Lanark. Owen found that many 'were idle, intemperate, dishonest [and] devoid of truth' (quoted in Butt, 1971). Evening patrols were introduced to stop drunkenness, and there were rules about keeping the residential areas clean and free of rubbish. He also had 'to deal with slack managers who had tolerated widespread theft and embezzlement, immorality and drunkenness' (Butt, 1971).

During Owen's time at the mill it usually employed about 1500 people, and soon after taking over he stopped employing children under 10. He introduced other social innovations: a store at which employees could buy goods more cheaply than elsewhere (a model for the Co-operative Movement), and a school which looked after children from the age of 1 – enabling their mothers to work in the mills. Owen actively managed the links between his business and the wider world. On buying the mills he quickly became part of the Glasgow business establishment, and was closely involved in the activities of the Chamber of Commerce. He took a prominent role in the social and political life of the city. He used these links in particular to argue the case for reforms in the educational and economic systems, and was critical of the effect that industrialisation was having upon working-class life.

Owen believed that education in useful skills would help to release working-class children from poverty and promoted the case for wider educational provision. He also developed several experiments in co-operation and community building, believing that the basis of his successful capitalist enterprise at New Lanark (education, good working conditions and a harmonious community) could be applied to society as a whole.

Sources: Butt (1971); McLaren (1990); Royle (1998); Donachie (2000).

Questions

1 Refer to Section 2.2, and make notes on which theory may have (implicitly) guided Owen's approach to business.

2 What 'rational goal' practices did he use at New Lanark? (Refer to Section 2.4.)

3 What 'human relations' practices did he use? (Refer to Section 2.6.)

4 Draw a systems diagram showing the main inputs, transformation and outputs of Robert Owen's mill. (Refer to Section 2.7, especially Figure 2.3.)

Communication

SPOTLIGHT: *Manager at Work*

Tweets. Twittering. Prior to 2006, the only definition we would have known for these words would have involved birds and the sounds they make. Now, practically everyone knows that Twitter is also an online service—as of early 2012 with 500 million registered users, 340 million tweets daily, and 1.6 billion daily search queries—used to trade short messages of 140 characters or less via the Web, cell phones, and other devices.[1] According to its founders (Evan Williams, Biz Stone, and Jack Dorsey; see photo next page), Twitter is many things: a messaging service, a customer-service tool to reach customers, real-time search, and microblogging. And as the numbers show, it's become quite popular!

One place where Twitter has caught on is the sports world, especially in college sports. For instance, Les Miles, head football coach at Louisiana State University calls himself "a Twittering kind of guy." He understands the power of instant communication. Miles wants to stay ahead of the competition, especially when it comes to recruiting and keeping fans informed. He said, "It (Twittering) allows us to communicate blasts of information to those people that subscribe. And it's also an opportunity for those recruiting prospects that subscribe to communicate to us." On game days, he Twitters (via a staff assistant) before games, at halftime, and after games. If it's okay for coaches to tweet, what about student athletes? That's often a different story.

Many universities and college coaches are monitoring and, in some cases, banning athletes' use of social media. "They're nervous because an ill-considered tweet can embarrass the program, draw the ire of administrators and boosters, and possibly violate NCAA recruitment rules." Here are a couple

Source: Cal Sport Media via AP Images

From Chapter 16 of *Management*, 12/e. Stephen P. Robbins and Mary Coulter. © Pearson Education Limited 2014. All rights reserved.

Source: Kevin Mazur/Getty Images

of tweeting slip-ups: a Western Kentucky running back was suspended after he tweeted critical comments about the team's fans; the NCAA pulled 15 football scholarships after an investigation based on a player's tweet; and a Lehigh

One place where Twitter has caught on is the sports world, especially in college sports.

University wide receiver was suspended for re-tweeting a racial slur. We even saw how tweeting backfired at the London Olympics. The first "casualty"—a Greek triple jumper—was banned from the Games over some racially charged tweets. That seems to be good reason for the managers (i.e., coaches and administrators) of these programs to attempt to control

the information flow. But is banning the answer? Some analysts say no. They argue that those setting up rules and regulations don't understand what social media is all about and the value it provides as a marketing and recruiting tool, and they argue that it's necessary to understand First Amendment rights (part of which includes freedom of speech). Rather than

---

MyManagementLab®

⭐ **Improve Your Grade!**

Over 10 million students improved their results using the Pearson MyLabs.
Visit **www.mymanagementlab.com** for simulations, tutorials, and end-of-chapter problems.

LEARNING OUTCOMES

16.1	**Define** the nature and function of communication.
16.2	**Compare** and contrast methods of interpersonal communication.
16.3	**Identify** barriers to effective interpersonal communication and how to overcome them.
16.4	**Explain** how communication can flow most effectively in organizations.
16.5	**Describe** how technology affects managerial communication and organizations.
16.6	**Discuss** contemporary issues in communication.

*banning the use of social media, many universities are hiring companies to monitor athletes' posts. This, however, requires athletes to give access to their accounts, which some call an invasion of privacy. **What do you think? How is this relevant to managers in business organizations?***

Ahhhh...welcome to the new world of communication! In this "world," managers are going to have to understand both the importance and the drawbacks of communication—all forms of communication. Communication between managers and employees is important because it provides the information necessary to get work done in organizations. Thus, there's no doubt that communication is fundamentally linked to managerial performance.[2]

16.1 **Define** the nature and function of communication.

THE NATURE and Function of Communication

Southwest Airlines suspended a pilot who accidentally broadcast a vulgar criticism that was picked up on an air traffic control frequency and heard by air traffic controllers and other pilots.[3] In the middle of the pilot's profanity-laced rant about the flight attendants on his plane, a Houston air-traffic controller interrupted and said, "Whoever's transmitting, better watch what you're saying." The Federal Aviation Administration sent the audio recording to Southwest, calling it "inappropriate." Southwest suspended the 12-year veteran pilot without pay for an undisclosed amount of time for making comments that were contrary to employee policy and sent him to sensitivity training. This example shows why it's important for managers to understand the impact of communication.

The ability to communicate effectively is a skill that must be mastered by any manager who wants to be an effective manager. The importance of effective communication for managers can't be overemphasized for one specific reason: Everything a manager does involves communicating. Not *some* things, but everything! A manager can't make a decision without information. That information has to be communicated. Once a decision is made, communication must again take place. Otherwise, no one would know that a decision was made. The best idea, the most creative suggestion, the best plan, or the most effective job redesign can't take shape without communication.

What Is Communication?

communication
The transfer and understanding of meaning

Communication is the transfer and understanding of meaning. Note the emphasis on the *transfer* of meaning: If information or ideas have not been conveyed, communication hasn't taken place. The speaker who isn't heard or the writer whose materials aren't read hasn't communicated. More importantly, however, communication involves the *understanding* of meaning. For communication to be successful, the meaning must be imparted and understood. A letter written in Spanish addressed to a person who doesn't read Spanish can't be considered communication until it's translated into a language the person does read and understand. Perfect communication, if such a thing existed, would be when a transmitted thought or idea was received and understood by the receiver exactly as it was envisioned by the sender.

Another point to keep in mind is that *good* communication is often erroneously defined by the communicator as *agreement* with the message instead of clear understanding of the message.[4] If someone disagrees with us, we assume that the person just didn't fully understand our position. In other words, many of us define good communication as having someone accept our views. But I can clearly understand what you mean and just *not* agree with what you say.

interpersonal communication
Communication between two or more people

organizational communication
All the patterns, networks, and systems of communication within an organization

The final point we want to make about communication is that it encompasses both **interpersonal communication**—communication between two or more people—and **organizational communication**, which is all the patterns, networks, and systems of communication within an organization. Both types are important to managers.

47

Functions of Communication

Irene Lews, CEO of SAIT Polytechnic, a Calgary, Alberta, Canada-based technical institute, was awarded the 2012 Excellence in Communication Leadership (EXCEL) Award by the International Association of Business Communicators. This award recognizes leaders who foster excellence in communication and contribute to the development and support of organizational communication. The selection committee noted Lewis' leadership and commitment to communication and her impact on SAIT's reputation and growth. "She is involved in a wide variety of issues and uses communications wisely to engage relevant stakeholders."[5]

Communication with new employees at Columbus Company, Ltd., a shoe care products company in Tokyo, serves the functions of information, motivation, and socialization. During their initiation, college graduates first attend a lecture to learn about the company's polishing creams and other shoe supplies. Then they are paired with a senior master polisher who teaches them how to shine shoes with the spirit of "polishing shoes is like polishing the heart." The new recruits also polish their mentors' shoes and receive feedback about their performance. Communication also provides a release for emotional expressions and feelings as new recruits interact socially with each other and senior staff members.
Source: Everett Kennedy Brown/EPA/Newscom

Throughout SAIT Polytechnic and many other organizations, communication serves four major functions: control, motivation, emotional expression, and information.[6] Each function is equally important.

Communication acts to *control* employee behavior in several ways. As we know from Chapter 11, organizations have authority hierarchies and formal guidelines that employees are expected to follow. For instance, when employees are required to communicate any job-related grievance to their immediate manager, to follow their job description, or to comply with company policies, communication is being used to control. Informal communication also controls behavior. When a work group teases a member who's ignoring the norms by working too hard, they're informally controlling the member's behavior.

Next, communication acts to *motivate* by clarifying to employees what is to be done, how well they're doing, and what can be done to improve performance if it's not up to par. As employees set specific goals, work toward those goals, and receive feedback on progress toward goals, communication is required.

For many employees, their work group is a primary source of social interaction. The communication that takes place within the group is a fundamental mechanism by which members share frustrations and feelings of satisfaction. Communication, therefore, provides a release for *emotional expression* of feelings and for fulfillment of social needs.

Finally, individuals and groups need information to get things done in organizations. Communication provides that *information.*

METHODS of Interpersonal Communication

Compare *and contrast* **16.2**
methods of interpersonal communication.

Before communication can take place, a purpose, expressed as a **message** to be conveyed, must exist. It passes between a source (the sender) and a receiver. The message is converted to symbolic form (called **encoding**) and passed by way of some medium (**channel**) to the receiver, who retranslates the sender's message (called **decoding**). The result is the transfer of meaning from one person to another.[7]

Exhibit 16-1 illustrates the elements of the **communication process**. Note that the entire process is susceptible to **noise**—disturbances that interfere with the transmission, receipt, or feedback of a message. Typical examples of noise include illegible print, phone static, inattention by the receiver, or background sounds of machinery or coworkers. However, anything that interferes with understanding can be noise, and noise can create distortion at any point in the communication process.

A personal written letter from a U.S. Army commander in Afghanistan to his troops assured them that they are "contributing to the overall success of the mission" here. Colonel David Haight, of the 10th Mountain Division's 3rd Brigade Combat team, sent the letter to each of the 3,500 men and women after two of their fellow soldiers were killed in combat and his chaplains reported that many were disillusioned about the war. In that letter, Haight said it's important for a leader to explain why certain tasks are important to the accomplishment of the overall mission. Communicating in that way ensures that the mission is not only accomplished, but is accomplished in

message
A purpose to be conveyed

encoding
Converting a message into symbols

channel
The medium a message travels along

decoding
Retranslating a sender's message

communication process
The seven elements involved in transferring meaning from one person to another

noise
Any disturbances that interfere with the transmission, receipt, or feedback of a message

Exhibit 16-1

The Interpersonal Communication Process

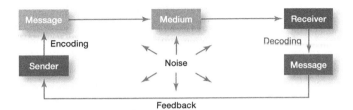

an exemplary way.[8] Here's a manager who understands the role of communication and how best to communicate to his subordinates.

You need to communicate to your employees the organization's new policy on sexual harassment; you want to compliment one of your workers on the extra hours she's put in to help your team complete a customer's order; you must tell one of your employees about changes to his job; or you would like to get employees' feedback on your proposed budget for next year. In each of these instances, how would you communicate? Managers have a wide variety of communication methods from which to choose and can use 12 questions to help them evaluate these methods.[9]

1. *Feedback:* How quickly can the receiver respond to the message?
2. *Complexity capacity:* Can the method effectively process complex messages?
3. *Breadth potential:* How many different messages can be transmitted using this method?
4. *Confidentiality:* Can communicators be reasonably sure their messages are received only by those intended?
5. *Encoding ease:* Can sender easily and quickly use this channel?
6. *Decoding ease:* Can receiver easily and quickly decode messages?
7. *Time-space constraint:* Do senders and receivers need to communicate at the same time and in the same space?
8. *Cost:* How much does it cost to use this method?
9. *Interpersonal warmth:* How well does this method convey interpersonal warmth?
10. *Formality:* Does this method have the needed amount of formality?
11. *Scanability:* Does this method allow the message to be easily browsed or scanned for relevant information?
12. *Time of consumption:* Does the sender or receiver exercise the most control over when the message is dealt with?

Exhibit 16-2 provides a comparison of various communication methods. Which method a manager ultimately chooses should reflect the needs of the sender, the attributes of the message, the attributes of the channel, and the needs of the receiver. For instance, if you need to communicate to an employee about the changes being made in her job, face-to-face communication would be a better choice than a memo because you want to be able to address immediately any questions and concerns she might have.

An important part of interpersonal communication is **nonverbal communication**—that is, communication transmitted without words. Some of the most meaningful communications are neither spoken nor written. When a college instructor is teaching a class, she doesn't need words to tell her that students are tuned out when they begin to read a newspaper in the middle of class. Similarly, when students start putting their book, papers, and notebooks away, the message is clear: Class time is about over. The size of a person's office or the clothes he or she wears also convey messages to others. Among these various forms of nonverbal communication, the best-known types are body language and verbal intonation.

Body language refers to gestures, facial expressions, and other body movements that convey meaning. A person frowning "says" something different from one who's smiling. Hand motions, facial expressions, and other gestures can communicate

nonverbal communication
Communication transmitted without words

body language
Gestures, facial configurations, and other body movements that convey meaning

High Feedback Potential
- Face-to-face
- Telephone
- Computer conference

High Complexity Capacity
- Face-to-face

High Breadth Potential
- Face-to-face
- Bulletin boards
- E-mail

High Confidentiality
- Face-to-face
- Voice mail

High Encoding Ease
- Face-to-face
- Telephone

High Time-Decoding Ease
- Face-to-face
- Telephone
- Hotlines
- Voice mail

High Space Constraint
- Face-to-face
- Group meetings
- ¹Formal presentations

High Cost
- Group meetings
- Formal presentations
- Videoconference

High Personal Warmth
- Face-to-face

High Formality
- Postal mail
- Publications

High Scanability
- Memos
- Postal mail
- Fax
- Publications
- Bulletin boards

Low Feedback Potential
- Publications

Low Complexity Capacity
- Bulletin boards

Low Breadth Potential
- Postal mail
- Audio-videotapes

Low Confidentiality
- Publications
- Bulletin boards
- Audio-videotapes
- Teleconference

Low Encoding Ease
- Publications

Low Time-Decoding Ease
- Memos
- Postal mail
- Fax
- Publications

Low Space Constraint
- Memos
- Postal mail
- Fax
- Publications
- Voice mail

Low Cost
- Bulletin boards

Low Personal Warmth
- Memos
- Bulletin boards

Low Formality
- Face-to-face
- Telephone
- Voice mail

Low Scanability
- Formal presentations
- Face-to-face
- Telephone
- Group meetings
- Audio-videotapes
- Hotlines
- E-mail
- Computer conference
- Voice mail
- Teleconference
- Videoconference

Exhibit 16-2
Comparison of Communication Methods

Source: Based on P. G. Clampitt, *Communicating for Managerial Effectiveness* (Newbury Park, CA: Sage Publications, 1991), p. 136.

LEADER *who made a* **DIFFERENCE**

Zappos, the quirky Las Vegas-based online shoe retailer (now a part of Amazon.com, which purchased the company for $1.2 billion), has a reputation for being a fun place to work.[11] Much of that is due to its CEO Tony Hsieh, who also understands the power of communication. And one thing that's communicated well and frequently is the company's values. He says that maintaining that corporate culture is "the number one priority." At the company's headquarters, employees use only one entrance and exit to encourage them to "literally run into" each other in the lobby. Hsieh believes that's a way to encourage opportune interactions to share ideas. His next project? Revitalizing downtown Las Vegas by using his own money to buy property, subsidize schools, and fund new business ventures. What can you learn from this leader who made a difference?

emotions or temperaments such as aggression, fear, shyness, arrogance, joy, and anger. Knowing the meaning behind someone's body moves and learning how to put forth your best body language can help you personally and professionally.[10]

Verbal intonation refers to the emphasis someone gives to words or phrases in order to convey meaning. To illustrate how intonations can change the meaning of a message, consider the student who asks the instructor a question. The instructor replies, "What do you mean by that?" The student's reaction will vary, depending on the tone of the instructor's response. A soft, smooth vocal tone conveys interest and creates a different meaning from one that is abrasive and puts a strong emphasis on saying the last word. Most of us would view the first intonation as coming from someone sincerely interested in clarifying the student's concern, whereas the second suggests that the person resents the question.

verbal intonation
An emphasis given to words or phrases that conveys meaning

Managers need to remember that as they communicate, the nonverbal component usually carries the greatest impact. It's not *what* you say, but *how* you say it.

16.3 *Identify barriers to effective interpersonal communication and how to overcome them.*

EFFECTIVE **Interpersonal Communication**

A company with 100 employees can expect to lose approximately $450,000 a year, or more, because of e-mail blunders, inefficiencies, and misunderstandings.[12] The chief executive of a marketing firm in New York was in a meeting with a potential client. For the entire hour-and-a-half meeting, the client was fiddling with his iPhone. Doing what? Playing a racing game, although he did glance up occasionally and ask questions.[13] Research done by an HR consulting firm found that U.S. and U.K. employees cost their businesses $37 billion every year because they don't really understand their jobs.[14]

Somewhere, somehow communication isn't being as effective as it needs to be. One reason is that managers face barriers that can distort the interpersonal communication process. Let's look at these barriers to effective communication.

Barriers to Communication

filtering
The deliberate manipulation of information to make it appear more favorable to the receiver

FILTERING **Filtering** is the deliberate manipulation of information to make it appear more favorable to the receiver. For example, when a person tells his or her manager what the manager wants to hear, information is being filtered. Or if information being communicated up through organizational levels is condensed by senders, that's filtering.

How much filtering takes place tends to be a function of the number of vertical levels in the organization and the organizational culture. The more vertical levels in an organization, the more opportunities there are for filtering. As organizations use more collaborative, cooperative work arrangements, information filtering may become less of a problem. In addition, e-mail reduces filtering because communication is more direct. Finally, the organizational culture encourages or discourages filtering by the type of behavior it rewards. The more that organizational rewards emphasize style and appearance, the more managers may be motivated to filter communications in their favor.

EMOTIONS How a receiver feels when a message is received influences how he or she interprets it. Extreme emotions are most likely to hinder effective communication.

In such instances, we often disregard our rational and objective thinking processes and substitute emotional judgments.

INFORMATION OVERLOAD   A marketing manager goes on a week-long sales trip to Spain where he doesn't have access to his e-mail, and he faces 1,000 messages on his return. It's not possible to fully read and respond to each message without facing **information overload**, which is when information exceeds our processing capacity. Today's employees frequently complain of information overload. Statistics show that 87 percent of employees use e-mail and that the average business e-mail user devotes 107 minutes a day to e-mail—about 25 percent of the workday. Other statistics show that employees send and receive an average of 112 e-mail messages every day. And the number of worldwide e-mail messages (not just workplace e-mails) sent daily is a staggering 294 billion.[15] The demands of keeping up with e-mail, text messages, phone calls, faxes, meetings, and professional reading create an onslaught of data. What happens when individuals have more information than they can process? They tend to ignore, pass over, forget, or selectively choose information. Or they may stop communicating. Regardless, the result is lost information and ineffective communication.

information overload
When information exceeds our processing capacity

DEFENSIVENESS   When people feel they're being threatened, they tend to react in ways that hinder effective communication and reduce their ability to achieve mutual understanding. They become defensive—verbally attacking others, making sarcastic remarks, being overly judgmental, or questioning others' motives.[16]

LANGUAGE   Conservative author/journalist Ann Coulter and rapper Nelly both speak English, but the language each uses is vastly different. Words mean different things to different people. Age, education, and cultural background are three of the more obvious variables that influence the language a person uses and the definitions he or she gives to words.

In an organization, employees come from diverse backgrounds and have different patterns of speech. Even employees who work for the same organization but in different departments often have different **jargon**—specialized terminology or technical language that members of a group use to communicate among themselves.

jargon
Specialized terminology or technical language that members of a group use to communicate among themselves

NATIONAL CULTURE   For technological and cultural reasons, the Chinese people dislike voice mail.[17] This general tendency illustrates how communication differences can arise from national culture as well as different languages. For example, let's compare countries that value individualism (such as the United States) with countries that emphasize collectivism (such as Japan).[18]

In an individualistic country like the United States, communication is more formal and is clearly spelled out. Managers rely heavily on reports, memos, and other formal forms of communication. In a collectivist country like Japan, more interpersonal contact takes place, and face-to-face communication is encouraged. A Japanese manager extensively consults with subordinates over an issue first and draws up a formal document later to outline the agreement that was made.

Overcoming the Barriers

On average, an individual must hear new information seven times before he or she truly understands.[19] In light of this fact and the communication barriers just described, what can managers do to be more effective communicators?

USE FEEDBACK   Many communication problems are directly attributed to misunderstanding and inaccuracies. These problems are less likely to occur if the manager gets feedback, both verbal and nonverbal.

A manager can ask questions about a message to determine whether it was received and understood as intended. Or the manager can ask the receiver to restate the message in his or her own words. If the manager hears what was intended, understanding and accuracy should improve. Feedback can also be more subtle, and general comments can give a manager a sense of the receiver's reaction to a message.

Feedback also doesn't have to be verbal. If a sales manager e mails information about a new monthly sales report that all sales representatives will need to complete and some of them don't turn it in, the sales manager has received feedback. This feedback suggests that the sales manager needs to clarify the initial communication. Similarly, managers can look for nonverbal cues to tell whether someone's getting the message.

SIMPLIFY LANGUAGE Because language can be a barrier, managers should consider the audience to whom the message is directed and tailor the language to them.[20] Remember, effective communication is achieved when a message is both received and *understood*. For example, a hospital administrator should always try to communicate in clear, easily understood terms and to use language tailored to different employee groups. Messages to the surgical staff should be purposefully different from those used with office employees. Jargon can facilitate understanding if it's used within a group that knows what it means, but can cause problems when used outside that group.

LISTEN ACTIVELY When someone talks, we hear, but too often we don't listen. Listening is an active search for meaning, whereas hearing is passive. In listening, the receiver is also putting effort into the communication.

Many of us are poor listeners. Why? Because it's difficult, and most of us would rather do the talking. Listening, in fact, is often more tiring than talking. Unlike hearing, **active listening**, which is listening for full meaning without making premature judgments or interpretations, demands total concentration. The average person normally speaks at a rate of about 125 to 200 words per minute. However, the average listener can comprehend up to 400 words per minute.[21] The difference leaves lots of idle brain time and opportunities for the mind to wander.

Active listening is enhanced by developing empathy with the sender—that is, by putting yourself in the sender's position. Because senders differ in attitudes, interests, needs, and expectations, empathy makes it easier to understand the actual content of a message. An empathetic listener reserves judgment on the message's content and carefully listens to what is being said. The goal is to improve one's ability to get the full meaning of a communication without distorting it by premature judgments or interpretations. Other specific behaviors that active listeners demonstrate are listed in Exhibit 16-3. As you can see, active listening takes effort, but it can help make communication much more effective.

active listening
Listening for full meaning without making premature judgments or interpretations

Exhibit 16-3
Active Listening Behaviors

Sources: Based on J. V. Thill and C. L. Bovee, *Excellence in Business Communication,* 9th ed. (Upper Saddle River, NJ: Prentice Hall, 2011), pp. 48–49; and S. P. Robbins and P. L. Hunsaker, *Training in Interpersonal Skills,* 5th ed. (Upper Saddle River, NJ: Prentice Hall, 2009), pp. 90–92.

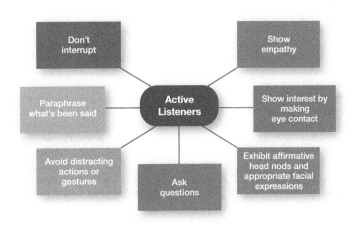

let's get REAL

The Scenario:

Jason Broughton manages a diverse team of corporate security system installers. On his most recent evaluation, his boss told him that his employees have complained that he never listens to what they're telling him. Because Jason hopes to eventually move into positions with more responsibility, he knows he needs to work on this.

Source: Julie Colon

Julie Colon
Creative Project Manager

What advice would you give Jason?

I would advise Jason to start working on creating a better forum between him and his employees for listening to their feedback. It could be that he listens but does not follow up; and to an employee, this can feel like they were not heard. He may want to implement a monthly meeting to update his team on the business, any structural changes in the company and also as a check in to hear any issues that may have come up. An open door policy can help his team to get more time with Jason and feel comfortable approaching him with issues.

CONSTRAIN EMOTIONS It would be naïve to assume that managers always communicate in a rational manner. We know that emotions can cloud and distort communication. A manager who's upset over an issue is more likely to misconstrue incoming messages and fail to communicate his or her outgoing messages clearly and accurately. What to do? The simplest answer is to calm down and get emotions under control before communicating.

WATCH NONVERBAL CUES If actions speak louder than words, then it's important to make sure your actions align with and reinforce the words that go along with them. An effective communicator watches his or her nonverbal cues to ensure that they convey the desired message.

ORGANIZATIONAL Communication

Explain how 16.4
communication can flow most effectively in organizations.

The European economic crisis has employees everywhere on edge. So when all 1,300 workers at Aviva Investors, the asset management division of a United Kingdom insurance company, opened their e-mail one morning, they found out they'd been fired. Except—it was a mistake. Only one unfortunate employee was supposed to get the message. Can you imagine the stunned silence in that office? A spokesman for the company said an apology was quickly issued for the mistaken e-mail message, but had damage already been done?[22]

Maybe you've had the experience of sitting in an employee meeting with managers when they ask if anyone has any questions—only to be met with deafening silence.[23] Communication can be an interesting thing, especially in organizations. As we've seen, managerial communication is important, but it is a two-way street. An understanding of managerial communication isn't possible without looking at organizational communication. In this section, we look at several important aspects of organizational communication, including formal versus informal communication, the flow patterns of communication, formal and informal communication networks, and workplace design.

Formal Versus Informal Communication

formal communication
Communication that takes place within prescribed organizational work arrangements

informal communication
Communication that is not defined by the organization's structural hierarchy

Communication within an organization is described as formal or informal. **Formal communication** refers to communication that takes place within prescribed organizational work arrangements. For example, when a manager asks an employee to complete a task, that's formal communication. Another example of formal communication occurs when an employee communicates a problem to his or her manager.

Informal communication is organizational communication not defined by the organization's structural hierarchy. When employees talk with each other in the lunch room, as they pass in hallways, or as they're working out at the company wellness facility, they engage in informal communication. Employees form friendships and communicate with each other. The informal communication system fulfills two purposes in organizations: (1) it permits employees to satisfy their need for social interaction, and (2) it can improve an organization's performance by creating alternative, and frequently faster and more efficient, channels of communication.

Direction of Communication Flow

Let's look at the ways that organizational communication can flow: downward, upward, laterally, or diagonally.

DOWNWARD Every morning and often several times a day, managers at UPS package delivery facilities gather workers for mandatory meetings that last precisely three minutes. During those 180 seconds, managers relay company announcements and go over local information like traffic conditions or customer complaints. Then, each meeting ends with a safety tip. The three-minute meetings have proved so successful that many of the company's office workers are using the idea.[24] CEOs at companies such as Starbucks and Apple use **town hall meetings** to communicate with employees. These town hall meetings are informal public meetings where top executives relay information, discuss issues, or bring employees together to celebrate accomplishments. These are examples of **downward communication** which is communication that flows from a manager to employees. It's used to inform, direct, coordinate, and evaluate employees. When managers assign goals to their employees, they're using downward communication. They're also using downward communication when providing employees with job descriptions, informing them of organizational policies and procedures, pointing out problems that need attention, or evaluating their performance. Downward communication can take place through any of the communication methods we described earlier.

town hall meeting
Informal public meetings where information can be relayed, issues can be discussed, or just as a way to bring employees together to celebrate accomplishments

downward communication
Communication that flows downward from a manager to employees

UPWARD COMMUNICATION Managers rely on their employees for information. For instance, reports are given to managers to inform them of progress toward goals or to report any problems. **Upward communication** is communication that flows from employees to managers. It keeps managers aware of how employees feel about their jobs, their coworkers, and the organization in general. Managers also rely on upward communication for ideas on how things can be improved. Some examples of upward communication include performance reports prepared by employees, suggestion boxes, employee attitude surveys, grievance procedures, manager-employee discussions, and informal group sessions in which employees have the opportunity to discuss problems with their manager or representatives of top-level management.

How much upward communication is used depends on the organizational culture. If managers have created a climate of trust and respect and use participative decision making or empowerment, considerable upward communication will occur as employees provide input to decisions. In a more highly structured and authoritarian environment, upward communication still takes place, but is limited.

upward communication
Communication that flows upward from employees to managers

lateral communication
Communication that takes place among any employees on the same organizational level

LATERAL COMMUNICATION Communication that takes place among employees on the same organizational level is called **lateral communication**. In today's dynamic environment, horizontal communications are frequently needed to save time and facilitate coordination. Cross-functional teams, for instance, rely heavily on this form of communication interaction. However, conflicts can arise if employees don't keep their managers informed about decisions they've made or actions they've taken.

DIAGONAL COMMUNICATION **Diagonal communication** is communication that crosses both work areas *and* organizational levels. A credit analyst who communicates directly with a regional marketing manager about a customer's problem—note the different department and different organizational level—uses diagonal communication. Because of its efficiency and speed, diagonal communication can be beneficial. Increased e-mail use facilitates diagonal communication. In many organizations, any employee can communicate by e-mail with any other employee, regardless of organizational work area or level, even with upper-level managers. In many organizations, CEOs have adopted an "open inbox" e-mail policy. For example, William H. Swanson, head of defense contractor Raytheon Company, figures he has received and answered more than 150,000 employee e-mails. And Henry McKinnell Jr., former CEO of Pfizer, says the approximately 75 internal e-mails he received every day were "an avenue of communication I didn't otherwise have."[25] However, diagonal communication also has the potential to create problems if employees don't keep their managers informed.

diagonal communication
Communication that cuts across work areas and organizational levels

Organizational Communication Networks

The vertical and horizontal flows of organizational communication can be combined into a variety of patterns called **communication networks**. Exhibit 16-4 illustrates three common communication networks.

communication networks
The variety of patterns of vertical and horizontal flows of organizational communication

TYPES OF COMMUNICATION NETWORKS In the *chain* network, communication flows according to the formal chain of command, both downward and upward. The *wheel* network represents communication flowing between a clearly identifiable and strong leader and others in a work group or team. The leader serves as the hub through whom all communication passes. Finally, in the *all-channel* network, communication flows freely among all members of a work team.

Which form of network you should use depends on your goal. Exhibit 16-4 also summarizes each network's effectiveness according to four criteria: speed, accuracy, the probability that a leader will emerge, and the importance of member satisfaction. One observation is immediately apparent: No single network is best for all situations.

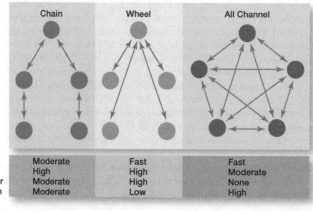

Exhibit 16-4
Organizational Communication Networks

CRITERIA	Chain	Wheel	All Channel
Speed	Moderate	Fast	Fast
Accuracy	High	High	Moderate
Emergence of leader	Moderate	High	None
Member satisfaction	Moderate	Low	High

let's get REAL

The Scenario:

Alexandra Pavlou has a delicate, potentially touchy issue she needs to discuss with her team of real estate appraisers. How can she approach this discussion with care and yet address the issue frankly?

What advice would you give Alexandra?

The discussion should be held in a private setting with all the facts at hand. Alexandra should be prepared to address any concerns as to how this will directly affect each of her team members. Depending on the severity, she should consider individual conversations, instead of a group meeting.

Kelly Osorio
Human Resources Manager

grapevine
The informal organizational communication network

THE GRAPEVINE We can't leave our discussion of communication networks without discussing the **grapevine**—the informal organizational communication network. The grapevine is active in almost every organization. Is it an important source of information? You bet! One survey reported that 63 percent of employees say they hear about important matters first through rumors or gossip on the grapevine.[26]

Certainly, the grapevine is an important part of any communication network and well worth understanding.[27] Acting as both a filter and a feedback mechanism, it pinpoints those bewildering issues that employees consider important. More importantly, from a managerial point of view, it *is* possible to analyze what is happening on the grapevine—what information is being passed, how information seems to flow, and what individuals seem to be key information conduits. By staying aware of the grapevine's flow and patterns, managers can identify issues that concern employees and in turn use the grapevine to disseminate important information. Because the grapevine can't be eliminated, managers should "manage" it as an important information network.

Rumors that flow along the grapevine also can never be eliminated entirely. However, managers can minimize the negative consequences of rumors. How? By communicating openly, fully, and honestly with employees, particularly in situations where employees may not like proposed or actual managerial decisions. Open and honest communication has positive benefits for an organization. A study by Towers Watson concluded that effective communication "connects employees to the business, reinforces the organization's vision, fosters process improvement, facilitates change, and drives business results by changing employee behavior." For those companies with effective communication, total returns to shareholders were 91 percent higher over a five-year period than for companies with less effective communication. This study also showed that companies that were highly effective communicators were four times as likely to report high levels of employee engagement as firms that communicated less effectively.[28]

Workplace Design and Communication

In addition to the direction of communication flow and organizational communication networks, another factor that influences organizational communication is workplace design. Despite all the information technology and associated employee mobility (which we'll discuss in the next section), much of an organization's communication still occurs in the workplace. In fact, some 74 percent of an employee's average workweek is spent in an office.[29] How that office workspace is designed and configured can affect the communication that occurs as well as influence an organization's overall performance. In fact, in a survey of American workers, 90 percent believed that better workplace design and layout result in better overall employee performance.[30]

Research shows that a workplace design should successfully support four types of employee work: focused work, collaboration, learning, and socialization.[31] Focused work is when an employee needs to concentrate on completing a task. In collaboration, employees need to work together to complete a task.

Learning is when employees are engaged in training or doing something new and could involve both focused work and collaboration. And socialization happens when employees informally gather to chat or to exchange ideas. A survey found that when workers had these types of "oases" or informal meeting places nearby, they had 102 percent more face-to-face communication than people who had only minimal access to such spots.[32] Because communication can and does take place in each of these settings, the workplace design needs to accommodate these organizational and interpersonal communications—all directions and all types—in order to be most effective.

As managers design the physical work environment, two common design elements have the greatest impact on communication.[33] First, the enclosures and barriers used in the workspace. Many organizational workplaces today—some 68 percent—are **open workplaces**; that is, they include few physical barriers and enclosures.[34] Research has shown both the merits and the drawbacks of an open workplace.[35] One of the things we know for sure about this type of arrangement and its effect on communication is *visibility*. People in open cubicles placed along main routes of circulation or adjacent to atria reported almost 60 percent more face-to-face communication with team members than did those in lower-visibility locations. Another thing is *density*. More people populating an immediate work area meant that more face-to-face interactions took place. Workspaces with a high density yielded 84 percent more team-member communication than did workspace arrangements with a low density. If it's important that employees communicate and collaborate, managers need to consider visibility and density in workplace design. Another consideration in any open workplace is making sure to have some area where sensitive discussions can take place when needed. For instance, when private personnel matters need to be addressed, those shouldn't take place where interruptions or "eavesdropping" can occur.

Another workplace design element is the availability of adjustable work arrangements, equipment, and furnishings. As organizations have moved toward nontraditional work arrangements, the adjustability and customizability of employee workspace have become essential and influence organizational communication. For instance, one study found that adjustable partitions were associated with both greater perceived privacy and better communication.

As companies shrink workspaces to save money, managers need to ensure that the smaller and generally more open workspaces are useful and contribute to efficient and effective work.[36] By providing workspaces where employees can have some privacy and still have opportunities for collaborative efforts, both interpersonal and organizational communication can flourish and contribute to the organization's overall performance.

Skype's business goal is to break down the barriers to communication by developing technology that is inventive, dependable, easy to use, and affordable. In support of this goal, open workplace designs at Skype's offices throughout the world provide a comfortable and relaxed environment that encourages concentration, productivity, and creativity and in which employees can easily communicate and collaborate with each other. Skype's core development team of engineers and designers work from offices in Tallinn, Estonia, shown here, where informal spaces support focused work, collaboration, learning, and socialization.
Source: Amruth/Caro Fotos/SIPA/Newscom

open workplaces
Workplaces with few physical barriers and enclosures

16.5 *Describe* how
technology affects
managerial
communication and
organizations.

INFORMATION Technology and Communication

Technology is changing the way we live and work. Take the following four examples: Chefs are using digital approaches to solve a kitchen crisis—recipe clutter. Japanese employees, managers, housewives, and teens use wireless interactive Web phones to send e-mail, surf the Web, swap photos, and play computer games. At DreamWorks Animation, a sophisticated videoconferencing system allows animators in three different locations to collaboratively edit films. Several thousand employees at Ford use cell phones exclusively at work. A recent survey of employees showed that 93 percent of those polled use the Internet at work. Employees at Lockheed Martin Corporation can access an internal social media site called Unity, which includes tools such as blogs, wikis, file-sharing, discussion forums, and social bookmarking.[37]

The world of communication isn't what it used to be! Although changing technology has been a significant source of the environmental uncertainty facing organizations, these same technological changes have enabled managers to coordinate employees' work efforts in more efficient and effective ways. Information technology (IT) now touches every aspect of almost every company's business. The implications for the ways managers communicate are profound.

How Technology Affects Managerial Communication

IT has radically changed the way organizational members communicate. For example, it has significantly improved a manager's ability to monitor individual and team performance, has allowed employees to have more complete information to make faster decisions, and has provided employees more opportunities to collaborate and share information. In addition, IT has made it possible for people in organizations to be fully accessible, any time, regardless of where they are. Employees don't have to be at their desk with their computer running to communicate with others in the

FUTURE VISION | Office of Tomorrow

The office of tomorrow is still likely to resemble the office of today. There probably won't be mail delivery by robots on hovercraft nor any teleportation devices. Most of the changes, however, will likely be in the way we communicate.[38] Employees will rely on multiple channels of communication with heavy reliance on social networks, text messaging, and instant messaging. Smartphones will be as powerful as today's mainframes, meaning employees will be able to do heavy computing on the go. Software will be able to track where employees are and blend that data with information about current projects and suggest potential collaborators. E-mail is likely to decline in popularity, largely because other channels are faster, more fluid, and more immediate.

Accurately forecasting tomorrow's technology is impossible. But several patterns seem to be evolving. For instance, the combining of functions in a single device is likely to result in employees having a single product that will combine phone, text messaging, Internet access, video camera, teleconferencing, and language translator. It will allow people to read proposals, legal papers, news, or almost any document digitally. It won't need a keyboard and will operate via voice commands. It's also likely not to be handheld but rather something akin to combining reading glasses and an earpiece. You'll read documents through the lenses of what look like normal reading glasses and the earpiece/microphone will make it hands-free.

Another outcome made possible by technology will be a significant decrease in business travel. Improvements in computer-mediated groupware will allow individuals to conduct meetings in environments that closely simulate face-to-face interactions. In settings where employees use different languages, real-time translations will be transcribed and displayed on screen and teleconferencers will be able to hear and see the words.

organization. Two IT developments that are most significant for managerial communication are networked systems and wireless capabilities.

NETWORKED SYSTEMS   In a networked system, an organization's computers are linked. Organizational members can communicate with each other and tap into information whether they're down the hall, across town, or halfway across the world. We're not looking at the mechanics of how a network system works, but some of its communication applications include e-mail; instant messaging; social media such as blogs, wikis, and Twitter; webinars; voice-mail; fax; teleconferencing and videoconferencing; and intranets.

WIRELESS CAPABILITIES   At Seattle-based Starbucks Corporation, district managers use mobile technology, giving them more time to spend in the company's stores. A company executive says, "These are the most important people in the company. Each has between 8 to 10 stores that he or she services. And while their primary job is outside of the office—and in those stores—they still need to be connected."[39] As this example shows, wireless communication technology has the ability to improve work for managers and employees. Even Internet access is available through Wi-Fi and WiMax hot spots, which are locations where users gain wireless access. The number of these hot spot locations continues to grow. With more than 50 million "mobile" workers in the United States, smartphones, notebook computers, computing devices such as iPad, and other pocket communication devices have generated whole new ways for managers to "keep in touch." And the number of mobile communication users keeps increasing.[40] Employees don't have to be at their desks to communicate with others in the organization. As wireless technology continues to improve, we'll see more organizational members using it as a way to collaborate and share information.

How Information Technology Affects Organizations

Monsanto Company wanted to raise the visibility of some projects and to make a stronger argument for bioengineered crops. Using a YouTube approach, the company sent camera crews to the Philippines, Australia, and other countries to film testimonials from farmers using Monsanto products to grow these crops. The clips were posted on a company Web site, which now attracts more than 15,000 visitors a month. The PR manager in charge of the project said, "When the people involved relate how their life has changed and you actually see it, it's more compelling."[41] That's the power of IT at work. Employees—working in teams or as individuals—need information to make decisions and to do their work. It's clear that technology *can* significantly affect the way that organizational members communicate, share information, and do their work.

IT technology has affected the communication and exchange of information among doctors, medical staff, and patients by removing the constraints of geography and time. Shown here is Doctor Nir Cohen working on his Apple iPad before visiting a patient at the Mayanei Hayeshua Medical Center in Bnei Brak, Israel. Using iPads enables Dr. Cohen and his medical staff to check patients' records, test results, and other medical information; to study high-resolution X-rays and CT scans from both within and outside the hospital; and to diagnose and prescribe treatment immediately at any time.
Source: Reuters/Nir Elias

Communication and the exchange of information among organizational members are no longer constrained by geography or time. Collaborative work efforts among widely dispersed individuals and teams, sharing of information, and integration of decisions and work throughout an entire organization have the potential to increase organizational efficiency and effectiveness. And while the economic benefits of IT are obvious, managers must not forget the psychological drawbacks.[42] For instance, what is the psychological cost of an employee always being accessible? Will it lead to increased pressure for employees to "check in" even during their off hours? How important is it for employees to separate their work and personal lives? These questions don't come with easy answers, and managers will have to face these and similar issues.

16.6 *Discuss*
contemporary issues in
communication.

COMMUNICATION Issues in Today's Organizations

"Pulse lunches." That's what managers at Citibank's offices throughout Malaysia used to address pressing problems of declining customer loyalty and staff morale and increased employee turnover. By connecting with employees and listening to their concerns—that is, taking their "pulse"—during informal lunch settings, managers were able to make changes that boosted both customer loyalty and employee morale by more than 50 percent and reduced employee turnover to nearly zero.[43]

Being an effective communicator in today's organizations means being connected—not only to employees and customers, but to any of the organization's stakeholders. In this section, we examine five communication issues of particular significance to today's managers: managing communication in an Internet world, managing the organization's knowledge resources, communicating with customers, getting employee input, and communicating ethically.

Managing Communication in an Internet World

Lars Dalgaard, founder and chief executive of SuccessFactors, a human resource management software company, recently sent an e-mail to his employees banning in-house e-mail for a week. His goal? Getting employees to "authentically address issues amongst each other."[44] And he's not alone. Other companies have tried the same thing. (See Case Application 1 at the end of the chapter.) As we discussed earlier, e-mail can consume employees, but it's not always easy for them to let go of it, even when they know it can be "intexticating." But e-mail is only one communication challenge in this Internet world. A recent survey found that 20 percent of employees at large companies say they contribute regularly to blogs, social networks, wikis, and other Web services.[45] Managers are learning, the hard way sometimes, that all this new technology has created special communication challenges. The two main ones are (1) legal and security issues, and (2) lack of personal interaction.

LEGAL AND SECURITY ISSUES Chevron paid $2.2 million to settle a sexual-harassment lawsuit stemming from inappropriate jokes being sent by employees over company e-mail. U.K. firm Norwich Union had to pay £450,000 in an out-of-court settlement after an employee sent an e-mail stating that their competitor Western Provident Association was experiencing financial difficulties. Whole Foods Market was investigated by federal regulators and its board after CEO John P. Mackey used a pseudonym to post comments on a blog attacking the company's rival Wild Oats Markets.[46]

Although e-mail, blogs, tweets, and other forms of online communication are quick and easy ways to communicate, managers need to be aware of potential legal problems from inappropriate usage. Electronic information is potentially admissible in court. For instance, during the Enron trial, prosecutors entered into evidence e-mails and other documents they say showed that the defendants defrauded investors. Says one expert, "Today, e-mail and instant messaging are the electronic equivalent of DNA evidence."[47] But legal problems aren't the only issue—security concerns are as well.

A survey addressing outbound e-mail and content security found that 26 percent of the companies surveyed saw their businesses affected by the exposure of sensitive or embarrassing information.[48] Managers need to ensure that confidential information is kept confidential. Employee e-mails and blogs should not communicate—inadvertently or purposely—proprietary information. Corporate computer and e-mail systems should be protected against hackers (people who try to gain unauthorized access) and spam (electronic junk mail). These serious issues must be addressed if the benefits of communication technology are to be realized.

PERSONAL INTERACTION   It may be called social media, but another communication challenge posed by the Internet age we live and work in is the lack of personal interaction.[49] Even when two people are communicating face-to-face, understanding is not always achieved. However, it can be especially challenging to achieve understanding and collaborate on getting work done when communication takes place in a virtual environment. In response, some companies have banned e-mail on certain days, as we saw earlier. Others have simply encouraged employees to collaborate more in-person. Yet, in some situations and at certain times, personal interaction isn't physically possible—your colleagues work across the continent or even across the globe. In those instances, real-time collaboration software (such as private workplace wikis, blogs, instant messengers, and other types of groupware) may be a better communication choice than sending an e-mail and waiting for a response.[50] Instead of fighting it, other companies are encouraging employees to utilize the power of social networks to collaborate on work and to build strong connections. This form of interaction is especially appealing to younger workers who are comfortable with this communication medium. Some companies have gone as far as creating their own in-house social networks. For instance, employees at Starcom MediaVest Group tap into SMG Connected to find colleague profiles that outline their jobs, list the brands they admire, and describe their values. A company vice president says, "Giving our employees a way to connect over the Internet around the world made sense because they were doing it anyway."[51]

Managing the Organization's Knowledge Resources

Kara Johnson is a materials expert at product design firm IDEO. To make finding the right materials easier, she's building a master library of samples linked to a database that explains their properties and manufacturing processes.[52] What Johnson is doing is managing knowledge and making it easier for others at IDEO to learn and benefit from her knowledge. That's what today's managers need to do with the organization's knowledge resources—make it easy for employees to communicate and share their knowledge so they can learn from each other ways to do their jobs more effectively and efficiently. One way organizations can do this is to build online information databases that employees can access. For example, William Wrigley Jr. Co. launched an interactive Web site that allows sales agents to access marketing data and other product information. The sales agents can question company experts about products or search an online knowledge bank. In its first year, Wrigley estimates that the site cut research time of the sales force by 15,000 hours, making them more efficient and effective.[53]

In addition to online information databases for sharing knowledge, companies could create communities of practice, a concept that we introduced in Chapter 12, as a type of internal collaboration. To make these communities of practice work, however, it's important to maintain strong human interactions through communication using such essential tools as interactive Web sites, e-mail, and videoconferencing. In addition, these groups face the same communication problems that individuals face—filtering, emotions, defensiveness, overdocumentation, and so forth. However, groups can resolve these issues by focusing on the same suggestions we discussed earlier.

The Role of Communication in Customer Service

You've been a customer many times; in fact, you probably find yourself in a customer service encounter several times a day. So what does this have to do with communication? As it turns out, a lot! *What* communication takes place and *how* it takes place can have a significant impact on a customer's satisfaction with the service and the likelihood of being a repeat customer. Managers in service organizations need to make sure that employees who interact with customers are communicating appropriately and effectively with those customers. How? By first recognizing the three components in any service delivery process: the customer, the service organization, and the individual service provider.[54] Each plays a role in whether communication is

datapoints[55]

53 percent of companies have a policy for managing employees' use of social media.

176 square feet is now the average office space per workers. In 2010, it was 225 square feet; in 2017, it's forecasted to be 151 square feet.

70 percent of executives ranked in-person meetings as most valuable for an initial interaction with a new team member.

83 percent of employers use e-mail to engage employees and foster productivity; 75 percent use their organization's intranet to do so.

45 percent of North American workers use their mobile devices during lunch; 44 percent use it before going to work.

38 percent of employees have a negative view of workers with a messy desk.

15 percent of employees say that if there were no consequences, they'd say to their boss that they need a chance to express their ideas.

28 percent of survey respondents said that phone calls were the most common workplace distraction; 23 percent cited e-mails.

1 of every 7 communications by managers is redundant with a previous communication using a different technology.

No. 1 form of evidence in any employment law dispute is . . . e-mail.

44 percent of the time, e-mails are misinterpreted.

working. Obviously, managers don't have a lot of control over what or how the customer communicates, but they can influence the other two.

An organization with a strong service culture already values taking care of customers—finding out what their needs are, meeting those needs, and following up to make sure that their needs were met satisfactorily. Each of these activities involves communication, whether face-to-face, by phone or e-mail, or through other channels. In addition, communication is part of the specific customer service strategies the organization pursues. One strategy that many service organizations use is personalization. For instance, at Ritz-Carlton Hotels, customers are provided with more than a clean bed and room. Customers who have stayed at a location previously and indicated that certain items are important to them—such as extra pillows, hot chocolate, or a certain brand of shampoo—will find those items waiting in their room at arrival. The hotel's database allows service to be personalized to customers' expectations. In addition, all employees are asked to communicate information related to service provision. For instance, if a room attendant overhears guests talking about celebrating an anniversary, he or she is supposed to relay the information so something special can be done.[56] Communication plays an important role in the hotel's customer personalization strategy.

Communication also is important to the individual service provider or contact employee. The quality of the interpersonal interaction between the customer and that contact employee does influence customer satisfaction, especially when the service encounter isn't up to expectations.[57] People on the front line involved with those "critical service encounters" are often the first to hear about or notice service failures or breakdowns. They must decide *how* and *what* to communicate during these instances. Their ability to listen actively and communicate appropriately with the customer goes a long way in whether the situation is resolved to the customer's satisfaction or spirals out of control. Another important communication concern for the individual service provider is making sure that he or she has the information needed to deal with customers efficiently and effectively. If the service provider doesn't personally have the information, some way needs to be devised to get the information easily and promptly.[58]

The opinions and ideas of employees are valued by sisters Jenny Briones (left) and Lisa De Bono (right), who, along with their mother, are owner-operators of nine McDonald's restaurants. Communication plays a big part in the growth and success of the family business. Jenny and Lisa engender trust and respect among their managers, employees, and customers by frequently visiting restaurants and encouraging everyone to voice their opinions and share information that will improve their business. In this photo, they seek out feedback from one of their managers about a new incentive plan for their restaurant crew members.
Source: ZUMA Press/Newscom

Getting Employee Input

Nokia recently set up an intranet soapbox known as Blog-Hub, opening it up to employee bloggers around the world. There, employees have griped about their employer, but rather than shutting it down, Nokia managers want them to "fire away." They feel that Nokia's growth and success can be attributed to a "history of encouraging employees to say whatever's on their minds, with faith that smarter ideas will result."[59]

In today's challenging environment, companies need to get input from their employees. Have you ever worked somewhere that had an employee suggestion box? When an employee had an idea about a new way of doing something—such as reducing costs, improving delivery time, and so forth—it went into the suggestion box where it usually sat until someone decided to empty the box. Businesspeople frequently joked about the suggestion box, and cartoonists lambasted the futility of putting ideas in the employee suggestion box. And unfortunately, this attitude about suggestion boxes still persists in many organizations, and it shouldn't. Managers do business in a world today where you can't afford to ignore such potentially valuable information. Exhibit 16-5 lists some suggestions for letting employees know that their opinions matter.

Exhibit 16-5
How to Let Employees Know Their
Input Matters

- *Hold town-hall meetings* where information is shared and input solicited.
- *Provide information* about what's going on, good and bad.
- *Invest in training* so that employees see how they impact the customer experience.
- *Analyze problems together*—managers and employees.
- *Make it easy* for employees to give input by setting up different ways for them to do so (online, suggestion box, preprinted cards, and so forth).

Communicating Ethically

It's particularly important today that a company's communication efforts be ethical. **Ethical communication** "includes all relevant information, is true in every sense, and is not deceptive in any way."[60] On the other hand, unethical communication often distorts the truth or manipulates audiences. What are some ways that companies communicate unethically? It could be by omitting essential information. For instance, not telling employees that an impending merger is going to mean some of them will lose their jobs is unethical. It's unethical to plagiarize, which is "presenting someone else's words or other creative product as your own."[61] It would also be unethical communication to selectively misquote, misrepresent numbers, distort visuals, and fail to respect privacy or information security needs. For instance, although British Petroleum attempted to communicate openly and truthfully about the Gulf Coast oil spill in the summer of 2010, the public still felt that much of the company's communication contained some unethical elements.

So how can managers encourage ethical communications? One thing is to "establish clear guidelines for ethical behavior, including ethical business communication.[62] In a global survey by the International Association of Business Communicators, 70 percent of communication professionals said their companies clearly define what is considered ethical and unethical behavior."[63] If no clear guidelines exist, it's important to answer the following questions:

- Has the situation been defined fairly and accurately?
- Why is the message being communicated?
- How will the people who may be affected by the message or who receive the message be impacted?
- Does the message help achieve the greatest possible good while minimizing possible harm?
- Will this decision that appears to be ethical now seem so in the future?
- How comfortable are you with your communication effort? What would a person you admire think of it?[64]

Remember that as a manager, you have a responsibility to think through your communication choices and the consequences of those choices. If you always operate with these two things in mind, you're likely to have ethical communication.

ethical communication
Communication that includes all relevant information, is true in every sense, and is not deceptive in any way

CHAPTER

PREPARING FOR: Exams/Quizzes
CHAPTER SUMMARY by Learning Outcomes

16.1 | LEARNING OUTCOME |

Define the nature and function of communication.

Communication is the transfer and understanding of meaning. Interpersonal communication is communication between two or more people. Organizational communication includes all the patterns, networks, and systems of communication within an organization.

The functions of communication include controlling employee behavior, motivating employees, providing a release for emotional expression of feelings and fulfillment of social needs, and providing information.

16.2 | LEARNING OUTCOME |

Compare and contrast methods of interpersonal communication.

The communication process contains seven elements. First, a *sender* has a message. A *message* is a purpose to be conveyed. *Encoding* converts a message into symbols. A *channel* is the medium a message travels along. *Decoding* happens when the *receiver* retranslates a sender's message. Finally, *feedback* occurs.

Managers can evaluate the various communication methods according to their feedback, complexity capacity, breadth potential, confidentiality, encoding ease, decoding ease, time-space constraint, cost, interpersonal warmth, formality, scanability, and time of consumption.

The communication methods include face-to-face, telephone, group meetings, formal presentations, memos, traditional mail, fax, employee publications, bulletin boards, other company publications, audio- and videotapes, hotlines, e-mail, computer conferencing, voice mail, teleconferences, and videoconferences.

16.3 | LEARNING OUTCOME |

Identify barriers to effective interpersonal communication and how to overcome them.

The barriers to effective communication include filtering, emotions, information overload, defensiveness, language, and national culture.

Managers can overcome these barriers by using feedback, simplifying language, listening actively, constraining emotions, and watching for nonverbal clues.

16.4 | LEARNING OUTCOME |

Explain how communication can flow most effectively in organizations.

Formal communication is communication that takes place within prescribed organizational work arrangements. Informal communication is not defined by the organization's structural hierarchy.

Communication in an organization can flow downward, upward, laterally, and diagonally.

The three communication networks include the chain, in which communication flows according to the formal chain of command; the wheel, in which communication flows between a clearly identifiable and strong leader and others in a work team; and the all-channel, in which communication flows freely among all members of a work team.

Managers should manage the grapevine as an important information network. The negative consequences of rumors can be minimized by communicating openly, fully, and honestly with employees.

Workplace design also influences organizational communication. That design should support four types of employee work: focused work, collaboration, learning, and socialization. In each of these circumstances, communication must be considered.

16.5 [LEARNING OUTCOME]   **Describe** how technology affects managerial communication and organizations.

Technology has radically changed the way organizational members communicate. It improves a manager's ability to monitor performance; it gives employees more complete information to make faster decisions; it has provided employees more opportunities to collaborate and share information; and it has made it possible for people to be fully accessible, anytime anywhere.

IT affects organizations by influencing the way that organizational members communicate, share information, and do their work.

16.6 [LEARNING OUTCOME]   **Discuss** contemporary issues in communication.

The two main challenges of managing communication in an Internet world are the legal and security issues and the lack of personal interaction.

Organizations can manage knowledge by making it easy for employees to communicate and share their knowledge, which can help them learn from each other ways to do their jobs more effectively and efficiently. One way is through online information databases and another way is through creating communities of practice.

Communicating with customers is an important managerial issue since *what* communication takes place and *how* it takes place can significantly affect a customer's satisfaction with the service and the likelihood of being a repeat customer.

It's important for organizations to get input from their employees. Such potentially valuable information should not be ignored.

Finally, a company's communication efforts need to be ethical. Ethical communication can be encouraged through clear guidelines and through answering questions that force a communicator to think through the communication choices made and the consequences of those choices.

REVIEW AND DISCUSSION QUESTIONS ✪

1. Define communication, interpersonal communication, and organizational communication. Why isn't effective communication synonymous with *agreement?*

2. What are the functions of communication?

3. Explain the components in the communication process.

4. What are the various communication methods managers can use? What criteria can managers use to evaluate those communication methods?

5. Contrast formal and informal communication.

6. Explain communication flow, the three common communication networks, and how managers should handle the grapevine.

7. Discuss the five contemporary communication issues facing managers.

8. Which do you think is more important for a manager: speaking accurately or listening actively? Why?

PREPARING FOR: My Career
ETHICS DILEMMA ✪

Social networking Web sites can be fun. Staying in touch with old friends or even family is one of the pleasures of joining. However, what happens when colleagues or even your boss want to "friend" you? Experts say that you should proceed with caution.[65] What do you think? Is it okay to provide people you know in a professional sense a "window into your personal life?" What ethical issues might arise in such a situation?

SKILLS EXERCISE Developing Your Active Listening Skill

About the Skill

Active listening requires you to concentrate on what is being said. It's more than just hearing the words. It involves a concerted effort to understand and interpret the speaker's message.

Steps in Practicing the Skill

1. *Make eye contact.* How do you feel when somebody doesn't look at you when you're speaking? If you're like most people, you're likely to interpret this behavior as aloofness or disinterest. Making eye contact with the speaker focuses your attention, reduces the likelihood that you will become distracted, and encourages the speaker.

2. *Exhibit affirmative nods and appropriate facial expressions.* The effective listener shows interest in what is being said through nonverbal signals. Affirmative nods and appropriate facial expressions, when added to good eye contact, convey to the speaker that you're listening.

3. *Avoid distracting actions or gestures that suggest boredom.* In addition to showing interest, you must avoid actions that suggest that your mind is somewhere else. When listening, don't look at your watch, shuffle papers, play with your pencil, or engage in similar distractions. They make the speaker feel that you're bored or disinterested or indicate that you aren't fully attentive.

4. *Ask questions.* The critical listener analyzes what he or she hears and asks questions. This behavior provides clarification, ensures understanding, and assures the speaker that you're listening.

5. *Paraphrase what's been said.* The effective listener uses phrases such as "What I hear you saying is…" or "Do you mean…?" Paraphrasing is an excellent control device to check on whether you're listening carefully and to verify that what you heard is accurate.

6. *Avoid interrupting the speaker.* Let the speaker complete his or her thought before you try to respond. Don't try to second-guess where the speaker's thoughts are going. When the speaker is finished, you'll know it.

7. *Stay motivated to listen.* Most of us would rather express our own ideas than listen to what someone else says. Talking might be more fun and silence might be uncomfortable, but you can't talk and listen at the same time. The good listener recognizes this fact and doesn't overtalk.

8. *Make smooth transitions between the roles of speaker and listener.* The effective listener makes transitions smoothly from speaker to listener and back to speaker. From a listening perspective, this means concentrating on what a speaker has to say and practicing not thinking about what you're going to say as soon as you get your chance.

Practicing the Skill

Ask a friend to tell you about his or her day and listen without interrupting. When your friend has finished speaking, ask two or three questions if needed to obtain more clarity and detail. Listen carefully to the answers. Now summarize your friend's day in no more than five sentences.

How well did you do? Let your friend rate the accuracy of your paraphrase (and try not to interrupt).

WORKING TOGETHER Team Exercise

We've all watched and laughed at the oddball videos on YouTube and other online video sites. But what about using online video for work purposes?[66] What uses do you see for online video at work? What would be the advantages and drawbacks of using online video?

Form small groups of three to four individuals. Your team's task is to look at these issues. Answer the questions and be prepared to share your answers with the class.

MY TURN TO BE A MANAGER

- Research the characteristics of a good communicator. Keeping these characteristics in mind, practice being a good communicator—both as a sender and a listener.

- For one day, keep track of the types of communication you use (see Exhibit 16-2 for a list of various types). Which do you use most? Least? Were your choices of communication methods effective? Why or why not? Could they have been improved? How?

- For one day, track nonverbal communication that you notice in others. What types did you observe? Was the nonverbal communication always consistent with the verbal communication taking place? Describe.

- Research new types of IT devices. Write a report describing these devices (at least three) and their applicability to employees and organizations. Be sure to look at both the positive and negative aspects.

- Survey five different managers for their advice on being a good communicator. Put this information in a bulleted list format and be prepared to present it in class.

- Steve's and Mary's recommended readings: Phillip G. Clampitt, *Communicating for Managerial Effectiveness,* 4th ed. (Sage Publications, 2009); John Baldoni, *Great Communication Secrets of Great Leaders* (McGraw-Hill, 2003); Robert Mai and Alan Akerson, *The Leader as Communicator* (AMACOM, 2003); Boyd Clarke, *The Leader's Voice: How Communication Can Inspire Action and Get Results!* (Select Books, 2002); Jo-Ellan Dimitrius and Mark Mazzarella, *Reading People* (Random House, 1998).

- Survey 10 office workers. Ask them: (1) the number of e-mail messages they receive daily, on average; (2) how many times in one day they check their e-mail; and (3) if they think a ban on e-mail messages one day a week would be a good idea and why or why not. Compile this information into a report.

- Pick one of the five topics addressed in the section on Communication Issues in Today's Organizations and do some additional research. Put your findings in a bulleted list and be prepared to discuss in class. Be sure to cite your sources!

- In your own words, write down three things you learned in this chapter about being a good manager.

- Self-knowledge can be a powerful learning tool. Go to www.mymanagementlab.com and complete these self-assessment exercises: What's My Face-to-Face Communication Style? How Good Are My Listening Skills? How Good Am I at Giving Performance Feedback? Am I a Gossip? Using the results of your assessments, identify personal strengths and weaknesses. What will you do to reinforce your strengths and improve your weaknesses?

CASE APPLICATION 1 E-Mail Ban

Believing that most internal e-mail messages are a waste of employees' time and wanting to work with the tools that the young generation is using, Atos CEO Thierry Breton has banned internal e-mails and is replacing them with communication tools that include social networks like Facebook, instant messaging, and microblogging.
Source: Sipa via AP Images

It's estimated that the average corporate user sends and received some 112 e-mails daily.[67] That's about 14 e-mails per hour and even if half of those don't require a lot of time and concentration, that level of e-mail volume can be stressful and lead to unproductive time. Once imagined to be a time-saver, has the inbox become a burden? Back in 2007, U.S. Cellular's executive vice president, Jay Ellison (who has since retired) implemented a ban on e-mail every Friday. In his memo announcing the change to employees, he told them to get out and meet the people they work with rather than sending an e-mail. That directive went over with a thud. One employee confronted him saying that Ellison didn't understand how much work had to get done and how much easier it was when using e-mail. Eventually, however, employees were won over. Forced to use the phone, one employee learned that a co-worker he thought was across the country, was instead, across the hall. Now, in 2012, other executives are discovering the benefits of banning e-mail.

Jessica Rovello, co-founder and president of Arkadium, which develops games, has described e-mail as "a form of business attention-deficit disorder." She found herself—and her employees—putting e-mail in the inbox ahead of everything else being worked on. What she decided to do was only check her e-mail four times a day and to turn off her e-mail notification. Another executive, Tim Fry of Weber Shandwick, a global public relations firm, spent a year preparing to "wean" his employees off their e-mail system. His goal: dramatically reduce how much e-mail employees send and receive. His approach started with the firm's interoffice communication system, which became an internal social network, with elements of Facebook, work group collaboration software, and an employee bulletin board. And then there's Thierry Breton, head of Europe's largest IT firm, Atos. He announced a "zero e-mail policy" to be replaced with a service more like Facebook and Twitter combined.

DISCUSSION QUESTIONS ✪

1. What do you think of this? Do you agree that e-mail can be unproductive in the workplace?
2. Were you surprised at the volume of e-mail an average employee receives daily? What are the challenges of dealing with this volume of e-mail? How much e-mail would you say you receive daily? Has your volume of e-mail increased? Have your had to change your e-mail habits?
3. What do you think of the e-mail "replacement" some businesses are using—more of a social media tool? In what ways might it be better? Worse?
4. What implications can you see for managers and communication from this story?

CASE APPLICATION 2 Neutralizing the Concordia Effect!

Communication has become crucial in Costa Cruises (the Italian cruise company owned by Carnival Corporation). In recent events, the *Costa Concordia* keeled over off the Italian coast near the island of Giglio in Tuscany, Italy, in January 2012 and the *Costa Allegra* was hit by fire and drifts in the Indian Ocean a few weeks later. Captain Schettino's preliminary abandoning of the *Costa Concordia* as well as his denial to return onboard the sinking ship brought into question the competence of the company crew as well as the effectiveness of recruitment procedures. After a few days of the company stressing that the complete responsibilities of the accident were attributed to the captain, Costa Cruises decided to suspend all social media activities as a sign of respect for the victims and as an attempt to prevent inappropriate comments.

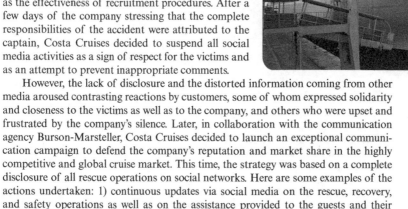

However, the lack of disclosure and the distorted information coming from other media aroused contrasting reactions by customers, some of whom expressed solidarity and closeness to the victims as well as to the company, and others who were upset and frustrated by the company's silence. Later, in collaboration with the communication agency Burson-Marsteller, Costa Cruises decided to launch an exceptional communication campaign to defend the company's reputation and market share in the highly competitive and global cruise market. This time, the strategy was based on a complete disclosure of all rescue operations on social networks. Here are some examples of the actions undertaken: 1) continuous updates via social media on the rescue, recovery, and safety operations as well as on the assistance provided to the guests and their families in order to document the status of relief efforts; 2) information on the strategy for the removal of the wreck; 3) the reduction of the environmental impact of the accident; and 4) diligent communication of the protection of the island's eco-system (seriously threatened by heavy fuel oil).

Costa Cruises was heavily criticized in the wake of the two disasters for its lack of transparent communication but with the help of a communication agency launched a campaign to defend the company.
Source: Vega Gonzalez/Shutterstock.com

The news of a friendly and successful negotiation for settling the initial compensation package for passengers of the shipwreck was promptly communicated with official press releases. The announcement of new safety measures was given during a ceremony celebrating the delivery of the company's new $665 million flagship *Costa Fascinosa*. Indeed, the number of bookings reserved four months later, showing an increase of 25 percent from what they were at the same time the year before was a big sigh of relief for Costa Cruises' executives.[68]

DISCUSSION QUESTIONS ✪

1. Beyond possible human error and tragedy responsibilities, what do you think of this situation from the perspective of managing communications?

2. Why do you think the company's executives decided to silence communication on social media? Was this an appropriate strategy?

3. In the first weeks, how could the communication have been better managed by the management?

4. The increase in the number of bookings seems to corroborate the success of the latter communication strategy of a complete disclosure on social media. Discuss the communication management implications.

This case is written by Marcello Russo, Assistant Professor, Rouen Business School, France.

Leadership

SPOTLIGHT: *Manager at Work*

A lot has been written about the late Steve Jobs.[1]
How he took Apple, a niche business, and turned it into the most valuable company in the world as measured by market capitalization. How he was extremely charismatic and extremely compelling in getting people to join with him and believe in his vision. But also how he was despotic, tyrannical, abrasive, uncompromising, and a perfectionist. So what is his leadership legacy?

Everything Jobs did and how he did it was motivated by his desire to have Apple make innovative products—products that were "insanely great"— "insanely" being one of his favorite descriptors. That singular focus shaped his leadership style which has been described as autocratic and yet persuasive. As one reporter said, Jobs "violated every rule of management. He was not a consensus builder but a dictator who listened mainly to his own intuition. He was a maniacal micromanager...He could be absolutely brutal in meetings." His verbal assaults on staff could be terrifying. The story is told that when Apple launched its first version of the iPhone that worked on 3G mobile networks, it included MobileMe, an email system that was supposed to provide seamless synchronization features similar to that used by the fanatical corporate users of Blackberrys. The problem: It didn't work well at all, and product reviews were quite critical. Since "Steve Jobs doesn't tolerate duds," it wasn't long after the launch that he gathered the MobileMe team in an auditorium on Apple's campus. According to a participant in that meeting, Jobs walked in—in his trademark black mock turtleneck and jeans—and "asked a simple

Source: © ZUMA Wire Service/Alamy

Source: Paul Sakuma/AP Photo

question: 'Can you tell me what MobileMe
is supposed to do?' Having received a
satisfactory answer, he responded, 'So
why the @#$% doesn't it do that?'" Then,
for the next 30 minutes, Jobs blasted
criticisms at the team. "You've tarnished
Apple's reputation. You should hate each

What is Steve Jobs' leadership legacy?

other for having let each other down."
Ouch. And this wasn't the only example
of his taking employees to task. He was
tough on the people around him. When
asked about his tendency to be rough
on people, Jobs responded, "Look at the
results. These are all smart people I work
with, and any of them could get a top job
at another place if they were truly feeling
brutalized. But they don't."

On the other hand, Steve Jobs could
be thoughtful, passionate, and "insanely"
charismatic. He could "push people
to do the impossible." And there's no
argument with the fact that the results
from the company he co-founded have
been market-changing. From the Macs and
iPods to the iPhones and iPads, Apple's
products have revolutionized industries
and created a fan base of consumers who

MyManagementLab®
⭐ **Improve Your Grade!**
Over 10 million students improved their results using the Pearson MyLabs.
Visit **www.mymanagementlab.com** for simulations, tutorials, and end-of-chapter problems.

LEARNING OUTCOMES

18.1 | ***Define*** *leader and leadership.*

18.2 | ***Compare*** *and contrast early theories of leadership.*

18.3 | ***Describe*** *the three major contingency theories of leadership.*

18.4 | ***Describe*** *contemporary views of leadership.*

18.5 | ***Discuss*** *contemporary issues affecting leadership.*

are very loyal to the Apple brand and employees who are very loyal to the company. **Would Steve Jobs' leadership approach work for others? What do you think?**

Steve Jobs of Apple provides a fascinating example of the what's and how's of leadership. His leadership approach and style is totally not what you'd read about in most books on leadership. Yet, how he led Apple probably wouldn't work in all situations, if any others. But leadership *is* needed in all organizations. Why? Because it's the leaders in organizations who make things happen.

<table><tr><td>18.1</td><td>**Define** leader and leadership.</td></tr></table>

leader
Someone who can influence others and who has managerial authority

leadership
A process of influencing a group to achieve goals

WHO Are Leaders and What Is Leadership?

Let's begin by clarifying who leaders are and what leadership is. Our definition of a **leader** is someone who can influence others and who has managerial authority. **Leadership** is a process of leading a group and influencing that group to achieve its goals. It's what leaders do.

Are all managers leaders? Because leading is one of the four management functions, yes, ideally, all managers *should* be leaders. Thus, we're going to study leaders and leadership from a managerial perspective.[2] However, even though we're looking at these from a managerial perspective, we're aware that groups often have informal leaders who emerge. Although these informal leaders may be able to influence others, they have not been the focus of most leadership research and are not the types of leaders we're studying in this chapter.

Leaders and leadership, like motivation, are organizational behavior topics that have been researched a lot. Most of that research has been aimed at answering the question: *What is an effective leader?* We'll begin our study of leadership by looking at some early leadership theories that attempted to answer that question.

<table><tr><td>18.2</td><td>**Compare** and contrast early theories of leadership.</td></tr></table>

EARLY Leadership Theories

People have been interested in leadership since they started coming together in groups to accomplish goals. However, it wasn't until the early part of the twentieth century that researchers actually began to study leadership. These early leadership theories focused on the *leader* (leadership trait theories) and how the *leader interacted* with his or her group members (leadership behavior theories).

Leadership Trait Theories

Researchers at the University of Cambridge in England recently reported that men with longer ring fingers, compared to their index fingers, tended to be more successful in the frantic high-frequency trading in the London financial district.[3] What does a study of the finger lengths of financial traders have to do with trait theories of leadership? Well, that's also what leadership trait theories have attempted to do—identify certain traits that all leaders have.

Leadership research in the 1920s and 1930s focused on isolating leader traits—that is, characteristics—that would differentiate leaders from nonleaders. Some of the traits studied included physical stature, appearance, social class, emotional stability, fluency of speech, and sociability. Despite the best efforts of researchers, it proved impossible to identify a set of traits that would *always* differentiate a leader (the person) from a nonleader. Maybe it was a bit optimistic to think that a set of consistent and unique traits would apply universally to all effective leaders, no matter whether they were in charge of Mondelez International (formerly Kraft Foods), the Moscow Ballet, the country of France, a local collegiate chapter of Alpha Chi Omega, Ted's Malibu Surf Shop, or Oxford University. However, later attempts to identify traits consistently associated with

Exhibit 18-1
Eight Traits Associated with
Leadership

1. *Drive.* Leaders exhibit a high effort level. They have a relatively high desire for achievement, they are ambitious, they have a lot of energy, they are tirelessly persistent in their activities, and they show initiative.

2. *Desire to lead.* Leaders have a strong desire to influence and lead others. They demonstrate the willingness to take responsibility.

3. *Honesty and integrity.* Leaders build trusting relationships with followers by being truthful or nondeceitful and by showing high consistency between word and deed.

4. *Self-confidence.* Followers look to leaders for an absence of self-doubt. Leaders, therefore, need to show self-confidence in order to convince followers of the rightness of their goals and decisions.

5. *Intelligence.* Leaders need to be intelligent enough to gather, synthesize, and interpret large amounts of information, and they need to be able to create visions, solve problems, and make correct decisions.

6. *Job-relevant knowledge.* Effective leaders have a high degree of knowledge about the company, industry, and technical matters. In-depth knowledge allows leaders to make well-informed decisions and to understand the implications of those decisions.

7. *Extraversion.* Leaders are energetic, lively people. They are sociable, assertive, and rarely silent or withdrawn.

8. *Proneness to guilt.* Guilt proneness is positively related to leadership effectiveness because it produces a strong sense of responsibility for others.

Sources: Based on S. A. Kirkpatrick and E. A. Locke, "Leadership: Do Traits Really Matter?" *Academy of Management Executive,* May 1991, pp. 48–60; T. A. Judge, J. E. Bono, R. Ilies, and M. W. Gerhardt, "Personality and Leadership: A Qualitative and Quantitative Review," *Journal of Applied Psychology,* August 2002, pp. 765–780; and R. L. Schaumberg and F. J. Flynn, "Uneasy Lies the Head That Wears the Crown: The Link Between Guilt Proneness and Leadership," *Journal of Personality and Social Psychology,* August 2012, pp. 327–342.

leadership (the process of leading, not the person) were more successful. The eight traits shown to be associated with effective leadership are described briefly in Exhibit 18-1.[4]

Researchers eventually recognized that traits alone were not sufficient for identifying effective leaders since explanations based solely on traits ignored the interactions of leaders and their group members as well as situational factors. Possessing the appropriate traits only made it more likely that an individual would be an effective leader. Therefore, leadership research from the late 1940s to the mid-1960s concentrated on the preferred behavioral styles that leaders demonstrated. Researchers wondered whether something unique in what effective leaders *did*—in other words, in their *behavior*—was the key.

Leadership Behavior Theories

Bill Watkins, former CEO of disk drive manufacturer Seagate Technology, once responded when asked how he handled his board of directors, "You never ask board members what they think. You tell them what you're going to do." In contrast, Joe Lee, CEO of Darden Restaurants during the aftermath of 9/11, was focused on only two things that morning: his Darden people who were traveling and his company's Muslim colleagues.[5] These two leaders of successful companies, as you can see, behaved in two very different ways. What do we know about leader behavior and how can it help us in our understanding of what an effective leader is?

Researchers hoped that the **behavioral theories** approach would provide more definitive answers about the nature of leadership than did the trait theories.[6] The four main leader behavior studies are summarized in Exhibit 18-2.

UNIVERSITY OF IOWA STUDIES The University of Iowa studies explored three leadership styles to find which was the most effective.[7] The **autocratic style** described

behavioral theories
Leadership theories that identify behaviors that differentiated effective leaders from ineffective leaders

autocratic style
A leader who dictates work methods, makes unilateral decisions, and limits employee participation

Exhibit 18-2
Behavioral Theories of Leadership

		Behavioral Dimension	Conclusion
	University of Iowa	*Democratic style:* involving subordinates, delegating authority, and encouraging participation	Democratic style of leadership was most effective, although later studies showed mixed results.
		Autocratic style: dictating work methods, centralizing decision making, and limiting participation	
		Laissez-faire style: giving group freedom to make decisions and complete work	
	Ohio State	*Consideration:* being considerate of followers' ideas and feelings	High–high leader (high in consideration and high in initiating structure) achieved high subordinate performance and satisfaction, but not in all situations
		Initiating structure: structuring work and work relationships to meet job goals	
	University of Michigan	*Employee oriented:* emphasized interpersonal relationships and taking care of employees' needs	Employee-oriented leaders were associated with high group productivity and higher job satisfaction.
		Production oriented: emphasized technical or task aspects of job	
	Managerial Grid	*Concern for people:* measured leader's concern for subordinates on a scale of 1 to 9 (low to high)	Leaders performed best with a 9,9 style (high concern for production and high concern for people).
		Concern for production: measured leader's concern for getting job done on a scale 1 to 9 (low to high)	

democratic style
A leader who involves employees in decision making, delegates authority, and uses feedback as an opportunity for coaching employees

laissez-faire style
A leader who lets the group make decisions and complete the work in whatever way it sees fit

a leader who dictated work methods, made unilateral decisions, and limited employee participation. The **democratic style** described a leader who involved employees in decision making, delegated authority, and used feedback as an opportunity for coaching employees. Finally, the **laissez-faire style** leader let the group make decisions and complete the work in whatever way it saw fit. The researchers' results seemed to indicate that the democratic style contributed to both good quantity and quality of work. Had the answer to the question of the most effective leadership style been found? Unfortunately, it wasn't that simple. Later studies of the autocratic and democratic styles showed mixed results. For instance, the democratic style sometimes produced higher performance levels than the autocratic style, but at other times, it didn't. However, more consistent results were found when a measure of employee satisfaction was used. Group members were more satisfied under a democratic leader than under an autocratic one.[8]

Now leaders had a dilemma! Should they focus on achieving higher performance or on achieving higher member satisfaction? This recognition of the dual nature of a leader's behavior—that is, focus on the task and focus on the people—was also a key characteristic of the other behavioral studies.

THE OHIO STATE STUDIES The Ohio State studies identified two important dimensions of leader behavior.[9] Beginning with a list of more than 1,000 behavioral dimensions, the researchers eventually narrowed it down to just two that accounted for most of the leadership behavior described by group members. The first was called **initiating structure**, which referred to the extent to which a leader defined his or her role and the roles of group members in attaining goals. It included behaviors that involved attempts to organize work, work relationships, and goals. The second was called **consideration**, which was defined as the extent to which a leader had work relationships characterized by mutual trust and respect for group members' ideas and feelings. A leader who was high in consideration helped group members with personal problems, was friendly and approachable, and treated all group members as equals. He or she showed concern for (was considerate of) his or her followers' comfort, well-being, status, and satisfaction. Research found that a leader who was high in both initiating structure and consideration (a **high–high leader**) sometimes achieved high group task performance and high group member satisfaction, but not always.

UNIVERSITY OF MICHIGAN STUDIES Leadership studies conducted at the University of Michigan at about the same time as those done at Ohio State also hoped to identify behavioral characteristics of leaders that were related to performance effectiveness. The Michigan group also came up with two dimensions of leadership behavior, which they labeled employee oriented and production oriented.[10] Leaders who were *employee oriented* were described as emphasizing interpersonal relationships. The *production-oriented* leaders, in contrast, tended to emphasize the task aspects of the job. Unlike the other studies, the Michigan researchers concluded that leaders who were employee oriented were able to get high group productivity and high group member satisfaction.

THE MANAGERIAL GRID The behavioral dimensions from these early leadership studies provided the basis for the development of a two-dimensional grid for appraising leadership styles. This **managerial grid** used the behavioral dimensions "concern for people" (the vertical part of the grid) and "concern for production" (the horizontal part of the grid) and evaluated a leader's use of these behaviors, ranking them on a scale from 1 (low) to 9 (high).[11] Although the grid had 81 potential categories into which a leader's behavioral style might fall, only five styles were named: impoverished management (1,1 or low concern for production, low concern for people), task management (9,1 or high concern for production, low concern for people), middle-of-the-road management (5,5 or medium concern for production, medium concern for people), country club management (1,9 or low concern for production, high concern for people), and team management (9,9 or high concern for production, high concern for people). Of these five styles, the researchers concluded that managers performed best when using a 9,9 style. Unfortunately, the grid offered no answers to the question of what made a manager an effective leader; it only provided a framework for conceptualizing leadership style. In fact, little substantive evidence supports the conclusion that a 9,9 style is most effective in all situations.[12]

Leadership researchers were discovering that predicting leadership success involved something more complex than isolating a few leader traits or preferable behaviors. They began looking at situational influences. Specifically, which leadership styles might be suitable in different situations and what were these different situations?

initiating structure
The extent to which a leader defines his or her role and the roles of group members in attaining goals

consideration
The extent to which a leader has work relationships characterized by mutual trust and respect for group members' ideas and feelings

high–high leader
A leader high in both initiating structure and consideration behaviors

managerial grid
A two-dimensional grid for appraising leadership styles

Chanda Kochhar is the managing director and chief executive officer of ICICI Bank in India. She is an employee-oriented leader whose behavior towards subordinates is compassionate, nurturing, and understanding. Kochhar sets high performance goals, encourages employees to work hard, motivates them to perform to the best of their abilities, and helps them realize their full potential. Her leadership behavior of emphasizing interpersonal relationships and being sensitive to employees has resulted in high group member satisfaction and high group productivity. Under her leadership, ICICI Bank has grown to become the largest private retail bank in India.
Source: Reuters/Vivek Prakash

CONTINGENCY **Theories of Leadership**

"The corporate world is filled with stories of leaders who failed to achieve greatness because they failed to understand the context they were working in."[13] In this section, we examine three contingency theories—Fiedler, Hersey-Blanchard, and path-goal. Each looks at defining leadership style and the situation, and attempts to answer the *if-then* contingencies (that is, *if* this is the context or situation, *then* this is the best leadership style to use).

The Fiedler Model

The first comprehensive contingency model for leadership was developed by Fred Fiedler.[14] The **Fiedler contingency model** proposed that effective group performance depended on properly matching the leader's style and the amount of control and influence in the situation. The model was based on the premise that a certain leadership style would be most effective in different types of situations. The keys were to (1) define those leadership styles and the different types of situations, and then (2) identify the appropriate combinations of style and situation.

Fiedler proposed that a key factor in leadership success was an individual's basic leadership style, either task oriented or relationship oriented. To measure a leader's style, Fiedler developed the **least-preferred coworker (LPC) questionnaire**. This questionnaire contained 18 pairs of contrasting adjectives—for example, pleasant–unpleasant, cold–warm, boring–interesting, or friendly–unfriendly. Respondents were asked to think of all the coworkers they had ever had and to describe that one person they *least enjoyed* working with by rating him or her on a scale of 1 to 8 for each of the 18 sets of adjectives (the 8 always described the positive adjective out of the pair and the 1 always described the negative adjective out of the pair).

If the leader described the least preferred coworker in relatively positive terms (in other words, a "high" LPC score—a score of 64 or above), then the respondent was primarily interested in good personal relations with coworkers, and the style would be described as *relationship oriented*. In contrast, if you saw the least preferred coworker in relatively unfavorable terms (a low LPC score—a score of 57 or below), you were primarily interested in productivity and getting the job done; thus, your style would be labeled as *task oriented*. Fiedler did acknowledge that a small number of people might fall in between these two extremes and not have a cut-and-dried leadership style. One other important point is that Fiedler assumed a person's leadership style was fixed regardless of the situation. In other words, if you were a relationship-oriented leader, you'd always be one, and the same for task-oriented.

After an individual's leadership style had been assessed through the LPC, it was time to evaluate the situation in order to be able to match the leader with the situation. Fiedler's research uncovered three contingency dimensions that defined the key situational factors in leader effectiveness.

- **Leader–member relations**: the degree of confidence, trust, and respect employees had for their leader; rated as either good or poor.
- **Task structure**: the degree to which job assignments were formalized and structured; rated as either high or low.
- **Position power**: the degree of influence a leader had over activities such as hiring, firing, discipline, promotions, and salary increases; rated as either strong or weak.

Each leadership situation was evaluated in terms of these three contingency variables, which when combined produced eight possible situations that were either favorable or unfavorable for the leader. (See the bottom of the chart in Exhibit 18-3.) Situations I, II, and III were classified as highly favorable for the leader. Situations IV, V, and VI were moderately favorable for the leader. And situations VII and VIII were described as highly unfavorable for the leader.

Fiedler contingency model
A leadership theory proposing that effective group performance depends on the proper match between a leader's style and the degree to which the situation allows the leader to control and influence

least-preferred coworker (LPC) questionnaire
A questionnaire that measures whether a leader is task or relationship oriented

leader–member relations
One of Fiedler's situational contingencies that describes the degree of confidence, trust, and respect employees had for their leader

task structure
One of Fiedler's situational contingencies that describes the degree to which job assignments are formalized and structured

position power
One of Fiedler's situational contingencies that describes the degree of influence a leader has over activities such as hiring, firing, discipline, promotions, and salary increases

Exhibit 18-3
The Fiedler Model

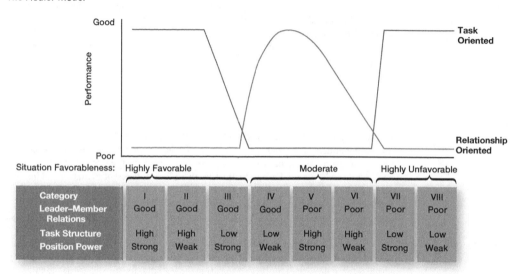

Category	I	II	III	IV	V	VI	VII	VIII
Leader–Member Relations	Good	Good	Good	Good	Poor	Poor	Poor	Poor
Task Structure	High	High	Low	Low	High	High	Low	Low
Position Power	Strong	Weak	Strong	Weak	Strong	Weak	Strong	Weak

Once Fiedler had described the leader variables and the situational variables, he had everything he needed to define the specific contingencies for leadership effectiveness. To do so, he studied 1,200 groups where he compared relationship-oriented versus task-oriented leadership styles in each of the eight situational categories. He concluded that task-oriented leaders performed better in very favorable situations and in very unfavorable situations. (See the top of Exhibit 18-3 where performance is shown on the vertical axis and situation favorableness is shown on the horizontal axis.) On the other hand, relationship-oriented leaders performed better in moderately favorable situations.

Because Fiedler treated an individual's leadership style as fixed, only two ways could improve leader effectiveness. First, you could bring in a new leader whose style better fit the situation. For instance, if the group situation was highly unfavorable but was led by a relationship-oriented leader, the group's performance could be improved by replacing that person with a task-oriented leader. The second alternative was to change the situation to fit the leader. This could be done by restructuring tasks; by increasing or decreasing the power that the leader had over factors such as salary increases, promotions, and disciplinary actions; or by improving the leader–member relations.

Research testing the overall validity of Fiedler's model has shown considerable evidence to support the model.[15] However, his theory wasn't without criticisms. The major one is that it's probably unrealistic to assume that a person can't change his or her leadership style to fit the situation. Effective leaders can, and do, change their styles. Another is that the LPC wasn't very practical. Finally, the situation variables were difficult to assess.[16] Despite its shortcomings, the Fiedler model showed that effective leadership style needed to reflect situational factors.

Hersey and Blanchard's Situational Leadership Theory

Paul Hersey and Ken Blanchard developed a leadership theory that has gained a strong following among management development specialists.[17] This model, called **situational leadership theory (SLT)**, is a contingency theory that focuses on followers' readiness. Before we proceed, two points need clarification: Why a leadership theory focuses on the followers and what is meant by the term *readiness*.

situational leadership theory (SLT)
A leadership contingency theory that focuses on followers' readiness

The emphasis on the followers in leadership effectiveness reflects the reality that it *is* the followers who accept or reject the leader. Regardless of what the leader does, the group's effectiveness depends on the actions of the followers. This important dimension has been overlooked or underemphasized in most leadership theories. And **readiness**, as defined by Hersey and Blanchard, refers to the extent to which people have the ability and willingness to accomplish a specific task.

readiness
The extent to which people have the ability and willingness to accomplish a specific task

SLT uses the same two leadership dimensions that Fiedler identified: task and relationship behaviors. However, Hersey and Blanchard go a step further by considering each as either high or low and then combining them into four specific leadership styles described as follows:

- *Telling* (high task–low relationship): The leader defines roles and tells people what, how, when, and where to do various tasks.
- *Selling* (high task–high relationship): The leader provides both directive and supportive behavior.
- *Participating* (low task–high relationship): The leader and followers share in decision making; the main role of the leader is facilitating and communicating.
- *Delegating* (low task–low relationship): The leader provides little direction or support.

The final component in the model is the four stages of follower readiness:

- *R1:* People are both *unable and unwilling* to take responsibility for doing something. Followers aren't competent or confident.
- *R2*: People are *unable but willing* to do the necessary job tasks. Followers are motivated but lack the appropriate skills.
- *R3:* People are *able but unwilling* to do what the leader wants. Followers are competent, but don't want to do something.
- *R4*: People are both *able and willing* to do what is asked of them.

path-goal theory
A leadership theory that says the leader's job is to assist followers in attaining their goals and to provide direction or support needed to ensure that their goals are compatible with the goals of the group or organization

SLT essentially views the leader–follower relationship as like that of a parent and a child. Just as a parent needs to relinquish control when a child becomes more mature and responsible, so too should leaders. As followers reach higher levels of readiness, the leader responds not only by decreasing control over their activities but also decreasing relationship behaviors. The SLT says if followers are at R1 (*unable* and *unwilling* to do a task), the leader needs to use the telling style and give clear and specific directions; if followers are at R2 (*unable* and *willing*), the leader needs to use the selling style and display high task orientation to compensate for the followers' lack of ability and high relationship orientation to get followers to "buy into" the leader's desires; if followers are at R3 (*able* and *unwilling*), the leader needs to use the participating style to gain their support; and if employees are at R4 (both *able* and *willing*), the leader doesn't need to do much and should use the delegating style.

Meg Whitman, CEO and president of Hewlett-Packard and formerly president and CEO of eBay, can be described as a supportive leader who is friendly and shows concern for the needs of followers. Believing that people are basically good, she trusts her subordinates, emotionally supports them, and treats them with care and respect. During her ten years at eBay, she led the company to incredible success, expanding it from 30 employees and $4 million in sales to 15,000 employees and $8 billion in sales. Her supportive leadership at eBay resulted in high employee performance and satisfaction.
Source: LiPo Ching/MCT/Newscom

SLT has intuitive appeal. It acknowledges the importance of followers and builds on the logic that leaders can compensate for ability and motivational limitations in their followers. However, research efforts to test and support the theory generally have been disappointing.[18] Possible explanations include internal inconsistencies in the model as well as problems with research methodology. Despite its appeal and wide popularity, we have to be cautious about any enthusiastic endorsement of SLT.

Path-Goal Model

Another approach to understanding leadership is **path-goal theory**, which states that the leader's job is to assist followers in attaining their goals and to provide direction or support needed to ensure that their goals are compatible with the goals of the group or organization. Developed by Robert House, path-goal theory takes key elements from the expectancy theory of motivation.[19] The term *path-goal* is derived from the belief that effective leaders remove the roadblocks and pitfalls so that followers have a clearer path to help them get from where they are to the achievement of their work goals.

House identified four leadership behaviors:

- *Directive leader:* Lets subordinates know what's expected of them, schedules work to be done, and gives specific guidance on how to accomplish tasks.
- *Supportive leader:* Shows concern for the needs of followers and is friendly.
- *Participative leader:* Consults with group members and uses their suggestions before making a decision.
- *Achievement oriented leader:* Sets challenging goals and expects followers to perform at their highest level.

In contrast to Fiedler's view that a leader couldn't change his or her behavior, House assumed that leaders are flexible and can display any or all of these leadership styles depending on the situation.

As Exhibit 18-4 illustrates, path-goal theory proposes two situational or contingency variables that moderate the leadership behavior–outcome relationship: those in the *environment* that are outside the control of the follower (factors including task structure, formal authority system, and the work group) and those that are part of the personal characteristics of the *follower* (including locus of control, experience, and perceived ability). Environmental factors determine the type of leader behavior required if subordinate outcomes are to be maximized; personal characteristics of the follower determine how the environment and leader behavior are interpreted. The theory proposes that a leader's behavior won't be effective if it's redundant with what the environmental structure is providing or is incongruent with follower characteristics. For example, some predictions from path-goal theory are:

- Directive leadership leads to greater satisfaction when tasks are ambiguous or stressful than when they are highly structured and well laid out. The followers aren't sure what to do, so the leader needs to give them some direction.
- Supportive leadership results in high employee performance and satisfaction when subordinates are performing structured tasks. In this situation, the leader only needs to support followers, not tell them what to do.
- Directive leadership is likely to be perceived as redundant among subordinates with high perceived ability or with considerable experience. These followers are quite capable, so they don't need a leader to tell them what to do.

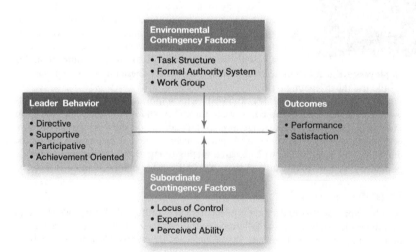

Exhibit 18-4
Path-Goal Model

- The clearer and more bureaucratic the formal authority relationships, the more leaders should exhibit supportive behavior and deemphasize directive behavior. The organizational situation has provided the structure as far as what is expected of followers, so the leader's role is simply to support.
- Directive leadership will lead to higher employee satisfaction when there is substantive conflict within a work group. In this situation, the followers need a leader who will take charge.
- Subordinates with an internal locus of control will be more satisfied with a participative style. Because these followers believe they control what happens to them, they prefer to participate in decisions.
- Subordinates with an external locus of control will be more satisfied with a directive style. These followers believe that what happens to them is a result of the external environment, so they would prefer a leader who tells them what to do.
- Achievement-oriented leadership will increase subordinates' expectancies that effort will lead to high performance when tasks are ambiguously structured. By setting challenging goals, followers know what the expectations are.

Testing path-goal theory has not been easy. A review of the research suggests mixed support.[20] To summarize the model, however, an employee's performance and satisfaction are likely to be positively influenced when the leader chooses a leadership style that compensates for shortcomings in either the employee or the work setting. However, if the leader spends time explaining tasks that are already clear or when the employee has the ability and experience to handle them without interference, the employee is likely to see such directive behavior as redundant or even insulting.

18.4 ⎰ ***Describe*** *contemporary views of leadership.*

CONTEMPORARY **Views of Leadership**

What are the latest views of leadership? We want to look at four of these views: leader–member exchange theory, transformational-transactional leadership, charismatic-visionary leadership, and team leadership.

Leader–Member Exchange (LMX) Theory

leader–member exchange theory (LMX)
The leadership theory that says leaders create in-groups and out-groups and those in the in-group will have higher performance ratings, less turnover, and greater job satisfaction

Have you ever been in a group in which the leader had "favorites" who made up his or her in-group? If so, that's the premise behind leader–member exchange (LMX) theory.[21] **Leader–member exchange theory (LMX)** says leaders create in-groups and out-groups and those in the in-group will have higher performance ratings, less turnover, and greater job satisfaction.

LMX theory suggests that early on in the relationship between a leader and a given follower, a leader will implicitly categorize a follower as an "in" or as an "out." That relationship tends to remain fairly stable over time. Leaders also encourage LMX by rewarding those employees with whom they want a closer linkage and punishing those with whom they do not.[22] For the LMX relationship to remain intact, however, both the leader and the follower must "invest" in the relationship.

It's not exactly clear how a leader chooses who falls into each category, but evidence shows that in-group members have demographic, attitude, personality, and even gender similarities with the leader or they have a higher level of competence than out-group members.[23] The leader does the choosing, but the follower's characteristics drive the decision.

Research on LMX has been generally supportive. It appears that leaders do differentiate among followers; that these disparities are not random; and followers with in-group status will have higher performance ratings, engage in more helping or "citizenship" behaviors at work, and report greater satisfaction with their boss.[24] This probably shouldn't be surprising since leaders invest their time and other resources in those whom they expect to perform best.

Transformational-Transactional Leadership

Many early leadership theories viewed leaders as **transactional leaders**; that is, leaders who lead primarily by using social exchanges (or transactions). Transactional leaders guide or motivate followers to work toward established goals by exchanging rewards for their productivity.[26] But another type of leader—a **transformational leader**—stimulates and inspires (transforms) followers to achieve extraordinary outcomes. Examples include Jim Goodnight of SAS Institute and Andrea Jung of Avon. They pay attention to the concerns and developmental needs of individual followers; they change followers' awareness of issues by helping those followers look at old problems in new ways; and they are able to excite, arouse, and inspire followers to exert extra effort to achieve group goals.

Transactional and transformational leadership shouldn't be viewed as opposing approaches to getting things done.[27] Transformational leadership develops from transactional leadership. Transformational leadership produces levels of employee effort and performance that go beyond what would occur with a transactional approach alone. Moreover, transformational leadership is more than charisma because the transformational leader attempts to instill in followers the ability to question not only established views but those views held by the leader.[28]

The evidence supporting the superiority of transformational leadership over transactional leadership is overwhelmingly impressive. For instance, studies that looked at managers in different settings, including the military and business, found that transformational leaders were evaluated as more effective, higher performers, more promotable than their transactional counterparts, and more interpersonally sensitive.[29] In addition, evidence indicates that transformational leadership is strongly correlated with lower turnover rates and higher levels of productivity, employee satisfaction, creativity, goal attainment, follower well-being, and corporate entrepreneurship, especially in start-up firms.[30]

LEADER who made a DIFFERENCE

Ajay Banga, CEO of MasterCard, has had well-rounded leadership experiences.[25] Born in India, Banga honed his leadership skills at Nestlé and PepsiCo before moving to Citigroup to head up its Asia-Pacific division. Citigroup was a challenging situation as he found a vast banking group that "worked fluidly in its product clusters but lacked coordination, synergy, or vision." Banga undertook the painful process of breaking down those "silos and stitching them together again under a single umbrella structure." When he was offered a position at MasterCard as president and chief operating officer, Banga jumped at the chance. Now as CEO, Banga is the company's cheerleader, shaking up the company's low-key corporate culture with hugs and fist bumps in the hallways. One analyst describes him as "energetic, open, and engaging." What can you learn from this leader who made a difference?

Source: Reuters/Keith Bedford

transactional leaders
Leaders who lead primarily by using social exchanges (or transactions)

transformational leaders
Leaders who stimulate and inspire (transform) followers to achieve extraordinary outcomes

Charismatic-Visionary Leadership

Jeff Bezos, founder and CEO of Amazon.com, is a person who exudes energy, enthusiasm, and drive.[31] He's fun-loving (his legendary laugh has been described as a flock of Canadian geese on nitrous oxide), but has pursued his vision for Amazon with serious intensity and has demonstrated an ability to inspire his employees through the ups and downs of a rapidly growing company. Bezos is what we call a **charismatic leader**—that is, an enthusiastic, self-confident leader whose personality and actions influence people to behave in certain ways.

Several authors have attempted to identify personal characteristics of the charismatic leader.[32] The most comprehensive analysis identified five such characteristics: they have a vision, the ability to articulate that vision, a willingness to take risks to achieve that vision, a sensitivity to both environmental constraints and follower needs, and behaviors that are out of the ordinary.[33]

An increasing body of evidence shows impressive correlations between charismatic leadership and high performance and satisfaction among followers.[34] Although one study found that charismatic CEOs had no impact on subsequent organizational performance, charisma is still believed to be a desirable leadership quality.[35]

charismatic leader
An enthusiastic, self-confident leader whose personality and actions influence people to behave in certain ways

If charisma is desirable, can people learn to be charismatic leaders? Or are charismatic leaders born with their qualities? Although a small number of experts still think that charisma can't be learned, most believe that individuals can be trained to exhibit charismatic behaviors.[36] For example, researchers have succeeded in teaching undergraduate students to "be" charismatic. How? They were taught to articulate a far-reaching goal, communicate high performance expectations, exhibit confidence in the ability of subordinates to meet those expectations, and empathize with the needs of their subordinates; they learned to project a powerful, confident, and dynamic presence; and they practiced using a captivating and engaging voice tone. The researchers also trained the student leaders to use charismatic nonverbal behaviors, including leaning toward the follower when communicating, maintaining direct eye contact, and having a relaxed posture and animated facial expressions. In groups with these "trained" charismatic leaders, members had higher task performance, higher task adjustment, and better adjustment to the leader and to the group than did group members who worked in groups led by noncharismatic leaders.

One last thing we should say about charismatic leadership is that it may not always be necessary to achieve high levels of employee performance. It may be most appropriate when the follower's task has an ideological purpose or when the environment involves a high degree of stress and uncertainty.[37] This distinction may explain why, when charismatic leaders surface, it's more likely to be in politics, religion, or wartime or when a business firm is starting up or facing a survival crisis. For example, Martin Luther King Jr. used his charisma to bring about social equality through nonviolent means, and Steve Jobs achieved unwavering loyalty and commitment from Apple's technical staff in the early 1980s by articulating a vision of personal computers that would dramatically change the way people lived.

Although the term *vision* is often linked with charismatic leadership, **visionary leadership** is different; it's the ability to create and articulate a realistic, credible, and attractive vision of the future that improves on the present situation.[38] This vision, if properly selected and implemented, is so energizing that it "in effect jump-starts the future by calling forth the skills, talents, and resources to make it happen."[39]

An organization's vision should offer clear and compelling imagery that taps into people's emotions and inspires enthusiasm to pursue the organization's goals. It should be able to generate possibilities that are inspirational and unique and offer new ways of doing things that are clearly better for the organization and its members. Visions that are clearly articulated and have powerful imagery are easily grasped and accepted. For instance, Michael Dell (Dell Computer) created a vision of a business that sells and delivers customized PCs directly to customers in less than a week. The late Mary Kay Ash's vision of women as entrepreneurs selling products that improved their self-image gave impetus to her cosmetics company, Mary Kay Cosmetics.

visionary leadership
The ability to create and articulate a realistic, credible, and attractive vision of the future that improves upon the present situation

This young man is a team leader who manages the bakery department at a Whole Foods Market store. As leader of a 13-member team, he needs to possess good communication skills, work well with others, and convey enthusiasm. He serves as a coach in training and motivating team members to excellence in all aspects of the department, from maintaining good relationships with each other and with vendors to achieving team goals for sales, growth, and productivity. Whole Foods is completely organized around employee teams, with team leaders for each store department. Team leaders in each store also function as a team, store leaders in each region are a team, and regional presidents work as a team.
Source: © Daily Mail/Rex/Alamy

Team Leadership

Because leadership is increasingly taking place within a team context and more organizations are using work teams, the role of the leader in guiding team members has become increasingly important. The role of team leader *is* different from the traditional leadership role, as J. D. Bryant, a supervisor at Texas Instruments' Forest Lane plant in Dallas, discovered.[40] One day he was contentedly overseeing a staff of 15 circuit board assemblers. The next day, he was told that the company was going to use employee teams and he was to become a "facilitator." He said, "I'm supposed to teach the teams everything I know and then let them make their own decisions." Confused about his new role, he admitted, "There was no clear plan on what I was supposed to do." What *is* involved in being a team leader?

Many leaders are not equipped to handle the change to employee teams. As one consultant noted, "Even the most capable managers have trouble making the transition because all the command-and-control type things they were encouraged to do before are no longer appropriate. There's no reason to have any skill or sense of this."[42] This same consultant estimated that "probably 15 percent of managers are natural team leaders; another 15 percent could never lead a team because it runs counter to their personality—that is, they're unable to sublimate their dominating style for the good of the team. Then there's that huge group in the middle: Team leadership doesn't come naturally to them, but they can learn it."[43]

The challenge for many managers is learning how to become an effective team leader. They have to learn skills such as patiently sharing information, being able to trust others and to give up authority, and understanding when to intervene. And effective team leaders have mastered the difficult balancing act of knowing when to leave their teams alone and when to get involved. New team leaders may try to retain too much control at a time when team members need more autonomy, or they may abandon their teams at times when the teams need support and help.[44]

One study looking at organizations that reorganized themselves around employee teams found certain common responsibilities of all leaders. These leader responsibilities included coaching, facilitating, handling disciplinary problems, reviewing team and individual performance, training, and communication.[45] However, a more meaningful way to describe the team leader's job is to focus on two priorities: (1) managing the team's external boundary and (2) facilitating the team process.[46] These priorities entail four specific leadership roles, which are identified in Exhibit 18-5.

let's get | REAL

The Scenario:

Linda Bustamante owns a thriving company that manufactures scented potpourris and other products. She's getting ready to expand her sales team again and wants to promote one of the current sales reps to team leader. This is a big step, and Linda desperately wants that person to succeed because it would take a load off her shoulders.

What advice could Linda give her newly appointed team leader?

Linda should advise her newly promoted team leader to meet with her team members one-on-one and let each know she is there to support them to achieve individual and department goals. Linda should devote time during her first few weeks in her new position to observe and listen to her team and their clients before implementing any major changes. She should take advantage of all of the training available within the company and look for a mentor she will feel comfortable working with.

Shawn Linett
Sales Manager

Source: Shawn Linett

Exhibit 18-5
Team Leadership Roles

Discuss contemporary
issues affecting
leadership.

LEADERSHIP **Issues in the Twenty-First Century**

It's not easy being a chief information officer (CIO) today. The person responsible for managing a company's information technology activities will find that the task comes with a lot of external and internal pressures. Technology continues to change rapidly—almost daily, it sometimes seems. Business costs continue to rise. Rob Carter, CIO of FedEx, is on the hot seat facing such challenges.[47] He's responsible for all the computer and communication systems that provide around-the-clock and around-the-globe support for FedEx's products and services. If anything goes wrong, you know who takes the heat. However, Carter has been an effective leader in this seemingly chaotic environment.

Leading effectively in today's environment is likely to involve such challenging circumstances for many leaders. In addition, twenty-first-century leaders do face some important leadership issues. In this section, we look at these issues that include managing power, developing trust, empowering employees, leading across cultures, and becoming an effective leader.

Managing Power

Where do leaders get their power—that is, their right and capacity to influence work actions or decisions? Five sources of leader power have been identified: legitimate, coercive, reward, expert, and referent.[48]

legitimate power
The power a leader has as a result of his or her position in the organization

Legitimate power and authority are the same. Legitimate power represents the power a leader has as a result of his or her position in the organization. Although people in positions of authority are also likely to have reward and coercive power, legitimate power is broader than the power to coerce and reward.

coercive power
The power a leader has to punish or control

Coercive power is the power a leader has to punish or control. Followers react to this power out of fear of the negative results that might occur if they don't comply. Managers typically have some coercive power, such as being able to suspend or demote employees or to assign them work they find unpleasant or undesirable.

reward power
The power a leader has to give positive rewards

Reward power is the power to give positive rewards. A reward can be anything a person values such as money, favorable performance appraisals, promotions, interesting work assignments, friendly colleagues, and preferred work shifts or sales territories.

expert power
Power that's based on expertise, special skills, or knowledge

Expert power is power based on expertise, special skills, or knowledge. If an employee has skills, knowledge, or expertise that's critical to a work group, that person's expert power is enhanced.

referent power
Power that arises because of a person's desirable resources or personal traits

Finally, **referent power** is the power that arises because of a person's desirable resources or personal traits. If I admire you and want to be associated with you, you can exercise power over me because I want to please you. Referent power develops out of admiration of another and a desire to be like that person.

Most effective leaders rely on several different forms of power to affect the behavior and performance of their followers. For example, the commanding officer of one of Australia's state-of-the-art submarines, the HMAS *Sheean,* employs different types of power in managing his crew and equipment. He gives orders to the crew (legitimate), praises them (reward), and disciplines those who commit infractions (coercive). As an effective leader, he also strives to have expert power (based on his expertise and knowledge) and referent power (based on his being admired) to influence his crew.

Developing Trust

Christine Day joined Lululemon Athletica as CEO in 2008 (after 20 years at Starbucks) and helped the company grow by trusting her employees to make decisions.[49] In today's uncertain environment, an important consideration for leaders is building trust and credibility, both of which can be extremely fragile. Before we can discuss ways leaders can build trust and credibility, we have to know what trust and credibility are and why they're so important.

The main component of credibility is honesty. Surveys show that honesty is consistently singled out as the number one characteristic of admired leaders. "Honesty is absolutely essential to leadership. If people are going to follow someone willingly, whether it be into battle or into the boardroom, they first want to assure themselves that the person is worthy of their trust."[50] In addition to being honest, credible leaders are competent and inspiring. They are personally able to effectively communicate their confidence and enthusiasm. Thus, followers judge a leader's **credibility** in terms of his or her honesty, competence, and ability to inspire.

credibility
The degree to which followers perceive someone as honest, competent, and able to inspire

Trust is closely entwined with the concept of credibility, and, in fact, the terms are often used interchangeably. **Trust** is defined as the belief in the integrity, character, and ability of a leader. Followers who trust a leader are willing to be vulnerable to the leader's actions because they are confident that their rights and interests will not be abused.[51] Research has identified five dimensions that make up the concept of trust:[52]

trust
The belief in the integrity, character, and ability of a leader

- *Integrity:* honesty and truthfulness
- *Competence:* technical and interpersonal knowledge and skills
- *Consistency:* reliability, predictability, and good judgment in handling situations
- *Loyalty:* willingness to protect a person, physically and emotionally
- *Openness:* willingness to share ideas and information freely

Of these five dimensions, integrity seems to be the most critical when someone assesses another's trustworthiness.[53] Both integrity and competence were seen in our earlier discussion of leadership traits found to be consistently associated with leadership. Workplace changes have reinforced why such leadership qualities are important. For instance, the trends toward empowerment and self-managed work teams have reduced many of the traditional control mechanisms used to monitor employees. If a work team is free to schedule its own work, evaluate its own performance, and even make its own hiring decisions, trust becomes critical. Employees have to trust managers to treat them fairly, and managers have to trust employees to conscientiously fulfill their responsibilities.

Also, leaders have to increasingly lead others who may not be in their immediate work group or may even be physically separated—members of cross-functional or virtual teams, individuals who work for suppliers or customers, and perhaps even people who represent other organizations through strategic alliances. These situations don't allow leaders the luxury of falling back on their formal positions for influence. Many of these relationships, in fact, are fluid and fleeting. So the ability to quickly develop trust and sustain that trust is crucial to the success of the relationship.

Why is it important that followers trust their leaders? Research has shown that trust in leadership is significantly related to positive job outcomes including job

Exhibit 18-6
Building Trust

> Practice openness.
> Be fair.
> Speak your feelings.
> Tell the truth.
> Show consistency.
> Fulfill your promises.
> Maintain confidences.
> Demonstrate competence.

performance, organizational citizenship behavior, job satisfaction, and organizational commitment.[54] Given the importance of trust to effective leadership, how can leaders build trust? Exhibit 18-6 lists some suggestions. (Also, see the Building Your Skill exercise in Chapter 5.)[55]

Now, more than ever, managerial and leadership effectiveness depends on the ability to gain the trust of followers.[56] Downsizing, financial challenges, and the increased use of temporary employees have undermined employees' trust in their leaders and shaken the confidence of investors, suppliers, and customers. A survey found that only 39 percent of U.S. employees and 51 percent of Canadian employees trusted their executive leaders.[57] Today's leaders are faced with the challenge of rebuilding and restoring trust with employees and with other important organizational stakeholders.

Empowering Employees

Employees at DuPont's facility in Uberaba, Brazil, planted trees to commemorate the site's 10th anniversary. Although they had several things to celebrate, one of the most important was the fact that since production began, the facility has had zero environmental incidents and no recordable safety violations. The primary reason for

let's get REAL

The Scenario:

Adhita Chopra is stumped. Three months ago, he was assigned to lead a team of phone app designers, and although no one has come out and said anything directly, he feels like his team doesn't trust him. They have been withholding information and communicating only selectively when asked questions. And they have persistently questioned the team's goals and strategies and even Adhita's actions and decisions. How can he build trust with his team?

What advice would you give Adhita?

To inspire and build trust, trust needs to be extended through communication and clarification of the team's goals and expectations. Adhita's actions and decisions need to be transparent and consistent and should demonstrate a commitment to achieving the team's objectives.

Susan Mathew
Program Manager

Source: Susan Mathew

this achievement was the company's STOP (Safety Training Observation Program) program—a program in which empowered employees were responsible for observing one another, correcting improper procedures, and encouraging safe procedures.[58]

As we've described in different places throughout the text, managers are increasingly leading by empowering their employees. As we've said before, empowerment involves increasing the decision-making discretion of workers. Millions of individual employees and employee teams are making the key operating decisions that directly affect their work. They're developing budgets, scheduling workloads, controlling inventories, solving quality problems, and engaging in similar activities that until very recently were viewed exclusively as part of the manager's job.[59] For instance, at The Container Store, any employee who gets a customer request has permission to take care of it. Garret Boone, chairman emeritus, says, "Everybody we hire, we hire as a leader. Anybody in our store can take an action that you might think of typically being a manager's action."[60]

One reason more companies are empowering employees is the need for quick decisions by those people who are most knowledgeable about the issues—often those at lower organizational levels. If organizations want to successfully compete in a dynamic global economy, employees have to be able to make decisions and implement changes quickly. Another reason is that organizational downsizings left many managers with larger spans of control. In order to cope with the increased work demands, managers had to empower their people. Although empowerment is not a universal answer, it can be beneficial when employees have the knowledge, skills, and experience to do their jobs competently.

Leading Across Cultures

"In the United States, leaders are expected to look great, sound great, and be inspiring. In other countries—not so much."[61] In this global economy, how can managers account for cross-cultural differences as they lead?

One general conclusion that surfaces from leadership research is that effective leaders do not use a single style. They adjust their style to the situation. Although not mentioned explicitly, national culture is certainly an important situational variable in determining which leadership style will be most effective. What works in China isn't likely to be effective in France or Canada. For instance, one study of Asian leadership styles revealed that Asian managers preferred leaders who were competent decision makers, effective communicators, and supportive of employees.[62]

National culture affects leadership style because it influences how followers will respond. Leaders can't (and shouldn't) just choose their styles randomly. They're constrained by the cultural conditions their followers have come to expect. Exhibit 18-7 provides some findings from selected examples of cross-cultural leadership studies. Because most leadership theories were developed in the United States, they have an American bias. They emphasize follower responsibilities rather than rights; assume self-gratification rather than commitment to duty or altruistic motivation; assume centrality of work and democratic value orientation; and stress rationality rather than spirituality, religion, or superstition.[63] However, the GLOBE research program, which we first introduced in Chapter 3, is the most extensive and comprehensive cross-cultural study of leadership ever undertaken. The GLOBE study found that leadership has some universal aspects. Specifically, a number of elements of transformational leadership appear to be associated with effective leadership regardless of what country the leader is in.[64] These elements include vision, foresight, providing encouragement, trustworthiness, dynamism, positiveness, and proactiveness. The results led two members of the GLOBE team to conclude that "effective business leaders in any country are expected by their subordinates to provide a powerful and proactive vision to guide the company into the future, strong motivational skills to stimulate all employees to fulfill the vision, and excellent planning skills to assist in implementing the vision."[65] Some people suggest that the universal appeal of these transformational

Exhibit 18-7
Cross-Cultural Leadership

- Korean leaders are expected to be paternalistic toward employees.
- Arab leaders who show kindness or generosity without being asked to do so are seen by other Arabs as weak.
- Japanese leaders are expected to be humble and speak frequently.
- Scandinavian and Dutch leaders who single out individuals with public praise are likely to embarrass, not energize, those individuals.
- Effective leaders in Malaysia are expected to show compassion while using more of an autocratic than a participative style.
- Effective German leaders are characterized by high performance orientation, low compassion, low self-protection, low team orientation, high autonomy, and high participation.

Sources: Based on J. C. Kennedy, "Leadership in Malaysia: Traditional Values, International Outlook," *Academy of Management Executive*, August 2002, pp. 15–17; F. C. Brodbeck, M. Frese, and M. Javidan, "Leadership Made in Germany: Low on Compassion, High on Performance," *Academy of Management Executive*, February 2002, pp. 16–29; M. F. Peterson and J. G. Hunt, "International Perspectives on International Leadership," *Leadership Quarterly*, Fall 1997, pp. 203–231; R. J. House and R. N. Aditya, "The Social Scientific Study of Leadership: Quo Vadis?" *Journal of Management*, vol. 23, no. 3, 1997, p. 463; and R. J. House, "Leadership in the Twenty-First Century," in A. Howard (ed.), *The Changing Nature of Work* (San Francisco: Jossey-Bass, 1995), p. 442.

As part of their leadership training, some 300 executives of Samsung Heavy Industries Ship Construction attended a one-week military training camp at an airbase in South Korea. Developing effective leaders who will act as agents of change is a top priority for Samsung in executing its plan of reaching $400 billion in revenue and becoming one of the world's top five brands by 2020. Through military-style training, participants learn how to develop mentally, physically, and emotionally; how to become a source of influence to inspire others through vision, courage, and commitment; and how to motivate others to attain higher levels of performance.
Source: Reuters/Handout

leader characteristics is due to the pressures toward common technologies and management practices, as a result of global competitiveness and multinational influences.

Becoming an Effective Leader

Organizations need effective leaders. Two issues pertinent to becoming an effective leader are leader training and recognizing that sometimes being an effective leader means *not* leading. Let's take a look at these issues.

LEADER TRAINING   Organizations around the globe spend billions of dollars, yen, and euros on leadership training and development.[66] These efforts take many forms—from $50,000 leadership programs offered by universities such as Harvard to sailing experiences at the Outward Bound School. Although much of the money spent on leader training may provide doubtful benefits, our review suggests that managers can do some things to get the maximum effect from such training.[67]

First, let's recognize the obvious. Some people don't have what it takes to be a leader. Period. For instance, evidence indicates that leadership training is more likely to be successful with individuals who are high self-monitors than with low self-monitors. Such individuals have the flexibility to change their behavior as different situations may require. In addition, organizations may find that individuals with higher levels of a trait called motivation to lead are more receptive to leadership development opportunities.[68]

What kinds of things can individuals learn that might be related to being a more effective leader? It may be a bit optimistic to think that "vision-creation" can be taught, but implementation skills can be taught. People can be trained to develop "an understanding about content themes critical to effective visions."[69] We can also teach skills such as trust-building and mentoring. And leaders can be taught situational analysis skills. They can learn how to evaluate situations, how to modify situations to make them fit better with their style, and how to assess which leader behaviors might be most effective in given situations.

SUBSTITUTES FOR LEADERSHIP   Despite the belief that some leadership style will always be effective regardless of the situation, leadership may not always be important! Research indicates that, in some situations, any behaviors a leader exhibits are irrelevant. In other words, certain individual, job, and organizational variables can act as "substitutes for leadership," negating the influence of the leader.[70]

For instance, follower characteristics such as experience, training, professional orientation, or need for independence can neutralize the effect of leadership. These characteristics can replace the employee's need for a leader's support or ability to create structure and reduce task ambiguity. Similarly, jobs that are inherently unambiguous and routine or intrinsically satisfying may place fewer demands on leaders. Finally, such organizational characteristics as explicit formalized goals, rigid rules and procedures, or cohesive work groups can substitute for formal leadership.

CHAPTER **18**

PREPARING FOR: Exams/Quizzes

CHAPTER SUMMARY by Learning Outcomes

18.1 LEARNING OUTCOME

Define leader and leadership.

A leader is someone who can influence others and who has managerial authority. Leadership is a process of leading a group and influencing that group to achieve its goals. Managers should be leaders because leading is one of the four management functions.

18.2 LEARNING OUTCOME

Compare and contrast early theories of leadership.

Early attempts to define leader traits were unsuccessful although later attempts found eight traits associated with leadership.

The University of Iowa studies explored three leadership styles. The only conclusion was that group members were more satisfied under a democratic leader than under an autocratic one. The Ohio State studies identified two dimensions of leader behavior—initiating structure and consideration. A leader high in both those dimensions at times achieved high group task performance and high group member satisfaction, but not always. The University of Michigan studies looked at employee-oriented leaders and production-oriented leaders. They concluded that leaders who were employee oriented could get high group productivity and high group member satisfaction. The Managerial Grid looked at leaders' concern for production and concern for people and identified five leader styles. Although it suggested that a leader who was high in concern for production and high in concern for people was the best, there was no substantive evidence for that conclusion.

As the behavioral studies showed, a leader's behavior has a dual nature: a focus on the task and a focus on the people.

18.3 LEARNING OUTCOME

Describe the three major contingency theories of leadership.

Fiedler's model attempted to define the best style to use in particular situations. He measured leader style—relationship oriented or task oriented—using the least-preferred coworker questionnaire. Fiedler also assumed a leader's style was fixed. He measured three contingency dimensions: leader–member relations, task structure, and position power. The model suggests that task-oriented leaders performed best in very favorable and very unfavorable situations, and relationship-oriented leaders performed best in moderately favorable situations.

Hersey and Blanchard's situational leadership theory focused on followers' readiness. They identified four leadership styles: telling (high task–low relationship), selling (high task–high relationship), participating (low task–high relationship), and delegating (low task–low relationship). They also identified four stages of readiness: unable and unwilling (use telling style), unable but willing (use selling style), able but unwilling (use participative style), and able and willing (use delegating style).

The path-goal model developed by Robert House identified four leadership behaviors: directive, supportive, participative, and achievement-oriented. He assumed that a leader can and should be able to use any of these styles. The two situational contingency variables were found in the environment and in the follower. Essentially the path-goal model says that a leader should provide direction and support as needed; that is, structure the path so the followers can achieve goals.

18.4 LEARNING OUTCOME

Describe contemporary views of leadership.

Leader–member exchange theory (LMX) says that leaders create in-groups and out-groups and those in the in-group will have higher performance ratings, less turnover, and greater job satisfaction.

A transactional leader exchanges rewards for productivity where a transformational leader stimulates and inspires followers to achieve goals.

A charismatic leader is an enthusiastic and self-confident leader whose personality and actions influence people to behave in certain ways. People can learn to be charismatic. A visionary leader is able to create and articulate a realistic, credible, and attractive vision of the future.

A team leader has two priorities: manage the team's external boundary and facilitate the team process. Four leader roles are involved: liaison with external constituencies, troubleshooter, conflict manager, and coach.

18.5 LEARNING OUTCOME

Discuss contemporary issues affecting leadership.

The five sources of a leader's power are legitimate (authority or position), coercive (punish or control), reward (give positive rewards), expert (special expertise, skills, or knowledge), and referent (desirable resources or traits).

Today's leaders face the issues of managing power, developing trust, empowering employees, leading across cultures, and becoming an effective leader.

REVIEW AND DISCUSSION QUESTIONS ✪

1. What does each of the four behavioral leadership theories say about leadership?

2. Explain Fiedler's contingency model of leadership.

3. How do situational leadership theory and path-goal theory each explain leadership?

4. What is leader–member exchange theory, and what does it say about leadership?

5. Differentiate between transactional and transformational leaders and between charismatic and visionary leaders.

6. What are the five sources of a leader's power?

7. Do you think most managers in real life use a contingency approach to increase their leadership effectiveness? Explain.

8. Do the followers make a difference in whether a leader is effective? Discuss.

PREPARING FOR: My Career

ETHICS DILEMMA ✪

Have you ever watched the show *Undercover Boss?* It features a company's "boss" working undercover in his or her own company to find out how the organization really works. Typically, the executive works undercover for a week, and then the employees the leader has worked with are summoned to company headquarters and either rewarded or punished for their actions. Bosses from organizations ranging from Waste Management and White Castle to NASCAR and Yankee Candle have participated. What do you think? Is it ethical for a leader to go undercover in his or her organization? Why or why not? What ethical issues could arise?

SKILLS EXERCISE Developing Your Choosing an Effective Leadership Style Skill

About the Skill

Effective leaders are skillful at helping the groups they lead be successful as the group goes through various stages of development. No leadership style is consistently effective. Situational factors, including follower characteristics, must be taken into consideration in the selection of an effective leadership style. The key situational factors that determine leadership effectiveness include stage of group development, task structure, position power, leader–member relations, the work group, employee characteristics, organizational culture, and national culture.

Steps in Practicing the Skill

You can choose an effective leadership style if you use the following six suggestions.

1. *Determine the stage in which your group or team is operating: forming, storming, norming, or performing.* Because each team stage involves specific and different issues and behaviors, it's important to know in which stage your team is. *Forming* is the first stage of group development during which people join a group and then help define the group's purpose, structure, and leadership. *Storming* is the second stage characterized by intragroup conflict. *Norming* is the third stage characterized by close relationships and cohesiveness. *Performing* is the fourth stage when the group is fully functional.

2. *If your team is in the forming stage, you want to exhibit certain leader behaviors.* These include making certain that all team members are introduced to one another, answering member questions, working to establish a foundation of trust and openness, modeling the behaviors you expect from the team members, and clarifying the team's goals, procedures, and expectations.

3. *If your team is in the storming stage, you want to exhibit certain leader behaviors.* These behaviors include identifying sources of conflict and adopting a mediator role, encouraging a win-win philosophy, restating the team's vision and its core values and goals, encouraging open discussion, encouraging an analysis of team processes in order to identify ways to improve, enhancing team cohesion and commitment, and providing recognition to individual team members as well as the team.

4. *If your team is in the norming stage, you want to exhibit certain leader behaviors.* These behaviors include clarifying the team's goals and expectations, providing performance feedback to individual team members and the team, encouraging the team to articulate a vision for the future, and finding ways to publicly and openly communicate the team's vision.

5. *If your team is in the performing stage, you want to exhibit certain leader behaviors.* These behaviors include providing regular and ongoing performance feedback, fostering innovation and innovative behavior, encouraging the team to capitalize on its strengths, celebrating achievements (large and small), and providing the team whatever support it needs to continue doing its work.

6. *Monitor the group for changes in behavior and adjust your leadership style accordingly.* Because a group is not a static entity, it will go through up periods and down periods. You should adjust your leadership style to the needs of the situation. If the group appears to need more direction from you, provide it. If it appears to be functioning at a high level on its own, provide whatever support is necessary to keep it functioning at that level.

Practicing the Skill

The following suggestions are activities you can do to practice the behaviors in choosing an effective leadership style.

1. Think of a group or team to which you currently belong or of which you have been a part. What type of leadership style did the leader of this group appear to exhibit? Give some specific examples of the types of leadership behaviors he or she used. Evaluate the leadership style. Was it appropriate for the group? Why or why not? What would you have done differently? Why?

2. Observe a sports team (either college or professional) that you consider extremely successful and one that you would consider not successful. What leadership styles appear to be used in these team situations? Give some specific examples of the types of leadership behaviors you observe. How would you evaluate the leadership style? Was it appropriate for the team? Why or why not? To what degree do you think leadership style influenced the team's outcomes?

WORKING TOGETHER Team Exercise

Everybody's probably had at least one experience with a *bad boss*. But what *is* a bad boss? And more importantly, what can you do in such a situation?

Break into small groups of three to four other class members. Come up with a bulleted list of characteristics and behaviors you believe a bad boss would have or exhibit. Then, come up with another bulleted list of what you can do if you find yourself in a situation with a bad boss. Be realistic about your suggestions; that is, don't suggest tampering with the person's coffee or slashing the person's tires!

MY TURN TO BE A MANAGER

- Think of the different organizations to which you belong. Note the different styles of leadership used by the leaders in these organizations. Write a paper describing these individual's style of leading (no names, please) and evaluate the styles being used.

- Write down three people you consider effective leaders. Make a bulleted list of the characteristics these individuals exhibit that you think make them effective leaders.

- Think about the times you have had to lead. Describe your own personal leadership style. What could you do to improve your leadership style? Come up with an action plan of steps you can take. Put all this information into a brief paper.

- Managers say that increasingly they must use influence to get things done. Do some research on the art of persuasion. Make a bulleted list of suggestions you find on how to improve your skills at influencing others.

- Here's a list of leadership skills. Choose two and develop a training exercise that will help develop or improve that skill: building employee communities; building teams; coaching and motivating others; communicating with impact, confidence, and energy; leading change; making decisions; providing direction and focus; and valuing diversity.

- Steve's and Mary's recommended readings: Stephen M. R. Covey with Rebecca Merrell, *The Speed of Trust: The One Thing That Changes Everything* (Free Press, 2006); Nancy S. Ahlrichs, *Manager of Choice* (Davies-Black Publishing, 2003); John H. Zenger and Joseph Folkman, *The Extraordinary Leader: Turning Good Managers into Great Leaders* (McGraw-Hill, 2002); Robert H. Rosen, *Leading People* (Viking Penguin Publishing, 1996); Margaret J. Wheatley, *Leadership and the New Science* (Berrett-Koehler Publishers, 1994); Max DePree, *Leadership Jazz* (Dell Publishing, 1992); and Max DePree, *Leadership Is an Art* (Dell Publishing, 1989).

- Select one of the topics in the section on leadership issues in the twenty-first century. Do some additional research on the topic, and put your findings in a bulleted list that you are prepared to share in class. Be sure to cite your sources.

- Interview three managers about what they think it takes to be a good leader. Write up your findings in a report and be prepared to present it in class.

- In your own words, write down three things you learned in this chapter about being a good manager.

- Self-knowledge can be a powerful learning tool. Go to www.mymanagementlab.com and complete these self-assessment exercises: What's My Leadership Style? What Is My LPC Score? How Charismatic Am I? Do I Trust Others? Do Others See Me as Trustworthy? How Good Am I at Building and Leading a Team? Am I an Ethical Leader? Using the results of your assessments, identify personal strengths and weaknesses. What will you do to reinforce your strengths and improve your weaknesses?

CASE APPLICATION 1

Women Leaders in the Arab World: The Case of Sheikha Lubna Al Qasimi

Sheikha Lubna became the first woman to hold a cabinet position in the United Arab Emirates when she was appointed Minister of Economy in 2004. She encourages women to seek education and knowledge to develop their careers.
Source: epa european pressphoto agency b.v./Alamy

Is it tough to be a woman leader in the Arab World? Ask Sheikha Lubna Al Qasimi. In 2010, Sheikha Lubna, the minister of foreign trade of the United Arab Emirates (UAE), was voted the most powerful Arab woman by *Forbes* magazine. She was also ranked the 92nd most powerful woman in the world in its 2012 annual list of the most influential females in politics, business, media, and lifestyle.

In 1999, Sheikha Lubna was awarded the coveted "Distinguished Government Employee Award" and was later appointed as the head of "Tejari," the Middle East's premier electronic business-to-business marketplace at its launch in 2000. The firm, now one of Dubai World's most successful units, has franchises across the Middle East. Prior to managing Tejari, Sheikha Lubna was the senior manager of the Information Systems Department at the Dubai Ports Authority (DPA) and Jebel Ali Free Zone, a position she held for more than seven years. She was appointed to her first ministerial post in November 2004, becoming Minister of Economy and Planning, before taking the Minister of Foreign Trade.

Sheikha Lubna believes in women leadership and wants to act as a role model for the younger generations in a country where more than three-quarters of students attending institutions of higher education and two-third of civil servants in the government sector are women. In the Gulf Cooperation Council (GCC) states where 48 percent of the combined population of 36 million are women the figures are even more compelling. Female participation in the economy of the GCC states stands at 19.2 percent only, or about one-fifth of the total workforce.

According to the *Forbes* profile, Sheikha Lubna is a regional power in her own right. The magazine said her pursuit of an open trade and economic diversification is helping put Dubai, whose economy suffered from the bursting of the property bubble in 2008, back on the road to recovery.

Drawing on the success of Sheikha Lubna and other women leaders, the Arab world has made significant advances in furthering women's leadership. Nevertheless, compared to the rest of the world, the region has a long way to go, and there is considerable scope for improvement. An enabling environment and a change in the mentalities are important to advance the agenda of Arab women leaders and to allow for the development of future generations of aspiring women in the region.

On a positive note, the likelihood of these changes taking place in the future is high as decision makers are aware that female business leaders in the Middle East seize opportunities for professional and societal advancement and that Arab women are at the forefront of an economic transformation throughout the Middle East, acting as agents of change in business, government, and society as a whole. Arab women now are more visible at every level in society and are demonstrating their leadership skills as executives across the region. There is an increasing awareness that the skills and talents of half the population have been underutilized for too long and that this should change. Women are a key human resource whose potential has not been maximized.

On a more negative note, women business leaders in the Middle East still face external challenges such as lack of financing, exclusion from informal business networks in which men operate, and the persistence of the old mentality that business is a male activity. Despite the numerous obstacles, women such as Sheikha Lubna and many others continue to move forward and pave the way to the next generations of Arab women leaders.[71]

DISCUSSION QUESTIONS ✪

1. Describe the leadership style of Sheikha Lubna as she is seen by many other women as a role model.
2. Why did Sheikha Lubna succeed where others have failed?
3. Do you see the future of women leadership in the Arab world as gloomy or bright? Why?

CASE APPLICATION 2 Leading the Skies - AirAsia

Tony Fernandes as the CEO of AirAsia does not believe in taking no for an answer and that you can achieve anything through hard work and perseverance. By relying on this motto, he was determined and bought the debt-ridden airline, AirAsia, for the sum of $0.26. Miraculously, he has settled all the debt within a year. Although the world's airline industry was severely affected by the tragedy on September 11, 2001, Tony took the challenge to reduce flight costs and unnecessary expenses to promote low-cost flights for everyone by throwing the idea of having luxury services in flight, with the tagline "now everyone can fly." Many businessmen feel that Tony will collapse with this low-cost model, but they are wrong because Tony is able to shift his thought quickly to exploit market opportunities, react to challenges, and not give up easily. Tony sacrifices everything to run the airline, committed to his work and a strong belief in his projects,

Tony Fernandes is an inspirational leader. He puts the success of AirAsia down to culture, focus, and discipline.
Source: Kevpix/Alamy

although the environment is not favorable for his business situation. As a result, AirAsia manages to be the world's best low-cost airline company and continues to flourish today.

At AirAsia, Tony is admired by his employees. His easygoing manner is translated into management style that focuses on outcomes, not form. Everyone is equal, the hierarchy is flat, decision making is decentralized, and the employees are empowered—practices that are alien in most Asian companies. From Tony's participative management approach, AirAsia has experienced many innovative concepts, namely online booking and check-in, travel insurance, and holiday packages. Underlying his leadership style is the concept of employees come first, customers come second. If you have a happy workforce, they will look after your customers. According to Tony, his employees are his ultimate asset. He recognizes every one of them by name, and they share the same passion. Tony's line of thought is considered as the latest fad in modern management thinking in which the bottom line of his concept is to turn the conventional management pyramid upside down.

Why did Tony decide to embrace this leadership style, and does it work? Tony deemed that it was the best way to transform the company from unyielding to a flexible and lucrative business practice in order to survive in a dynamic environment. Seeing is believing![72]

DISCUSSION QUESTIONS ✪

1. Explain Tony Fernandes's leadership style. What are the benefits and drawbacks of his style?
2. Based on Tony Fernades's radical approach, how does it foster or hinder his effort to transform AirAsia into a healthy and money-generating company?
3. How could future leaders be picked in this organization? Would leadership development be important to this organization? Discuss.
4. What could other businesses learn from Tony Fernandes's approach to leadership?

PLANNING

Learning outcomes

When you have read this chapter you should be able to:

1 Explain the purposes of planning and the content of different types of plan

2 Compare planning processes, and say when each may be most suitable

3 Outline the seven iterative steps in planning, and some techniques used in each

4 Explain how the goals in a plan affect motivation to achieve them

5 Assess the completeness of a plan

6 Use ideas from the chapter to comment on the management issues in the Crossrail case study

Activity 6.1 What is 'planning'?

Before reading this chapter, write some notes on what you understand by the term 'planning'.

Choose the organisation or people who may be able help you to learn about the topic. You may find it helpful to discuss it with a manager you know, or use an activity you have managed.

- Identify a planning issue you can use for this activity, and make a brief note about it.
- What types of plan do managers in the company make?
- How do they typically develop their plans – can they describe their planning process?
- Can they explain some of the planning techniques they use?

Keep these notes as you will be able to use them later.

6.1 Introduction

Crossrail is an example of a major project which managers can only achieve by doing a great deal of planning. From the early political processes to secure support from many interested parties – some in favour of the project, some against – through raising capital and securing public consent, managers have been planning what to do. That continues, as completing the project depends on the ever more detailed planning required to drive a new railway through a crowded capital city. The case will illustrate how Crossrail's managers deal with these challenges, some of which are unforeseen.

Perhaps paradoxically, as business conditions become more unstable, companies plan more, not less. Change creates uncertainty, and planning helps people adapt to this by clarifying objectives, specifying how to achieve them and monitoring progress. Plans include both ends (what to do) and means (how to do it).

Informal plans (not written down, nor widely shared) work perfectly well in many situations – but as the number of people involved in an activity increases they need something more to guide them. That is the focus here – on more formal plans, which record the goals of a business or unit, and who will do what to achieve them. When senior managers at Hiscox, a small but rapidly growing insurance company, decided to add an online service to its traditional way of doing business through insurance brokers, it needed a plan for the website AND a plan to reassure the brokers they still had a role. When two entrepreneurs decided to create the City Inn hotel chain they planned in detail the kind of hotels they would be – contemporary, city centre, newly built, 'active and open' atmosphere and a consistent room design across the group.

Figure 6.1 provides an overview of the themes. At the centre are seven generic tasks in planning – but people vary the order and how much attention they give to each. The chapter outlines the benefits of planning and their content. Later sections describe the process of planning and outlines some of the techniques that people use to create a plan which will help them achieve their objectives.

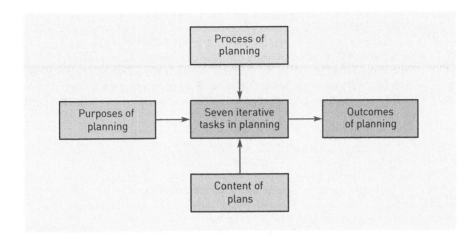

Figure 6.1
An overview
of the chapter

6.2 Purposes of planning

Planning is the iterative task of setting goals, specifying how to achieve them, implementing the plan and evaluating the results.

A **goal** (or **objective**) is a desired future state for an activity or organisational unit.

A planner is an individual contemplating future actions: the activity of **planning** involves establishing the **goals (or objectives)** for the task, specifying how to achieve them, implementing the plan and evaluating the results. Goals are the desired future state of an activity or organisational unit, and planning to meet them typically includes allocating resources and specifying what people need to do to meet the goals.

If people plan well it helps them to:

- clarify direction;
- motivate people;
- use resources efficiently; and
- increase control, as they can measure progress against goals.

The act of planning may in itself add value, by ensuring that people base decisions on a wider range of evidence than if there was no planning system. Giraudeau (2008) shows how the planning process in one of Renault's divisions enhanced debate among managers, and stimulated their strategic imagination. By observing the company's planners as they developed their plan to build a plant in Brazil, the author shows how providing detailed draft plans to other managers (many of whom were unfamiliar with that country) led them to see opportunities they had not considered. If done badly, planning has the opposite effect, leading to confusion and waste.

Good plans give direction to the people whose work contributes to their achievement. If everyone knows the purpose of an activity and how their task contributes, they work more effectively. They adjust their work to the plan (or vice versa), and co-operate and co-ordinate with others. It helps them cope with uncertainty: if they know the end result they can respond to unexpected changes, without waiting to be told. People like to know how their task fits the bigger picture, as it adds interest and enables them to take more responsibility.

Management in practice   Maersk – planning key to strategy   www.maersk.com

Maersk is the world's largest container operator, and depends on planning. Mark Cornwall, Operations Manager, explains:

> Maersk operates 470 container ships with 1.9 million individual containers that are all travelling around the world, and our job is to build efficiencies into the system – moving the cargo to the customer on time.
> Part of our strategy is to deliver unmatched reliability, and operations is key to that. From the top of the company right down to the clerks on the desk, everybody's focused on meeting deadlines and the

requirements of the customer every step of the way. So whether it's a ship arriving in a port on time, or a container loading on a ship on time, or a truck delivery to a warehouse, everybody's focused all the way through the chain on making sure that everything happens against the deadline as planned.

Efficiency's all about making the best use of your assets, so whether it's putting as many containers as possible on a ship, or maximising your utilisation of a particular train, or getting as many miles out of a truck as you can during a shift, it's all about planning your assets to get the biggest use out of them during that period.

Source: Interview with Mark Cornwall.

Planning reduces overlap and at the same time ensures that someone is responsible for each activity. A plan helps people co-ordinate their separate tasks, so saving time and resources; without a plan they may work at cross-purposes. If people are clear on the goal they can spot inefficiencies or unnecessary delays and act to fix them.

Setting final and interim goals lets people know how well they are progressing and when they have finished. Comparing actual progress against the intended progress enables people to adjust the goal or change the way they are using resources.

The content of a plan is the subject – *what* aspect of business it deals with: strategic, business unit, operational, tactical or special purpose. The next section deals with those topics, while Section 6.4 deals with *how* – the planning process.

6.3 The content of plans

People starting a new business or expanding an existing one prepare a **business plan** – a document that sets out the markets the business intends to serve, how it will do so and what finance they require. It does so in considerable detail, as it needs to convince potential investors to lend money. Managers seeking capital investment or other corporate resources need to convince senior managers to allocate them – which they do by presenting a convincing plan. People in the public sector do the same – a director of roads (for example) needs to present a plan to convince the chief executive or elected members that planned expenditure on roads will be a better use of resources than competing proposals from (say) the director of social work. Service managers inevitably compete with each other for limited resources and develop business plans to support their case.

> A **business plan** is a document which sets out the markets the business intends to serve, how it will do so and what finance they require.

Strategic plans apply to the whole organisation. They set out the overall direction and cover major activities – markets and revenues, together with plans for marketing, human resources and production. Strategy is concerned with deciding what business an organisation should be in, where it wants to be and how it is going to get there. These decisions involve major resource commitments and usually require several consequential operational decisions.

> A **strategic plan** sets out the overall direction for the business, is broad in scope and covers all the major activities.

In a large business there are divisional plans for each major unit. If subsidiaries operate as autonomous **strategic business units** (SBUs) they develop their plans with limited inputs from the rest of the company, as they manage distinct products or markets.

> A **strategic business unit** consists of a number of closely related products for which it is meaningful to formulate a separate strategy.

| Management in practice | British Airways plans survival   www.ba.com   FT |

In 2009 British Airways reported that it expected to lose money for the second successive year, and said it was planning more cost reductions to help it survive an expected two-year recession. It was shrinking operations at Gatwick Airport reducing the aircraft fleet based there from 32 to 24.

Other plans included:

- cutting thousands of jobs across the business;
- negotiating a merger with Spain's Iberia to create Europe's third-largest aviation group;

- reducing absenteeism among staff;
- negotiating more efficient working practices for cabin staff;
- reducing capacity at London City Airport by a further 17 per cent from an earlier plan.

Source: Adapted from BA cuts costs as it anticipates two years of recession (Kevin Done), *Financial Times*, 6 March 2009.

Strategic plans usually set out a direction for several years, though in businesses with long lead times (energy production or aircraft manufacture) they look perhaps 15 years ahead. Ryanair plans to grow capacity to meet demand, and makes a plan showing the financial and other implications of enlarging the fleet, recruiting staff and opening new routes. Such plans are not fixed: managers regularly update them to take account of new conditions, so they are sometimes called 'rolling plans'.

Operational plans detail how the overall objectives are to be achieved, by specifying what senior management expects from specific departments or functions.

Operational plans detail how managers expect to achieve the strategic objectives. They are narrower in scope, indicating what departments or functions should do to support the strategy. So there may be a family of related plans forming a hierarchy – a strategic plan for the organisation and main divisions, and several operational plans for departments or teams. Sainsbury announced an aggressive expansion plan in 2009, with the aim of opening 50 new supermarkets and extending another 50, over the next two years. Justin King, chief executive, said that it would concentrate the expansion in areas where it was weak, such as the west of England, Wales and Scotland. Such plans will contain linked objectives and will become more specific as they move down the organisation – eventually dealing with small activities that need to be dealt with for each new store – but aiming to be consistent with the wider expansion strategy. Table 6.1 shows this hierarchical arrangement, and how the character of plans changes at each level.

Most organisations prepare annual plans which focus on finance and set budgets for the coming year – these necessarily include sales, marketing, production or technology plans as well. Activity plans are short-term plans which deal with immediate production or service delivery – a sheet scheduling which orders to deliver next week, or who is on duty tomorrow. Standing plans specify how to deal with routine, recurring issues like recruitment or customer complaints. Some use a method called **enterprise resource planning** to integrate the day-to-day work of complex production systems – Chapter 10 describes this technique in Section 10.5.

Enterprise resource planning (ERP) is a computer-based planning system which links separate databases to plan the use of all resources within the enterprise.

Managers also prepare special purpose plans. Disasters like the explosion in 2010 at BP's oil rig in the Gulf of Mexico severely damage a company's reputation, but a well-prepared and regularly rehearsed disaster recovery plan can limit the damage. They also prepare plans to organise and implement specific changes, such as introducing a new computer system or launching a new product. When The Royal Bank of Scotland took over NatWest Bank,

Table 6.1 A planning hierarchy

Type of plan	Strategic	Operational	Activity
Level	Organisation or business unit	Division, department, function or market	Work unit or team
Focus	Direction and strategy for whole organisation	Functional changes or market activities to support strategic plans	Actions needed to deliver current products or services
Nature	Broad, general direction	Detail on required changes	Specific detail on immediate goals and tasks
Timescale	Long-term (2–3 years?)	Medium (up to 18 months?)	Very short-term (hours to weeks?)

managers quickly developed over 160 interlocking plans to incorporate NatWest operations into those of RBS (Kennedy *et al.*, 2006). People starting a new business have to prepare business plans to persuade potential investors – even though the majority change their plans significantly in the first few years of trading.

6.4 The process of planning

The process of planning refers to how people plan – do they develop them at the top of the organisation, or do staff contribute ideas? How frequently do they revise them? Who monitors them? A **planning system** organises and co-ordinates these activities, thus shaping the quality and value of a plan. Designing and maintaining a suitable planning system is part of the planning task.

One issue is participation – who should take part in making the plan? One approach is to appoint a group of staff specialists to be responsible for producing plans, with or without consultation with the line managers or staff concerned. Others believe the quality and acceptability of the plan will be higher if staff who are familiar with local conditions help to create it.

> A **planning system** refers to the processes by which the members of an organisation produce plans, including their frequency and who takes part in the process.

Management in practice   A new planning process at Merck   www.merck.com   FT

In the early 1990s Merck was the world's leading pharmaceutical company, but by 2006 it was ranked only eighth. Dick Clark, the new Chief Executive, was charged with reviving a company: one of his first actions was to make radical changes in the company's planning process. Teams of employees were asked to present the business cases to senior managers to test possible directions for the company – such as whether to build a generic drugs business. This process was vital, said Mr Clark, as it showed the 200 senior executives that Merck would now operate in an atmosphere where assumptions would be openly questioned by anyone. He has also changed the way the company sets its earnings projections. Formerly set by top managers, projections are now set by lower-level teams. 'It wasn't like Dick Clark said "We're going to have double-digit growth, go out and find it!" We tested it and tweaked it . . . but it was legitimate and we believe in it, so let's go public with it. And that's the first time we'd done that as a company.'

Source: Adapted from The man who has to shake up Merck (by Christopher Bowe), *Financial Times*, 27 March 2006, p. 10.

Another issue is how fixed or flexible the planning should be. Some advocate a rational approach to planning, taking care to assemble all relevant data and information, and setting clear, fixed objectives and how they will be met. Others favour 'learning' or 'emergent' approaches. They believe that, in rapidly changing conditions, plans are essentially temporary and provisional, so that managers can adapt them to suit changing circumstances.

Planning and doing may seem like separate activities, and in stable conditions they may be. In volatile conditions, with markets or technologies changing quickly, people conduct them simultaneously. In their study of strategic planning, Whittington *et al.* (2006) conclude that strategising and organising:

> become very similar, or even common: in the heat of the moment practitioners may be unable to distinguish the two. (p. 618)

Jennings (2000) shows how companies change their approach to planning as conditions change. A study of the UK electricity generating company PowerGen (now owned by the German company E.on) traced the evolution of the company's corporate planning process since it was privatised in 1991. It had retained a formal process with a five-year planning horizon, but it is more devolved. A small central team focuses on overall strategy while business units develop local plans, quickly completing the planning cycle. These changes created a more adaptive style of planning which suited the (new) uncertainty of the business.

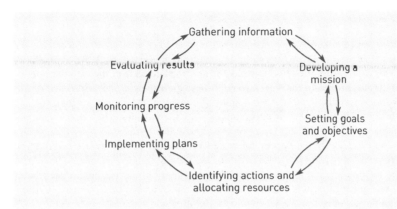

Figure 6.2
Seven iterative
tasks in making
a plan

Figure 6.2 shows the seven generic tasks which people can perform when they make a plan. They use them iteratively, often going back to an earlier stage when they find new information that implies, say, that they need to reshape the original goals. And they may miss a stage, or spend too little or too much time on them: the figure only indicates a way of analysing the stages of planning.

6.5   Gathering information

Any plan depends on information – including informal, soft information gained from casual encounters with colleagues, as well as formal analyses of economic and market trends.

Chapter 3 outlined the competitive and general environments, and planners usually begin by drawing on information about these. External sources include government economic and demographic statistics, industry surveys and business intelligence services. Managers also commission market research on, for example, individual shopping patterns, attitudes towards particular firms or brand names and satisfaction with existing products or services.

Management in practice   **Inamo – planning the start-up**   www.inamo-restaurant.com

Danny Potter, Managing Director, explained the information they needed before they started:

Well, in terms of market research, we looked into what other interactive ordering restaurants and concepts there might be, a lot of research on the world wide web and just going round London to various restaurants. We also looked at good guides which give you a quick summary. Also meeting people in the industry, going to shows and exhibitions are quick ways of learning a great deal. Also a few brainstorming sessions to get feedback on what people thought of the concept – one piece of feedback from that was that this would not fit a formal French dining environment, for example. We came to the conclusion that Oriental fusion was the appropriate cuisine type.

We spent a great deal of time finding the right location. We went through the government statistics database and built a database of our own, analysing demographics of the whole of London. What we found was that a very small area around central London is really where all the buzz happens, where all of the restaurants want to be. And then focused on finding the right location in this area.

Source: Interview with Danny Potter.

SWOT analysis

At a strategic level, planning will usually combine an analysis of external environmental factors with an internal analysis of the organisation's strengths and weaknesses. A **SWOT analysis** does this, bringing together the internal strengths and weaknesses and the external opportunities and threats. Internally, managers would analyse the strengths and weaknesses of the resources within, or available to, the organisation (Grant, 1991) – such as a firm's distinctive research capability or its skill in integrating acquired companies. The external analysis would probably be based on PESTEL and Porter's (1980a) five forces model (see Chapter 3). These tools help to identify the opportunities and threats that people believe could affect the business.

A **SWOT analysis** is a way of summarising the organisation's strengths and weaknesses relative to external opportunities and threats.

While the method appears to be a rational way of gathering information, its usefulness depends on recognising that it is a human representation of reality: participants will differ about the significance of factors – a debate which may itself add value to the process.

Critical success factors analysis

In considering whether to enter a new market, a widely used planning technique is to assess the **critical success factors** in that market. These are the things which customers most value about a product or service: some value price, others quality, others some unusual feature of the product – but in all cases they are things that a company must be able to do well to succeed in that market.

Critical success factors are those aspects of a strategy that *must* be achieved to secure competitive advantage.

Forecasting

Forecasts or predictions are usually based on an analysis of past trends in factors such as input prices (wages, components etc.), sales patterns or demographic trends. In relatively stable environments, people can reasonably assume that past trends will continue, but in uncertain conditions they need alternative assumptions. A new market might support rapid sales growth, whereas in a saturated market (basic foods, paid-for newspapers) it might be more realistic to assume a low or zero growth rate.

Forecasting is big business, with companies selling analyses to business and government, using formal techniques such as time-series analysis, econometric modelling and simulation. These become less useful as uncertainty increases. Grant (2003) reports that oil companies have reduced the resources they spend on forecasting oil demand and prices, preferring to rely on broader assumptions about possible trends.

Sensitivity analysis

One way to test assumptions is to make a **sensitivity analysis** of key variables in a plan. This may assume that the company will attain a 10 per cent share of a market within a year: what will be the effect on the calculations if they secure 5 per cent, or 15 per cent? What if interest rates rise, increasing the cost of financing the projects? Planners can then compare the robustness of the options and assess the relative risks.

A **sensitivity analysis** tests the effect on a plan of several alternative values of the key variables.

Scenario planning

An alternative to forecasting is to consider possible scenarios. **Scenario planning** typically begins by considering how external forces such as the internet, an ageing population or climate change might affect a company's business over the next 5–10 years. Doing so can bring managers new ideas about their environment enabling them to consider previously unthinkable possibilities. Advocates (Van der Heijden, 1996) claim that it encourages managers to develop their awareness of the business environment and of the most critical uncertainties they are likely to face. Few companies use the technique systematically, as it

Scenario planning is an attempt to create coherent and credible alternative stories about the future.

is time consuming and costly. A notable exception is Shell, which began developing the technique in 1971:

> Scenario thinking now underpins the established way of thinking at Shell. It has become a part of the culture, such that people throughout the company, dealing with significant decisions, normally will think in terms of multiple, but equally plausible futures to provide a context for decision making. (Van der Heijden, 1996, p. 21)

The company has a team of 14 staff based in the Netherlands developing scenarios, alongside the company's strategy analysts (*Financial Times*, 30 November 2010).

A combination of PESTEL and five forces analysis should ensure that managers recognise major external factors. Forecasting and scenario planning can help them to consider possible implications for the business.

6.6 Setting goals (or objectives)

A useful plan depends on being clear about the ultimate purpose of a task – whether this concerns the organisation or a unit. This seems obvious, but managers favour action above planning and often spend too little time on this (difficult) step.

Goals (or objectives)

Goals give focus to a task – what will we achieve, by when? Setting goals is difficult, as we need to look beyond a (relatively) known present to an unknown future. Goals provide the reference point for other decisions, and the criteria against which to measure performance. At the business level they include quantified financial objectives – earnings per share, return on shareholders' funds and cash flow. At the project level, the targets will be expressed in other ways – such as the energy performance of a building.

A hierarchy of goals

A way of relating goals to each other is to build them into a hierarchy, in which the overall goals are transformed into more specific goals for different parts of the organisation – such as marketing, finance, operations and human resources. Managers in those areas develop plans setting out the actions they must undertake to meet the overall goal. Figure 6.3 illustrates this by using IKEA's plan to expand in Japan. To meet its planned sales growth, managers decided to open many stores across Asia, of which the first were to be in Japan. That evolved into a plan for their probable location, and then into a precise plan for two near Tokyo. That in turn led managers to develop progressively more detailed plans for the thousands of details that will need to be in good order if the venture is to succeed.

Plans like this need to be flexible, as they will need to change between design and completion. Managers often stress their firm commitment to the highest level goals – but leave staff with more discretion about how to achieve lower level plans.

However convincingly set out, statements of goals only have value if they guide action. Effective goal setting involves balancing multiple goals, considering whether they meet the SMART criteria, and evaluating their likely motivational effects.

Single or multiple goals?

Company statements of goals – whether short- or long-term – are usually expressed in the plural, since a single measure cannot indicate success or failure. Emphasis on one goal, such as growth, ignores another, such as dividends. Managers balance multiple, possibly conflicting goals: Gerry Murphy, who became chief executive of Kingfisher (a UK DIY retailer), recalled:

> Alan Sheppard, my boss at Grand Metropolitan and one of my mentors, used to say that senior management shouldn't have the luxury of single point objectives. Delivering growth

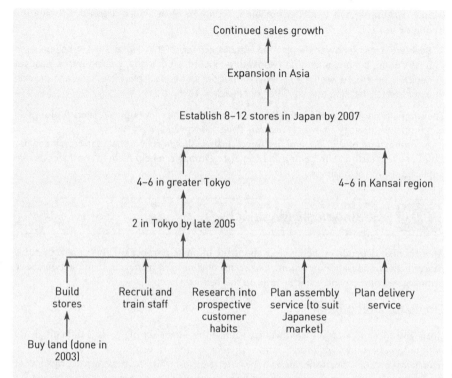

Figure 6.3
Developing a plan
for IKEA (Japan)

without returns or returns without growth is not something I find attractive or acceptable. Over time we are going to do both. (*Financial Times*, 28 April 2004, p. 23)

As senior managers try to take account of a range of stakeholders, they balance their diverse interests. This can lead to conflict between **stated goals**, as reflected in public announcements, and the **real goals** – those to which people pay most attention. The latter reflect senior managers' priorities, expressed through what they say and how they reward and discipline managers.

Stated goals are those which are prominent in company publications and websites.

Real goals are those to which people pay most attention.

Criteria for assessing goals

The SMART acronym summarises some criteria for assessing a set of goals. What form of each is effective depends on circumstances (specific goals are not necessarily better than directional ones). The list simply offers some measures against which to evaluate a statement of goals.

- **Specific** Does the goal set specific targets? People who are planning a meeting can set specific goals for what they hope to achieve, such as:

  By the end of the meeting we will have convinced them to withdraw their current proposal, and to have set a date (within the next two weeks) at which we will start to develop an alternative plan.

  Having a clear statement of what the meeting (or any other activity in a plan) is intended to achieve helps people to focus effort.

- **Measurable** Some goals may be quantified ('increase sales of product X by 5 per cent a year over the next three years') but others, equally important, are more qualitative ('to offer a congenial working environment'). Quantitative goals are not more useful than qualitative ones – what can be measured is not necessarily important. What matters is that goals are defined precisely enough to measure progress towards them.

- **Attainable** Goals should be challenging, but not unreasonably difficult. If people perceive a goal as unrealistic, they will not be committed. Equally, goals should not be too easy, as this too undermines motivation. Goal-setting theory (see Chapter 13, Section 13.5) predicts the motivational consequences of goal setting.
- **Rewarded** People need to see that attaining a goal will bring a reward – this gives meaning and helps ensure commitment.
- **Timed** Does the goal specify the time by which it will be achieved, and is that also a reasonable and acceptable standard?

6.7 Identifying actions and communicating the plan

This part of the planning process involves deciding what needs to be done, who will do it and communicating that. In a small activity like planning a project in a club, this would just mean listing the tasks and dividing them clearly among a few able and willing members. At the other extreme, Ford's plan to build a new car plant in China probably runs to several volumes.

Identifying what needs to be done – and by whom

Figure 1.3 (reproduced as Figure 6.4) provides a model to help envisage the implications of a goal, by enabling managers to ask what, if any, changes do they need to make to each element? If the goal is to launch a new product, the plan could identify which parts of the organisation will be affected (structure), what investment is needed (finance), how production will fit with existing lines (business processes) and so on. Computer projects often fail because planners pay too much attention to the technological aspects and too little to contextual elements such as structure, culture and people (Boddy *et al.*, 2009a). Each main heading will require further actions that people can identify and assign.

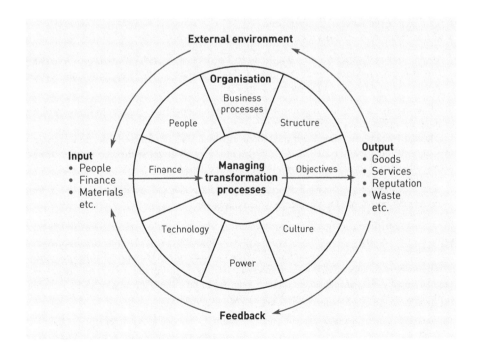

Figure 6.4
Possible action areas in a plan

Communicating the plan

In a small organisation or where the plan deals with only one area, communication in any formal way is probably unnecessary. Equally, those who have been involved in developing the objectives and plans will be well aware of it. However, in larger enterprises managers will probably invest time and effort in communicating both the objectives and the actions required throughout the areas affected. They do this to:

- Ensure that everyone understands the plan;
- Allow them to resolve any confusion and ambiguity;
- Communicate the judgements and assumptions that underlie the plan; and
- Ensure that activities around the organisation are co-ordinated in practice as well as on paper.

6.8 Implementing plans and monitoring results

However good the plan, nothing worthwhile happens until people implement it by making visible, physical changes to the organisation and the way people work within it. Many managers find this the most challenging part of the process – when plans, however well developed, are brought into contact with current ways of working. The plan then meets organisational and environmental obstacles – possibly showing that some of the assumptions in the plan are wrong.

Organisations are slower to change than plans are to prepare – so events may overtake the plan. Miller *et al.* (2004) tracked the long-term outcomes of 150 strategic plans to establish how managers put them into action and how that affected performance. They defined implementation as

> all the processes and outcomes which accrue to a strategic decision once authorisation has been given to . . . put the decision into practice. (Miller *et al.*, 2004, p. 203)

Their intention was to identify the conditions in which implementation occurs, the managerial activities involved in putting plans into practice, and the extent to which they achieved the objectives. They concluded that success was heavily influenced by:

- managers' experience of the issue, and
- **organisational readiness** for a change.

> Having relevant experience of what has to be done . . . enables managers to assess the objectives [and to] specify the tasks and resource implications appropriately, leading [those affected to accept the process]. (p. 206)

Readiness means a receptive organisational climate that enables managers to implement the change within a positive environment.

The statistical results were illustrated by cases which showed, for example, how managers in a successful company were able to implement a plan to upgrade their computer systems because they had *experience* of many similar changes. They were

> able to set targets, detail what needed doing and allocate the resources . . . That is, they could plan and control the implementation effectively. (p. 209)

In another illustration, a regional brewer extending into the London area had no directly relevant experience, and so was not able to set a specific plan. But people in the organisation were very *receptive* to new challenges, and could implement the move with little formal planning.

The authors concluded that the activities of planning do not in themselves lead to success, but are a means for gaining acceptance of what has to be done. Planning helps by inducing confidence in the process, leading to high levels of acceptability:

> Planning is a necessary part of this approach to success, but it is not sufficient in itself. (p. 210)

Organisational readiness refers to the extent to which staff are able to specify objectives, tasks and resource requirements of a plan appropriately, leading to acceptance.

The final stage in planning is to set up a system that allows people to monitor progress towards the goals. This happens at all levels of planning – from a project manager monitoring and controlling the progress of a discrete project to a board committee monitoring the progress of a broad strategic change that affects many parts of the business – such as integrating an acquisition or entering a new line of business. This is sometimes called a programme, and monitoring then focuses on the interdependencies between many smaller specific projects.

Project plans define and display every task and activity, but someone managing a programme of linked projects would soon become swamped with such detail. The programme manager needs to maintain a quick-to-understand snapshot of the programme. This should show progress to date, the main events being planned, interdependencies, issues and expected completion dates. This also helps the programme manager to communicate with senior executives and project managers.

Activity 6.2   What is 'planning'?

Having read the chapter, make brief notes summarising the main planning issues affecting the organisation.

- What types of plan do managers in the company make? (See Sections 6.2 and 6.3.)
- Can you describe their planning processes? (Refer to Section 6.4.)
- Which planning techniques did they use to gather information? (Refer to Section 6.5.)

Compare what you have found with other students on your course.

Summary

1 Explain the purposes of planning and the content of different types of plan

- Effective plans can clarify direction, motivate people, use resources efficiently and allow people to measure progress towards objectives.
- Plans can be at strategic, tactical and operational levels and, in new businesses, people prepare business plans to secure capital. Strategic business units also prepare plans relatively independently of the parent. There are also special-purpose or project plans, and standing plans. All can be either specific or directional in nature.

2 Compare alternative planning processes and say when each may be most suitable

- Plans can be formal/rational/top-down in nature, or they can be adaptable and flexible (logical incrementalism). Firms in volatile conditions are likely to use several methods.

3 Outline the seven iterative steps in planning and describe techniques used in each

- Recycling through the tasks of gathering information, developing a mission, setting goals, identifying actions and allocating resources, implementing plans, monitoring progress and evaluating results.
- Planners draw information from the general and competitive environments using tools such as Porter's five forces analysis. They can do this within the framework of a SWOT analysis, and also use forecasting, sensitivity analysis, critical success factors and scenario planning techniques.

4 Use theory to evaluate the quality of the goals stated in a plan

- Goals can also be evaluated in terms of whether they are specific, measurable, attainable, rewarded and timed.

5 Use a framework to evaluate whether a plan is sufficiently comprehensive

- The 'wheel' provides a model for recalling the likely areas in an organisation which a plan should cover, indicating the likely ripple effects of change in one area on others.

Review questions

1 What types of planning do you do in your personal life? Describe them in terms of whether they are (a) strategic or operational, (b) short- or long-term, (c) specific or directional.

2 What are four benefits that people in organisations may gain from planning?

3 What are the main sources of information that managers can use in planning? What models can they use to structure this information?

4 What are SMART goals?

5 In what ways can a goal be motivational? What practical things can people do in forming plans that take account of goal-setting theory?

6 What is meant by the term 'hierarchy of goals', and how can the idea help people to build a consistent plan?

7 Explain the term 'organisational readiness', and how people can use the idea in developing a plan that is likely to work.

8 What are the main ways to monitor progress on a plan, and why is this a vital task in planning?

Further reading

Sahlman, W. A. (1997), 'How to write a great business plan', *Harvard Business Review*, vol. 75, no. 4, pp. 98–108.

Valuable guidance by an experienced investor, relevant to start-ups and established businesses.

Weblinks

These websites have appeared in the chapter:

www.maersk.com
www.ba.com
www.merck.com
www.inamo-restaurant.com
www.crossrail.co.uk

Visit two of the sites in the list, and navigate to the pages dealing with corporate news, or investor relations.

- What planning issues are managers in the company likely to be dealing with?
- What kind of environment are they working in, and how may that affect their planning processes?

 Annotated weblinks, multiple choice questions and other useful resources can be found on **www.pearsoned.co.uk/boddy**

Case study   Crossrail   www.crossrail.co.uk

Crossrail is a new railway for London and the south east of England which will connect the City, Canary Wharf, the West End and Heathrow Airport to commuter areas east and west of the capital. It aims to be a world-class, affordable railway, with high frequency, convenient and accessible services across the capital. The plans are intended to:

- relieve congestion on many Underground and rail lines;
- provide new connections and new services;
- bring modern trains; and
- provide six new stations in central London.

By kind permission, Crossrail.

It will add 10 per cent to London's overall transport capacity and provide 40 per cent of the extra rail capacity London needs. Main construction of the railway began in 2010, with services commencing in 2018. Crossrail will make travelling in the area easier and quicker and reduce crowding on London's transport network. It will operate with main line size trains, each carrying more than 1500 passengers.

It is the largest civil engineering project in the UK and the largest single addition to the London transport network for over 50 years. It will run 118 km from Maidenhead and Heathrow in the west, through new twin-bore, 21 km tunnels under Central London out to Shenfield and Abbey Wood in the east, joining the Great Western and Great Eastern railway networks.

The project has a long history – it was first proposed in 1990, but amidst considerable opposition from other players it was cancelled in 1996. Support for building the line continued to grow, as many saw it a major contribution to solving London's transport problems: the company had wide support from businesses and from business organisations such as the CBI, London First and London Chamber of Commerce and Industry.

Political conditions changed again, and Royal Assent was given to the Crossrail Act in July 2008, giving the company authority to build the railway, and in December 2008 the Government and the Mayor of London signed the key funding agreements for Crossrail. The cost (estimated at £14.8 billion) will be met by UK Government, Transport for London and London businesses. Passengers will contribute towards the debt raised during construction by Transport for London and Network Rail will pay for using the line to run train services. Other beneficiaries will also contribute to the cost, including The City of London Corporation, British Airports Authority and property developers such as Canary Wharf Group.

By March 2010, the plan began to turn into reality as many of the smaller elements were implemented. For example, the company announced the award of contracts for what it calls enabling work such as various pieces of complex demolition work at several stations and their surrounding area. The company also announced that the Learning & Skills Council had agreed to provide £5 million towards the cost of a new tunnelling and underground construction academy. A senior manager said:

This is great news for the programme and great news for the tunnelling and underground construction industry. This decision means we can now progress our plans to build this fantastic training facility, which the industry so urgently needs. (private communication)

In 2009, the company published its outline plans for the station building and tunnelling work to be done – making it clear that as detailed design and development of the scheme progressed there would be increasing certainty over the exact times that works will start and finish at each location.

The two 21 km tunnels will present a particular challenge as they run at depths of up to 36m below the busy streets of London. In doing so, they will weave between existing underground railway tunnels, sewers and building foundations. In early 2011, the company indicated that the choice of tunnelling boring machines to use would depend on local circumstances. They estimated that the tunnelling work and the excavation of new stations would create 6 million tonnes of material: they plan to remove most of this by moving it along the tunnels to disposal sites, so avoiding as far as possible the need for lorry movements through central London.

At some locations, enabling works (such as the diversion of utilities like gas mains and demolition of existing buildings) will need to take place before main works. The sites may also be required after main works, for example to support fitting out of stations and tunnels. Enabling works for the station at Tottenham Court Road were planned to start in January 2009, construction in early 2010, and the works would be completed in 2016.

Work on stations and tracks on the existing surface railway to be served by Crossrail will be carried out by Network Rail.

Meanwhile, work was progressing on the timetable for the services to be offered. The unusual complexity of this task arises because the new services will, for much of their routes, run on the existing railway lines, so they will need to fit into the existing timetables. Crossrail is therefore working closely with Network Rail and freight and passenger companies to create a timetable for the new services. They have carried out extensive simulation of future services on the railway, showing that a high level of punctuality can be achieved with at least 24 trains an hour running in each direction at peak times.

Source: Company website and other published sources.

Questions

Visit the Crossrail website (see above).

1 What are the main items of recent news about the progress of the project?

2 What types of plan is the company likely to have made? (See Section 6.3.)

3 What planning processes will it probably have used? (Refer to Section 6.4.)

4 Which of the planning tools mentioned in Sections 6.5, 6.6 and 6.7 are they likely to have used?

SPOTLIGHT: *Manager at Work*

$10 billion. *That's how much Eli Lilly & Co. stands to lose in annual revenues between now and 2016 as three of its major drug patents expire.[1] Replacing that revenue is high on the list of "must-do's" for CEO John Lechleiter (see photo). The solution is speeding up the pace of drug development, but his challenge is: How?*

Unlike its global competitors that have addressed similar product development challenges by using large-scale mergers and acquisitions, Lechleiter's focus has been on acquiring smaller drug companies. He said large-scale combinations "provide short-term relief but don't fundamentally address the issue of innovation and how to make [product development] pipelines more productive." Developing new products and moving them forward as quickly as possible on the thorough and mandatory approval process, which can be agonizingly slow, is critical to the company's present and future success.

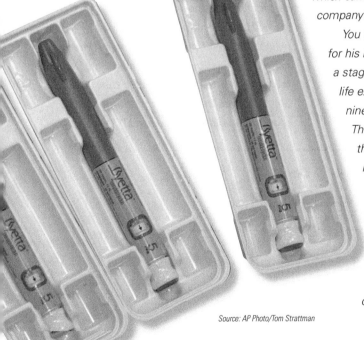

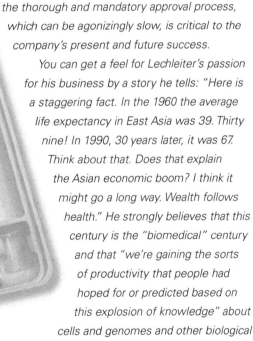

You can get a feel for Lechleiter's passion for his business by a story he tells: "Here is a staggering fact. In the 1960 the average life expectancy in East Asia was 39. Thirty nine! In 1990, 30 years later, it was 67. Think about that. Does that explain the Asian economic boom? I think it might go a long way. Wealth follows health." He strongly believes that this century is the "biomedical" century and that "we're gaining the sorts of productivity that people had hoped for or predicted based on this explosion of knowledge" about cells and genomes and other biological

Source: AP Photo/Tom Strattman

Source: Bloomberg via Getty Images

functioning. His optimism is tempered by what has happened in his company (and other pharmaceutical companies)—what he calls the "patent cliff—the intellectual-property expirations" that threaten research and development.

$10 billion. That's how much Eli Lilly & Co. stands to lose in annual revenues.

One action Lechleiter took was revamping the company's operational structure into five global business units: oncology, diabetes, established markets, emerging markets, and animal health. Part of the restructuring also involved creating an improved product research and development center. Another was encouraging the company's R&D unit to look at ways in which modern technology—improved communications, always-available

Internet, and high-bandwidth systems—could be harnessed as alternatives to how R&D had always been done. And despite the challenges, Lilly's operational performance has been steady. More than 60 percent of the company's project milestones were met or accelerated. **What other organizational design elements might Lechleiter use to ensure that Lilly achieves its goal of speeding up its product development process?**

MyManagementLab®
✪ Improve Your Grade!
Over 10 million students improved their results using the Pearson MyLabs.
Visit **www.mymanagementlab.com** for simulations, tutorials, and end-of-chapter problems.

LEARNING OUTCOMES

11.1 | ***Describe*** *six key elements in organizational design.*

11.2 | ***Contrast*** *mechanistic and organic structures.*

11.3 | ***Discuss*** *the contingency factors that favor either the mechanistic model or the organic model of organizational design.*

11.4 | ***Describe*** *traditional organizational designs.*

Replacing $10 billion in revenue can't and won't be easy. However, Lechleiter understands the importance of organizational structure and design, especially when it comes to the difficult product development challenges facing his company. His initial restructuring actions are ones that many companies undergo when faced with radical environmental challenges in an attempt to become a stronger, more successful organization. His actions also illustrate the importance of designing or redesigning a structure that helps an organization accomplish its goals efficiently and effectively. In this chapter, we'll look at what's involved with that.

DESIGNING Organizational Structure

11.1 *Describe* six key elements in organizational design.

A short distance south of McAlester, Oklahoma, employees in a vast factory complex make products that must be perfect. These people "are so good at what they do and have been doing it for so long that they have a 100 percent market share."[2] They make bombs for the U.S. military and doing so requires a work environment that's an interesting mix of the mundane, structured, and disciplined, coupled with high levels of risk and emotion. The work gets done efficiently and effectively here. Work also gets done efficiently and effectively at Cisco Systems although not in such a structured and formal way. At Cisco, some 70 percent of the employees work from home at least 20 percent of the time.[3] Both of these organizations get needed work done although each does so using a different structure.

Few topics in management have undergone as much change in the past few years as that of organizing and organizational structure. Managers are reevaluating traditional approaches to find new structural designs that best support and facilitate employees' doing the organization's work—designs that can achieve efficiency but are also flexible.[4]

The basic concepts of organization design formulated by early management writers, such as Henri Fayol and Max Weber, offered structural principles for managers to follow. (Those principles are described on pp. 55–57.) Over 90 years have passed since many of those principles were originally proposed. Given that length of time and all the changes that have taken place, you'd think that those principles would be pretty worthless today. Surprisingly, they're not. For the most part, they still provide valuable insights into designing effective and efficient organizations. Of course, we've also gained a great deal of knowledge over the years as to their limitations.

organizing
Arranging and structuring work to accomplish the organization's goals

organizational structure
The formal arrangement of jobs within an organization

organizational chart
The visual representation of an organization's structure

organizational design
Creating or changing an organization's structure

In Chapter 1, we defined **organizing** as arranging and structuring work to accomplish organizational goals. It's an important process during which managers design an organization's structure. **Organizational structure** is the formal arrangement of jobs within an organization. This structure, which can be shown visually in an **organizational chart**, also serves many purposes. (See Exhibit 11-1.) When managers create or change the structure, they're engaged in **organizational design**, a process that involves decisions about six key elements: work specialization, departmentalization, chain of command, span of control, centralization and decentralization, and formalization.[5]

Exhibit 11-1
Purposes of Organizing

- Divides work to be done into specific jobs and departments.
- Assigns tasks and responsibilities associated with individual jobs.
- Coordinates diverse organizational tasks.
- Clusters jobs into units.
- Establishes relationships among individuals, groups, and departments.
- Establishes formal lines of authority.
- Allocates and deploys organizational resources.

Work Specialization

At the Wilson Sporting Goods factory in Ada, Ohio, 150 workers (with an average work tenure exceeding 20 years) make every football used in the National Football League and most of those used in college and high school football games. To meet daily output goals, the workers specialize in job tasks such as molding, stitching and sewing, lacing, and so forth.[6] This is an example of **work specialization**, which is dividing work activities into separate job tasks. Individual employees "specialize" in doing part of an activity rather than the entire activity in order to increase work output. It's also known as division of labor, a concept we introduced in the Looking Back: The History of Management module.

Work specialization makes efficient use of the diversity of skills that workers have. In most organizations, some tasks require highly developed skills; others can be performed by employees with lower skill levels. If all workers were engaged in all the steps of, say, a manufacturing process, all would need the skills necessary to perform both the most demanding and the least demanding jobs. Thus, except when performing the most highly skilled or highly sophisticated tasks, employees would be working below their skill levels. In addition, skilled workers are paid more than unskilled workers, and, because wages tend to reflect the highest level of skill, all workers would be paid at highly skilled rates to do easy tasks—an inefficient use of resources. This concept explains why you rarely find a cardiac surgeon closing up a patient after surgery. Instead, doctors doing their residencies in open-heart surgery and learning the skill usually stitch and staple the patient after the surgeon has finished the surgery.

Early proponents of work specialization believed it could lead to great increases in productivity. At the beginning of the twentieth century, that generalization was reasonable. Because specialization was not widely practiced, its introduction almost always generated higher productivity. But, as Exhibit 11-2 illustrates, a good thing can be carried too far. At some point, the human diseconomies from division of labor—boredom, fatigue, stress, low productivity, poor quality, increased absenteeism, and high turnover—exceed the economic advantages.[7]

TODAY'S VIEW Most managers today continue to see work specialization as important because it helps employees be more efficient. For example, McDonald's uses

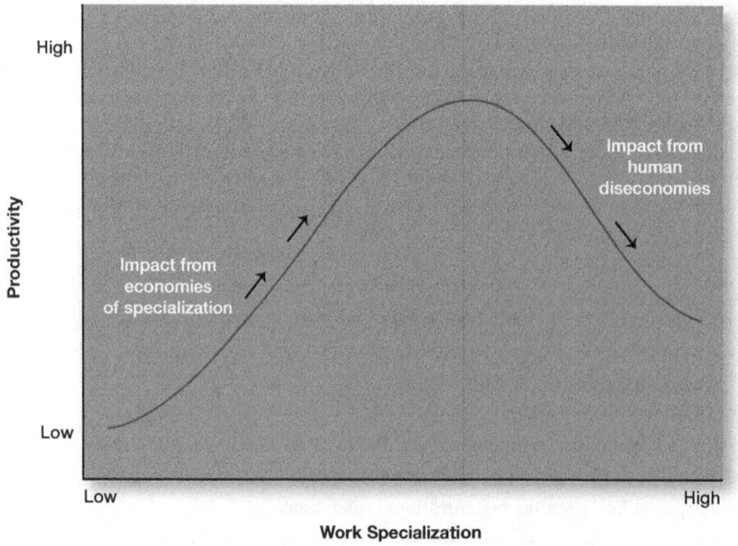

work specialization
Dividing work activities into separate job tasks

Exhibit 11-2
Economies and Diseconomies of Work Specialization

116

high work specialization to get its products made and delivered to customers efficiently and quickly—that's why it's called "fast" food. One person takes orders at the drive-through window, others cook and assemble the hamburgers, another works the fryer, another gets the drinks, another bags orders, and so forth. Such single-minded focus on maximizing efficiency has contributed to increasing productivity. In fact, at many McDonald's, you'll see a clock that times how long it takes employees to fill the order; look closer and you'll probably see posted somewhere an order fulfillment time goal. At some point, however, work specialization no longer leads to productivity. That's why companies such as Avery-Dennison, Ford Australia, Hallmark, and American Express use minimal work specialization and instead give employees a broad range of tasks to do.

Departmentalization

departmentalization
The basis by which jobs are grouped together

Does your college have a department of student services or financial aid department? Are you taking this course through a management department? After deciding what job tasks will be done by whom, common work activities need to be grouped back together so work gets done in a coordinated and integrated way. How jobs are grouped together is called **departmentalization**. Five common forms of departmentalization are used, although an organization may develop its own unique classification. (For instance, a hotel might have departments such as front desk operations, sales and catering, housekeeping and laundry, and maintenance.) Exhibit 11-3 illustrates each type of departmentalization as well as the advantages and disadvantages of each.

TODAY'S VIEW   Most large organizations continue to use combinations of most or all of these types of departmentalization. For example, a major Japanese electronics firm organizes its divisions along functional lines, its manufacturing units around processes, its sales units around seven geographic regions, and its sales regions into four customer groupings. Black & Decker organizes its divisions along functional lines, its manufacturing units around processes, its sales around geographic regions, and its sales regions around customer groupings.

cross-functional team
A work team composed of individuals from various functional specialties

One popular departmentalization trend is the increasing use of customer departmentalization. Because getting and keeping customers is essential for success, this approach works well because it emphasizes monitoring and responding to changes in customers' needs. Another popular trend is the use of teams, especially as work tasks have become more complex and diverse skills are needed to accomplish those tasks. One specific type of team that more organizations are using is a **cross-functional team**, a work team composed of individuals from various functional specialties. For instance, at Ford's material planning and logistics division, a cross-functional team of employees from the company's finance, purchasing, engineering, and quality control areas, along with representatives from outside logistics suppliers, has developed several work improvement ideas.[8] We'll discuss cross-functional teams (and all types of teams) more fully in Chapter 14.

Chain of Command

chain of command
The line of authority extending from upper organizational levels to the lowest levels, which clarifies who reports to whom

Suppose you were at work and had a problem with an issue that came up. What would you do? Who would you go to help you resolve that issue? People need to know who their boss is. That's what the chain of command is all about. The **chain of command** is the line of authority extending from upper organizational levels to lower levels, which clarifies who reports to whom. Managers need to consider it when organizing work because it helps employees with questions such as "Who do I report to?" or "Who do I go to if I have a problem?" To understand the chain of command, you have to understand three other important concepts: authority, responsibility, and unity of command. Let's look first at authority.

FUNCTIONAL DEPARTMENTALIZATION—Groups Jobs According to Function

Exhibit 11-3
The Five Common
Forms of
Departmentalization

Plant Manager

| Manager, Engineering | Manager, Accounting | Manager, Manufacturing | Manager, Human Resources | Manager, Purchasing |

+ Efficiencies from putting together similar specialties and people with common skills, knowledge, and orientations
+ Coordination within functional area
+ In-depth specialization
− Poor communication across functional areas
− Limited view of organizational goals

GEOGRAPHICAL DEPARTMENTALIZATION—Groups Jobs According to Geographic Region

Vice President for Sales

| Sales Director, Western Region | Sales Director, Southern Region | Sales Director, Midwestern Region | Sales Director, Eastern Region |

+ More effective and efficient handling of specific regional issues that arise
+ Serve needs of unique geographic markets better
− Duplication of functions
− Can feel isolated from other organizational areas

PRODUCT DEPARTMENTALIZATION—Groups Jobs by Product Line

Source: Bombardier Annual Report.

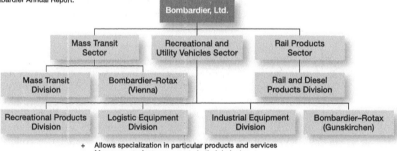

Bombardier, Ltd.

Mass Transit Sector — Recreational and Utility Vehicles Sector — Rail Products Sector

Mass Transit Division — Bombardier–Rotax (Vienna) — Rail and Diesel Products Division

Recreational Products Division — Logistic Equipment Division — Industrial Equipment Division — Bombardier–Rotax (Gunskirchen)

+ Allows specialization in particular products and services
+ Managers can become experts in their industry
+ Closer to customers
− Duplication of functions
− Limited view of organizational goals

PROCESS DEPARTMENTALIZATION—Groups Jobs on the Basis of Product or Customer Flow

Plant Superintendent

| Sawing Department Manager | Planing and Milling Department Manager | Assembling Department Manager | Lacquering and Sanding Department Manager | Finishing Department Manager | Inspection and Shipping Department Manager |

+ More efficient flow of work activities
− Can only be used with certain types of products

CUSTOMER DEPARTMENTALIZATION—Groups Jobs on the Basis of Specific and Unique Customers Who Have Common Needs

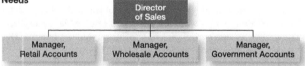

Director of Sales

| Manager, Retail Accounts | Manager, Wholesale Accounts | Manager, Government Accounts |

+ Customers' needs and problems can be met by specialists
− Duplication of functions
− Limited view of organizational goals

These waiters and waitresses stand in line while attending a meeting held by their managers before they start their work at a restaurant at the Beijing Airport. The managers have the authority to give employees instructions for their work day as it is an inherent right in their position as managers to tell people what to do and to expect them to do it. The concept of authority is part of the chain of command that extends from higher organizational levels to lower levels and clarifies who reports to whom. The concept of authority also includes the perspective that subordinates are willing to accept it when they understand what they are told to do and are able to perform the task.
Source: © Lou Linwei/Alamy

authority
The rights inherent in a managerial position to tell people what to do and to expect them to do it

acceptance theory of authority
The view that authority comes from the willingness of subordinates to accept it

line authority
Authority that entitles a manager to direct the work of an employee

AUTHORITY Authority was a major concept discussed by the early management writers; they viewed it as the glue that held an organization together. **Authority** refers to the rights inherent in a managerial position to tell people what to do and to expect them to do it.[9] Managers in the chain of command had authority to do their job of coordinating and overseeing the work of others. Authority could be delegated downward to lower-level managers, giving them certain rights while also prescribing certain limits within which to operate. These writers emphasized that authority was related to one's position within an organization and had nothing to do with the personal characteristics of an individual manager. They assumed that the rights and power inherent in one's formal organizational position were the sole source of influence and that if an order was given, it would be obeyed.

Another early management writer, Chester Barnard, proposed another perspective on authority. This view, the **acceptance theory of authority**, says that authority comes from the willingness of subordinates to accept it.[10] If an employee didn't accept a manager's order, there was no authority. Barnard contended that subordinates *will* accept orders only if the following conditions are satisfied:

1. They understand the order.
2. They feel the order is consistent with the organization's purpose.
3. The order does not conflict with their personal beliefs.
4. They are able to perform the task as directed.

Barnard's view of authority seems to make sense, especially when it comes to an employee's ability to do what he or she is told to do. For instance, if my manager (my department chair) came into my classroom and told me to do open-heart surgery on one of my students, the traditional view of authority said that I would have to follow that order. Barnard's view would say, instead, that I would talk to my manager about my lack of education and experience to do what he's asked me to do and that it's probably not in the best interests of the student (or our department) for me to follow that order. Yes, this is an extreme—and highly unrealistic—example. However, it does point out that simply viewing a manager's authority as total control over what an employee does or doesn't do is unrealistic also, except in certain circumstances like the military where soldiers are expected to follow their commander's orders. However, understand that Barnard believed most employees would do what their managers asked them to do if they were able to do so.

The early management writers also distinguished between two forms of authority: line authority and staff authority. **Line authority** entitles a manager to direct the work of an employee. It is the employer–employee authority relationship that extends from the top of the organization to the lowest echelon, according to the chain of command, as shown in Exhibit 11-4. As a link in the chain of command, a manager with line authority has the right to direct the work of employees and to make certain decisions without consulting anyone. Of course, in the chain of command, every manager is also subject to the authority or direction of his or her superior.

Keep in mind that sometimes the term *line* is used to differentiate line managers from staff managers. In this context, *line* refers to managers whose organizational function contributes directly to the achievement of organizational objectives. In a manufacturing firm, line managers are typically in the production and sales functions, whereas managers in human resources and payroll are considered staff managers with staff authority. Whether a manager's function is classified as line or staff depends on the organization's objectives. For example, at Staff Builders, a supplier of temporary employees, interviewers have a line function. Similarly, at the payroll firm of ADP, payroll is a line function.

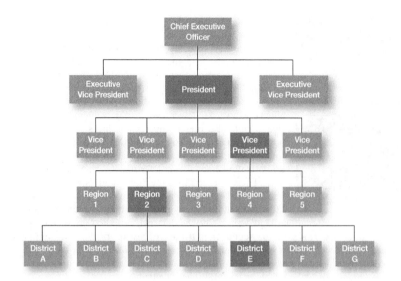

Exhibit 11-4
Chain of Command and Line Authority

As organizations get larger and more complex, line managers find that they do not have the time, expertise, or resources to get their jobs done effectively. In response, they create **staff authority** functions to support, assist, advise, and generally reduce some of their informational burdens. For instance, a hospital administrator who cannot effectively handle the purchasing of all the supplies the hospital needs creates a purchasing department, which is a staff function. Of course, the head of the purchasing department has line authority over the purchasing agents who work for him. The hospital administrator might also find that she is overburdened and needs an assistant, a position that would be classified as a staff position. Exhibit 11-5 illustrates line and staff authority.

staff authority
Positions with some authority that have been created to support, assist, and advise those holding line authority

RESPONSIBILITY   When managers use their authority to assign work to employees, those employees take on an obligation to perform those assigned duties. This obligation or expectation to perform is known as **responsibility**. And employees should be held accountable for their performance! Assigning work authority without

responsibility
The obligation or expectation to perform any assigned duties

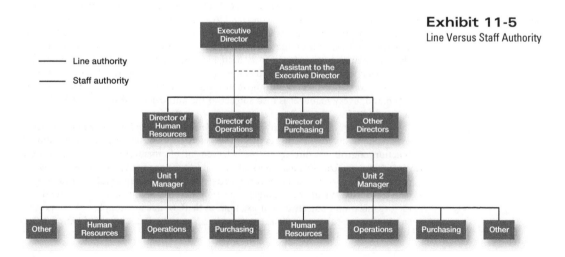

Exhibit 11-5
Line Versus Staff Authority

let's get REAL

Source: Paul Baranda

The Scenario:

Reid Lawson is a project manager for a lighting design company in Los Angeles. He's one of 30 project managers in the company, each with a team of between 10–15 employees. Although the company's top managers say they want employees to be "innovative" in their work, Reid and the other project managers face tight-fisted control from the top. Reid's already lost two of his most talented designers (who went to work for a competitor) because he couldn't get approval for a project because the executive team kept nit-picking the design these two had been working on.

Paul Baranda
Marketing Executive
Director

How can Reid and the other project managers get their bosses to loosen up the control? What would you suggest?

Innovation is the driving force to a successful business and is usually hindered by red tape in the workplace. It is important to examine internal processes to ensure company procedures are not creating road blocks. The project manager should work with the executive team to ensure their ability to empower their employees as well as keep them engaged and inspired. With the proper support and understanding of expectations from the executive team, the project managers can assure their teams that their ingenious ideas would be approved or implemented.

responsibility and accountability can create opportunities for abuse. Likewise, no one should be held responsible or accountable for work tasks over which he or she has no authority to complete those tasks.

unity of command
The management principle that each person should report to only one manager

UNITY OF COMMAND   Finally, the **unity of command** principle (one of Fayol's 14 management principles) states that a person should report to only one manager. Without unity of command, conflicting demands from multiple bosses may create problems as it did for Damian Birkel, a merchandising manager in the Fuller Brands division of CPAC, Inc. He found himself reporting to two bosses—one in charge of the department-store business and the other in charge of discount chains. Birkel tried to minimize the conflict by making a combined to-do list that he would update and change as work tasks changed.[11]

TODAY'S VIEW   Although early management theorists (Fayol, Weber, Taylor, Barnard, and others) believed that chain of command, authority (line and staff), responsibility, and unity of command were essential, times have changed.[12] Those elements are far less important today. For example, at the Michelin plant in Tours, France, managers have replaced the top-down chain of command with "birdhouse" meetings, in which employees meet for five minutes at regular intervals throughout the day at a column on the shop floor and study simple tables and charts to identify production bottlenecks. Instead of being bosses, shop managers are enablers.[13] Information technology also has made such concepts less relevant today. Employees can access information that used to be available only to managers in a matter of a few seconds. It also means that employees can communicate with anyone else in the organization without going through the chain of command. Also, many employees, especially in organizations where work revolves around projects, find themselves reporting to more than one boss, thus violating the unity of command principle. However, such arrangements can and do work if communication, conflict, and other issues are managed well by all involved parties.

Span of Control

How many employees can a manager efficiently and effectively manage? That's what **span of control** is all about. The traditional view was that managers could not—and should not—directly supervise more than five or six subordinates. Determining the span of control is important because to a large degree, it determines the number of levels and managers in an organization—an important consideration in how efficient an organization will be. All other things being equal, the wider or larger the span, the more efficient the organization. Here's why.

Assume two organizations both have approximately 4,100 employees. As Exhibit 11-6 shows, if one organization has a span of four and the other a span of eight, the organization with the wider span will have two fewer levels and approximately 800 fewer managers. At an average manager's salary of $42,000 a year, the organization with the wider span would save over $33 million a year! Obviously, wider spans are more efficient in terms of cost. However, at some point, wider spans may reduce effectiveness if employee performance worsens because managers no longer have the time to lead effectively.

TODAY'S VIEW The contemporary view of span of control recognizes there is no magic number. Many factors influence the number of employees a manager can efficiently and effectively manage. These factors include the skills and abilities of the manager and the employees and the characteristics of the work being done. For instance, managers with well-trained and experienced employees can function well with a wider span. Other contingency variables that determine the appropriate span include similarity and complexity of employee tasks, the physical proximity of subordinates, the degree to which standardized procedures are in place, the sophistication of the organization's information system, the strength of the organization's culture, and the preferred style of the manager.[14]

The trend in recent years has been toward larger spans of control, which is consistent with managers' efforts to speed up decision making, increase flexibility, get closer to customers, empower employees, and reduce costs. Managers are beginning to recognize that they can handle a wider span when employees know their jobs well and when those employees understand organizational processes. For instance, at PepsiCo's Gamesa cookie plant in Mexico, 56 employees now report to each manager. However, to ensure that performance doesn't suffer because of these wider spans, employees were thoroughly briefed on company goals and processes. Also, new pay systems reward quality, service, productivity, and teamwork.[15]

span of control
The number of employees a manager can efficiently and effectively manage

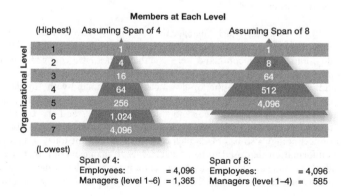

Exhibit 11-6
Contrasting Spans of Control

Centralization and Decentralization

One of the questions that needs to be answered when organizing is "At what organizational level are decisions made?" **Centralization** is the degree to which decision making takes place at upper levels of the organization. If top managers make key decisions with little input from below, then the organization is more centralized. On the other hand, the more that lower-level employees provide input or actually make decisions, the more **decentralization** there is. Keep in mind that centralization-decentralization is not an either-or concept. The decision is relative, not absolute—that is, an organization is never completely centralized or decentralized.

Early management writers proposed that the degree of centralization in an organization depended on the situation.[16] Their goal was the optimum and efficient use of employees. Traditional organizations were structured in a pyramid, with power and authority concentrated near the top of the organization. Given this structure, historically centralized decisions were the most prominent, but organizations today have become more complex and responsive to dynamic changes in their environments. As such, many managers believe decisions need to be made by those individuals closest to the problems, regardless of their organizational level. In fact, the trend over the past several decades—at least in U.S. and Canadian organizations—has been a movement toward more decentralization in organizations.[17] Exhibit 11-7 lists some of the factors that affect an organization's use of centralization or decentralization.[18]

TODAY'S VIEW   Today, managers often choose the amount of centralization or decentralization that will allow them to best implement their decisions and achieve organizational goals.[19] What works in one organization, however, won't necessarily work in another, so managers must determine the appropriate amount of decentralization for each organization and work units within it.

As organizations have become more flexible and responsive to environmental trends, there's been a distinct shift toward decentralized decision making.[20] This trend, also known as **employee empowerment**, gives employees more authority (power) to make decisions. (We'll address this concept more thoroughly in our discussion of leadership in Chapter 18.) In large companies especially, lower-level managers are "closer to the action" and typically have more detailed knowledge about problems and how best to solve them than top managers. For instance, at Terex Corporation, CEO Ron Defeo, a big proponent of decentralized management, tells his managers that, "You gotta' run the company you're given." And they have! The company generated revenues of more than $4 billion in 2009 with about 16,000 employees

centralization
The degree to which decision making is concentrated at upper levels of the organization

decentralization
The degree to which lower-level employees provide input or actually make decisions

employee empowerment
Giving employees more authority (power) to make decisions

Exhibit 11-7
Centralization or Decentralization

More Centralization	More Decentralization
• Environment is stable.	• Environment is complex, uncertain.
• Lower-level managers are not as capable or experienced at making decisions as upper-level managers.	• Lower-level managers are capable and experienced at making decisions.
• Lower-level managers do not want a say in decisions.	• Lower-level managers want a voice in decisions.
• Decisions are relatively minor.	• Decisions are significant.
• Organization is facing a crisis or the risk of company failure.	• Corporate culture is open to allowing managers a say in what happens.
• Company is large.	• Company is geographically dispersed.
• Effective implementation of company strategies depends on managers retaining say over what happens.	• Effective implementation of company strategies depends on managers having involvement and flexibility to make decisions.

let's get REAL

Source: Julie Colon

The Scenario:

An old saying goes like this: "If you want something done right, do it yourself." But Alicia Nunez, customer service manager at a party imports company in Guadalajara, Mexico, wants to do just the opposite! She wants to delegate tasks to her team of 25 customer service representatives. But she also wants to do it in a way that her team is still productive and functional.

Julie Colon
Creative Project Manager

What can Alicia do to make sure her employee delegation is successful?

It is most important in any business to delegate tasks to employees so they feel empowered to make decisions. This is essential for building teams that support their leader and feel like they have an important role to play within the organization. Delegating tasks gives the team ownership of the work and drives them to be more passionate about the work. Delegation must be done in a way that takes into account the skills of the team as well as consideration of what tasks will give them a challenge. When we are challenged, we tend to work smarter in order to solve issues that arise, and that can be a very rewarding result of delegation.

worldwide and a small corporate headquarters staff.[21] Another example can be seen at the General Cable plant in Piedras Negras, Coahuila, Mexico, where employees are responsible for managing nearly 6,000 active raw material SKUs (stock-keeping units) in inventory and on the plant floor. And company managers continue to look for ways to place more responsibility in the hands of workers.[22]

Formalization

Formalization refers to how standardized an organization's jobs are and the extent to which employee behavior is guided by rules and procedures. In highly formalized organizations, there are explicit job descriptions, numerous organizational rules, and clearly defined procedures covering work processes. Employees have little discretion over what's done, when it's done, and how it's done. However, where formalization is low, employees have more discretion in how they do their work.

formalization
How standardized an organization's jobs are and the extent to which employee behavior is guided by rules and procedures

TODAY'S VIEW Although some formalization is necessary for consistency and control, many organizations today rely less on strict rules and standardization to guide and regulate employee behavior. For instance, consider the following situation:

> A customer comes into a branch of a large national drug store and drops off a roll of film for same-day developing 37 minutes after the store policy cut-off time. Although the sales clerk knows he's supposed to follow rules, he also knows he could get the film developed with no problem and wants to accommodate the customer. So he accepts the film, violating policy, hoping that his manager won't find out.[23]

Has this employee done something wrong? He did "break" the rule. But by "breaking" the rule, he actually brought in revenue and provided good customer service.

Considering there are numerous situations where rules may be too restrictive, many organizations have allowed employees some latitude, giving them sufficient

mechanistic organization
An organizational design that's rigid and tightly controlled

organic organization
An organizational design that's highly adaptive and flexible

11.2 *Contrast* mechanistic and organic structures.

*data*points[29]

24 percent of job seekers said they preferred to work at a company with more than 1,000 employees; 27 percent they preferred a company with fewer than 200 employees.

80 percent of a company's total workforce is what typical frontline managers directly supervise.

34 percent of HR executives said they had retrained employees for new positions over the last six months.

68 percent of organizations said they've increased central- ization in the last five years.

51 percent of white-collar workers say teleworking is a good idea.

42 percent of U.S. companies offer some form of telework arrangement.

55 percent of workers believe their work quality is perceived the same when working remotely as when working in the office.

autonomy to make those decisions that they feel are best under the circumstances. It doesn't mean throwing out all organizational rules because there *will* be rules that are important for employees to follow—and these rules should be explained so employees understand why it's important to adhere to them. But for other rules, employees may be given some leeway.[24]

MECHANISTIC and Organic Structures

Stocking extra swimsuits in retail stores near water parks seems to make sense, right? And if size 11 women's shoes have been big sellers in Chicago, then stocking more size 11s seems to be a no-brainer. After suffering through 16 months of declining same-store sales, Macy's CEO Terry Lundgren decided it was time to restructure the organization to make sure these types of smart retail decisions are made.[25] He's mak- ing the company both more centralized and more locally focused. Although that may seem a contradiction, the redesign seems to be working. Lundgren centralized Macy's purchasing, planning, and marketing operations from seven regional offices to one office at headquarters in New York. He also replaced regional merchandise managers with more local managers—each responsible for a dozen stores—who spend more time figuring out what's selling. Designing (or redesigning) an organizational struc- ture that works is important. Basic organizational design revolves around two organi- zational forms, described in Exhibit 11-8.[26]

The **mechanistic organization** (or bureaucracy) was the natural result of com- bining the six elements of structure. Adhering to the chain-of-command principle ensured the existence of a formal hierarchy of authority, with each person controlled and supervised by one superior. Keeping the span of control small at increasingly higher levels in the organization created tall, impersonal structures. As the distance between the top and the bottom of the organization expanded, top management would increasingly impose rules and regulations. Because top managers couldn't con- trol lower-level activities through direct observation and ensure the use of standard practices, they substituted rules and regulations. The early management writers' belief in a high degree of work specialization created jobs that were simple, routine, and standardized. Further specialization through the use of departmentalization in- creased impersonality and the need for multiple layers of management to coordinate the specialized departments.[27]

The **organic organization** is a highly adaptive form that is as loose and flexible as the mechanistic organization is rigid and stable. Rather than having standardized jobs and regulations, the organic organization's loose structure allows it to change rapidly as required.[28] It has division of labor, but the jobs people do are not standard- ized. Employees tend to be professionals who are technically proficient and trained to handle diverse problems. They need few formal rules and little direct supervision because their training has instilled in them standards of professional conduct. For instance, a petroleum engineer doesn't need to follow specific procedures on how to locate oil sources miles offshore. The engineer can solve most problems alone or after conferring with colleagues. Professional standards guide his or her behavior. The organic organization is low in centralization so that the professional can respond quickly to problems and because top-level managers cannot be expected to possess the expertise to make necessary decisions.

Exhibit 11-8
Mechanistic Versus Organic Organizations

Mechanistic	Organic
• High specialization	• Cross-functional teams
• Rigid departmentalization	• Cross-hierarchical teams
• Clear chain of command	• Free flow of information
• Narrow spans of control	• Wide spans of control
• Centralization	• Decentralization
• High formalization	• Low formalization

CONTINGENCY Factors Affecting Structural Choice

Discuss the 11.3
contingency factors
that favor either the
mechanistic model or
the organic model of
organizational design.

When Carol Bartz took over the CEO position at Yahoo! from cofounder Jerry Yang, she found a company "hobbled by slow decision making and ineffective execution on those decisions."[30] Bartz said, "There's plenty that has bogged this company down." For a company that was once the darling of Web search, Yahoo! seemed to have lost its way, a serious misstep in an industry where change is continual and rapid. Bartz (who is no longer the CEO) implemented a new streamlined structure intended to "make the company a lot faster on its feet." Top managers typically put a lot of thought into designing an appropriate organizational structure. What that appropriate structure is depends on four contingency variables: the organization's strategy, size, technology, and degree of environmental uncertainty.

Strategy and Structure

An organization's structure should facilitate goal achievement. Because goals are an important part of the organization's strategies, it's only logical that strategy and structure are closely linked. Alfred Chandler initially researched this relationship.[31] He studied several large U.S. companies and concluded that changes in corporate strategy led to changes in an organization's structure that support the strategy.

Research has shown that certain structural designs work best with different organizational strategies.[32] For instance, the flexibility and free-flowing information of the organic structure works well when an organization is pursuing meaningful and unique innovations. The mechanistic organization with its efficiency, stability, and tight controls works best for companies wanting to tightly control costs.

Size and Structure

There's considerable evidence that an organization's size affects its structure.[33] Large organizations—typically considered to be those with more than 2,000 employees—tend to have more specialization, departmentalization, centralization, and rules and regulations than do small organizations. However, once an organization grows past a certain size, size has less influence on structure. Why? Essentially, once there are around 2,000 employees, it's already fairly mechanistic. Adding another 500 employees won't impact the structure much. On the other hand, adding 500 employees to an organization with only 300 employees is likely to make it more mechanistic.

Technology and Structure

Every organization uses some form of technology to convert its inputs into outputs. For instance, workers at Whirlpool's Manaus, Brazil, facility build microwave ovens and air conditioners on a standardized assembly line. Employees at FedEx Kinko's Office and Print Services produce custom design and print jobs for individual customers. And employees at Bayer's facility in Karachi, Pakistan, are involved in producing pharmaceuticals on a continuous-flow production line.

LEADER who made a DIFFERENCE

Source: Wang Jun/EyePress EPN/Newscom

As chairman and CEO of Haier Group, Zhang Ruimin runs a successful enterprise with annual revenues of more than $20 billion by turning it into one of China's first global brands.[34] Zhang is considered by many to be China's leading corporate executive. When he took over a floundering refrigerator plant in Qingdao, he quickly found out it produced terrible refrigerators. The story goes that he gave the workers sledgehammers and ordered them to destroy every one. His message: Poor quality would no longer be tolerated. Using his business training, Zhang successfully organized Haier for efficient mass production. But here in the twenty-first century, Zhang believes success requires a different competency. So he reorganized the company into self-managed groups, each devoted to a customer or group of similar customers. Zhang gets it! He understands clearly how an organization's design can help it be successful. What can you learn from this leader who made a difference?

Exhibit 11-9

Woodward's Findings on Technology and Structure

	Unit Production	Mass Production	Process Production
Structural characteristics:	Low vertical differentiation	Moderate vertical differentiation	High vertical differentiation
	Low horizontal differentiation	High horizontal differentiation	Low horizontal differentiation
	Low formalization	High formalization	Low formalization
Most effective structure:	Organic	Mechanistic	Organic

unit production

The production of items in units or small batches

mass production

The production of items in large batches

process production

The production of items in continuous processes

The initial research on technology's effect on structure can be traced to Joan Woodward, who studied small manufacturing firms in southern England to determine the extent to which structural design elements were related to organizational success.[35] She couldn't find any consistent pattern until she divided the firms into three distinct technologies that had increasing levels of complexity and sophistication. The first category, **unit production**, described the production of items in units or small batches. The second category, **mass production**, described large-batch manufacturing. Finally, the third and most technically complex group, **process production**, included continuous-process production. A summary of her findings is shown in Exhibit 11-9.

Other studies also have shown that organizations adapt their structures to their technology depending on how routine their technology is for transforming inputs into outputs.[36] In general, the more routine the technology, the more mechanistic the structure can be, and organizations with more nonroutine technology are more likely to have organic structures.[37]

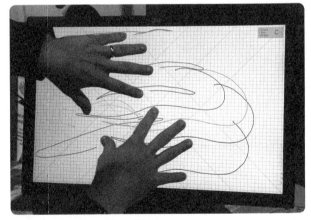

Facing the dynamic environmental forces of global competition and accelerated product innovation by competitors, 3M Company has a flexible and decentralized organic structure that enables it to respond quickly to customer demands for high quality products and fast service. Describing itself as "a global innovation company that never stops inventing," 3M has 35 business units that operate as small companies to keep the company agile and entrepreneurial. The 10-finger multi-touch screen shown in this photo is an innovation of 3M's Touch System business unit designed for customers in the medical and engineering industries. With its organic structure, 3M is poised to adapt quickly to the fast-growing demand for touch-screen products.
Source: Ethan Miller/Getty Images

Environmental Uncertainty and Structure

Some organizations face stable and simple environments with little uncertainty; others face dynamic and complex environments with a lot of uncertainty. Managers try to minimize environmental uncertainty by adjusting the organization's structure.[38] In stable and simple environments, mechanistic designs can be more effective. On the other hand, the greater the uncertainty, the more an organization needs the flexibility of an organic design. For example, the uncertain nature of the oil industry means that oil companies need to be flexible. Soon after he was named CEO of Royal Dutch Shell PLC, Jeroen van der Veer (now the former CEO) streamlined the corporate structure to counteract some of the industry volatility. One thing he did was eliminate the company's cumbersome, overly analytical process of making deals with OPEC countries and other major oil producers.[39]

TODAY'S VIEW The evidence on the environment-structure relationship helps explain why so many managers today are restructuring their organizations to be lean, fast, and flexible. Worldwide economic downturns, global competition, accelerated product innovation by competitors, and increased demands from customers for high quality and faster deliveries are examples of dynamic environmental forces. Mechanistic organizations are not equipped to respond to rapid environmental change and environmental uncertainty. As a result, we're seeing organizations become more organic.

TRADITIONAL **Organizational Designs**

Describe traditional | 11. 4
organizational designs.

They're a big hit with the elementary-school crowd, and millions of them were sold every month. Ever heard of Silly Bandz?[40] If you're over the age of 10, you probably haven't! These colorful rubber bands retain the shapes they're twisted in and kids love them. The small business that created Silly Bandz—BCP Imports of Toledo, Ohio—increased its employee count from 20 to 200 and added 22 phone lines to keep up with inquiries. The person behind those organizing decisions is company president Robert Croak. In making structural decisions, managers have some common designs from which to choose. In this chapter, we're going to describe the traditional organizational designs. In the next chapter, we'll be looking at more contemporary types of organizational designs.

When designing a structure, managers may choose one of the traditional organizational designs. These structures tend to be more mechanistic in nature. A summary of the strengths and weaknesses of each can be found in Exhibit 11-10.

Simple Structure

Most companies start as entrepreneurial ventures using a **simple structure**, an organizational design with low departmentalization, wide spans of control, authority centralized in a single person, and little formalization.[41] As employees are added, however, most don't remain as simple structures. The structure tends to become more specialized and formalized. Rules and regulations are introduced, work becomes specialized, departments are created, levels of management are added, and the organization becomes increasingly bureaucratic. At this point, managers might choose a functional structure or a divisional structure.

simple structure
An organizational design with low departmentalization, wide spans of control, centralized authority, and little formalization

Functional Structure

A **functional structure** is an organizational design that groups similar or related occupational specialties together. You can think of this structure as functional departmentalization applied to the entire organization.

functional structure
An organizational design that groups together similar or related occupational specialties

Divisional Structure

The **divisional structure** is an organizational structure made up of separate business units or divisions.[42] In this structure, each division has limited autonomy, with a division manager who has authority over his or her unit and is responsible for

divisional structure
An organizational structure made up of separate, semiautonomous units or divisions

Exhibit 11-10
Traditional Organizational Designs

Simple Structure
- Strengths: Fast; flexible; inexpensive to maintain; clear accountability.
- Weaknesses: Not appropriate as organization grows; reliance on one person is risky.

Functional Structure
- Strengths: Cost-saving advantages from specialization (economies of scale, minimal duplication of people and equipment); employees are grouped with others who have similar tasks.
- Weaknesses: Pursuit of functional goals can cause managers to lose sight of what's best for the overall organization; functional specialists become insulated and have little understanding of what other units are doing.

Divisional Structure
- Strengths: Focuses on results—division managers are responsible for what happens to their products and services.
- Weaknesses: Duplication of activities and resources increases costs and reduces efficiency.

performance. In divisional structures, however, the parent corporation typically acts as an external overseer to coordinate and control the various divisions, and often provides support services such as financial and legal. Walmart, for example, has two divisions: retail (Walmart Stores, International, Sam's Clubs, and others) and support (distribution centers).

Hopefully, you've seen in this chapter that organizational structure and design (or redesign) are important managerial tasks. Also, we hope that you recognize that organizing decisions aren't only important for upper-level managers. Managers at all levels may have to deal with work specialization or authority or span of control decisions. In the next chapter, we'll continue our discussion of the organizing function by looking at contemporary organizational designs.

CHAPTER

PREPARING FOR: Exams/Quizzes

CHAPTER SUMMARY by Learning Outcomes

 11.1 LEARNING OUTCOME

Describe six key elements in organizational design.

The key elements in organizational design are work specialization, chain of command, span of control, departmentalization, centralization-decentralization, and formalization. Traditionally, work specialization was viewed as a way to divide work activities into separate job tasks. Today's view is that it is an important organizing mechanism but it can lead to problems. The chain of command and its companion concepts—authority, responsibility, and unity of command—were viewed as important ways of maintaining control in organizations. The contemporary view is that they are less relevant in today's organizations. The traditional view of span of control was that managers should directly supervise no more than five to six individuals. The contemporary view is that the span of control depends on the skills and abilities of the manager and the employees and on the characteristics of the situation.

The various forms of departmentalization are as follows: *Functional* groups jobs by functions performed; *product* groups jobs by product lines; *geographical* groups jobs by geographical region; *process* groups jobs on product or customer flow; and *customer* groups jobs on specific and unique customer groups.

Authority refers to the rights inherent in a managerial position to tell people what to do and to expect them to do it. The acceptance view of authority says that authority comes from the willingness of subordinates to accept it. Line authority entitles a manager to direct the work of an employee. Staff authority refers to functions that support, assist, advise, and generally reduce some of managers' informational burdens. Responsibility is the obligation or expectation to perform assigned duties. Unity of command states that a person should report to only one manager. Centralization-decentralization is a structural decision about who makes decisions—upper-level managers or lower-level employees. Formalization concerns the organization's use of standardization and strict rules to provide consistency and control.

11.2 LEARNING OUTCOME

Contrast mechanistic and organic structures.

A mechanistic organization is a rigid and tightly controlled structure. An organic organization is highly adaptive and flexible.

11.3 LEARNING OUTCOME

Discuss the contingency factors that favor either the mechanistic model or the organic model of organizational design.

An organization's structure should support the strategy. If the strategy changes, the structure also should change. An organization's size can affect its structure up to a certain point. Once an organization reaches a certain size (usually around 2,000 employees), it's fairly mechanistic. An organization's technology can affect its structure. An organic structure is most effective with unit production and process production technology. A mechanistic structure is most effective with mass production technology. The more uncertain an organization's environment, the more it needs the flexibility of an organic design.

11.4 [LEARNING OUTCOME] **Describe** traditional organizational designs.
A simple structure is one with low departmentalization, wide spans of control, authority centralized in a single person, and little formalization. A functional structure groups similar or related occupational specialties together. A divisional structure is made up of separate business units or divisions.

REVIEW AND DISCUSSION QUESTIONS ✪

1. Discuss the traditional and contemporary views of each of the six key elements of organizational design.

2. Contrast mechanistic and organic organizations.

3. Would you rather work in a mechanistic or an organic organization? Why?

4. Contrast the three traditional organizational designs.

5. With the availability of advanced information technology that allows an organization's work to be done anywhere at any time, is organizing still an important managerial function? Why or why not?

6. Researchers are now saying that efforts to simplify work tasks actually have negative results for both companies and their employees. Do you agree? Why or why not?

PREPARING FOR: My Career
ETHICS DILEMMA ✪

Thomas Lopez, a lifeguard in the Miami area, was fired for leaving his assigned area to save a drowning man.[43] His employer, Jeff Ellis and Associates, which has a contract with the Florida city of Hallandale, said Lopez "left his patrol area unmonitored and exposed the company to legal liability." Lopez said he had no choice but to do what he did. "I'm not going to put my job over helping someone. I'm going to do what I felt was right, and I did." After this story hit the media, the company offered Lopez his job back, but he declined. What do you think? What ethical concerns do you see? What lessons can be applied to organizational design from this story?

SKILLS EXERCISE   Developing Your Empowering People (Delegating) Skill

About the Skill
Managers get things done through other people. Because there are limits to any manager's time and knowledge, effective managers need to understand how to delegate.[44] Delegation is the assignment of authority to another person to carry out specific duties. It allows an employee to make decisions. Delegation should not be confused with participation. In participative decision making, authority is shared. In delegation, employees make decisions on their own.

Steps in Practicing the Skill
A number of actions differentiate the effective delegator from the ineffective delegator. The following five behaviors are used by effective delegators.

1. *Clarify the assignment.* Determine *what* is to be delegated and *to whom.* You need to identify the person who's most capable of doing the task and then determine whether he or she has the time and motivation to do the task. If you have a willing and able employee, it's your responsibility to provide clear information on what is delegated, the results you expect, and any time or performance expectations you may have. Unless there's an overriding need to adhere to specific methods, you should delegate only the results expected. Get agreement on what is to be done and the results expected, but let the employee decide the best way to complete the task.

2. *Specify the employee's range of discretion.* Every situation of delegation comes with constraints. Although you're delegating to an employee the authority to perform some task or tasks, you're not delegating unlimited authority. You are delegating authority to act on certain issues within certain parameters. You need to specify what those parameters are so that employees know, without any doubt, the range of their discretion.

131

3. *Allow the employee to participate.* One of the best ways to decide how much authority will be necessary to accomplish a task is to allow the employee who will be held accountable for that task to participate in that decision. Be aware, however, that allowing employees to participate can present its own set of potential problems as a result of employees' self-interests and biases in evaluating their own abilities.

4. *Inform others that delegation has occurred.* Delegation shouldn't take place behind the scenes. Not only do the manager and employee need to know specifically what has been delegated and how much authority has been given, but so does anyone else who's likely to be affected by the employee's decisions and actions. This includes people inside and outside the organization. Essentially, you need to communicate what has been delegated (the task and amount of authority) and to whom.

5. *Establish feedback channels.* To delegate without establishing feedback controls is inviting problems. The establishment of controls to monitor the employee's performance increases the likelihood that important problems will be identified and that the task will be completed on time and to the desired specifications. Ideally, these controls should be determined at the time of the initial assignment. Agree on a specific time for the completion of the task and then set progress dates when the employee will report back on how well he or she is doing and any major problems that may have arisen. These controls can be supplemented with periodic checks to ensure that authority guidelines aren't being abused, organizational policies are being followed, proper procedures are being met, and the like.

Practicing the Skill
Read through the following scenario. Write a paper describing how you would handle the situation described. Be sure to refer to the five behaviors described for delegating.

Scenario
Ricky Lee is the manager of the contracts group of a large regional office supply distributor. His boss, Anne Zumwalt, has asked him to prepare by the end of the month the department's new procedures manual that will outline the steps followed in negotiating contracts with office products manufacturers who supply the organization's products. Because Ricky has another major project he's working on, he went to Anne and asked her if it would be possible to assign the rewriting of the procedures manual to Bill Harmon, one of his employees who's worked in the contracts group for about three years. Anne said she had no problems with Ricky reassigning the project as long as Bill knew the parameters and the expectations for the completion of the project. Ricky is preparing for his meeting in the morning with Bill regarding this assignment.

WORKING TOGETHER Team Exercise

An organizational chart can be a useful tool for understanding certain aspects of an organization's structure. Form small groups of three to four individuals. Among yourselves, choose an organization with which one of you is familiar (where you work, a student organization to which you belong, your college or university, etc.). Draw an organizational chart of this organization. Be careful to show departments (or groups) and especially be careful to get the chain of command correct. Be prepared to share your chart with the class.

MY TURN TO BE A MANAGER

- Find three different examples of an organizational chart. (Company's annual reports are a good place to look.) In a report, describe each of these. Try to decipher the organization's use of organizational design elements, especially departmentalization, chain of command, centralization-decentralization, and formalization.

- Survey at least 10 different managers as to how many employees they supervise. Also ask them whether they feel they could supervise more employees or whether they feel the number they supervise is too many. Graph your survey results and write a report describing what you found. Draw some conclusions about span of control.

- Using the organizational chart you created in the team exercise, redesign the structure. What structural changes might make this organization more efficient and effective? Write a report describing what you would do and why. Be sure to include an example of the original organizational chart as well as a chart of your proposed revision of the organizational structure.

- Steve's and Mary's suggested readings: Gary Hamel, *The Future of Management* (Harvard Business School Press, 2007); Thomas Friedman, *The World Is Flat 3.0* (Picador, 2007); Harold J. Leavitt, *Top Down: Why Hierarchies Are Here to Stay and How to Manage Them More Effectively*

(Harvard Business School Press, 2005); and Thomas W. Malone, *The Future of Work* (Harvard Business School Press, 2004).

- In your own words, write down three things you learned in this chapter about being a good manager.
- Self-knowledge can be a powerful learning tool. Go to www.mymanagementlab.com and complete these self-assessment exercises: How Well Do I Handle Ambiguity? What Type of Organizational Structure Do I Prefer? Do I Like Bureaucracy? How Good Am I at Playing Politics? How Willing Am I to Delegate? Using the results of your assessments, identify personal strengths and weaknesses. What will you do to reinforce your strengths and improve your weaknesses?

CASE APPLICATION 1   Ask Chuck

The Charles Schwab Corporation (Charles Schwab) is a San Francisco-based financial services company.[45] Like many companies in that industry, Charles Schwab struggled during the economic recession.

Founded in 1971 by its namesake as a discount brokerage, the company has now "grown up" into a full-service traditional brokerage firm, with more than 300 offices in some 45 states and in London and Hong Kong. It still offers discount brokerage services, but also financial research, advice, and planning; retirement plans; investment management; and proprietary financial products including mutual funds, mortgages, CDs, and other banking products through its Charles Schwab Bank unit. However, its primary business is still making stock trades for investors who make their own financial decisions. The company has a reputation for being conserva-

Effective communication with customers that helps them become "better investors" plays an important role in Charles Schwab's customer service strategy as the company strives to succeed in a challenging economic environment. Each day managers of the company's offices receive customer feedback reports and empower employees to respond quickly to customer concerns.
Source: AP Photo/Eric Risberg

tive, which helped it avoid the financial meltdown suffered by other investment firms. Founder Charles R. Schwab has a black bowling ball perched on his desk. "It's a memento of the long-forgotten bubble of 1961, when shares of bowling-pin companies, shoemakers, chalk manufacturers, and lane operators were thought to be can't-miss plays on the limitless potential of suburbia—and turned out to be duds." He keeps the ball as a reminder not to "buy into hype or take excessive risks."

Like many companies, Charles Schwab is fanatical about customer service. By empowering front-line employees to respond fast to customer issues and concerns, Cheryl Pasquale, a manager at one of Schwab's branches, is on the front line of Schwab's efforts to prosper in a "resource-challenged economy." Every workday morning, she pulls up a customer feedback report for her branch generated by a brief survey the investment firm e-mails out daily. The report allows her to review how well her six financial consultants handled the previous day's transactions. She's able to see comments of customers who gave both high and low marks and whether a particular transaction garnered praise or complaint. On one particular day, she notices that several customers commented on how difficult it was to use the branch's in-house information kiosks. "She decides she'll ask her team for insights about this in their weekly meeting." One thing that she pays particular attention to is a "manager alert—a special notice triggered by a client who has given Schwab a poor rating for a delay in posting a transaction to his account." And she's not alone. Every day, Pasquale and the managers at all the company's branches receive this type of customer feedback. It's been particularly important to have this information in the challenging economic climate of the last few years.

DISCUSSION QUESTIONS ✪

1. Describe and evaluate what Charles Schwab is doing.

2. How might the company's culture of not buying into hype and not taking excessive risks affect its organizational structural design?

3. What structural implications—good and bad—might Schwab's intense focus on customer feedback have?

4. Do you think this arrangement would work for other types of organizations? Why or why not?

CASE APPLICATION 2 A New Kind of Structure

After finding that employees were spending too much time on menial and time-consuming tasks, Pfizer created an arrangement called PfizerWorks for its global employees that helps them work more efficiently and effectively by allowing them to use the services of several Indian outsourcing firms for support work such as creating documents and manipulating data.
Source: Bloomberg via Getty Images

Admit it. Sometimes the projects you're working on (school, work, or both) can get pretty boring and monotonous. Wouldn't it be great to have a magic button you could push to get someone else to do that boring, time-consuming stuff? At Pfizer, that "magic button" is a reality for a large number of employees.[46]

As a global pharmaceutical company, Pfizer is continually looking for ways to help employees be more efficient and effective. The company's senior director of organizational effectiveness found that the "Harvard MBA staff we hired to develop strategies and innovate were instead Googling and making PowerPoints." Indeed, internal studies conducted to find out just how much time its valuable talent was spending on menial tasks was startling. The average Pfizer employee was spending 20 percent to 40 percent of his or her time on support work (creating documents, typing notes, doing research, manipulating data, scheduling meetings) and only 60 percent to 80 percent on knowledge work (strategy, innovation, networking, collaborating, critical thinking). And the problem wasn't just at lower levels. Even the highest-level employees were affected. Take, for instance, David Cain, an executive director for global engineering. He enjoys his job—assessing environmental real estate risks, managing facilities, and controlling a multimillion-dollar budget. But he didn't so much enjoy having to go through spreadsheets and put together PowerPoints. Now, however, with Pfizer's "magic button," those tasks are passed off to individuals outside the organization.

Just what is this "magic button?" Originally called the Office of the Future (OOF), the renamed PfizerWorks allows employees to shift tedious and time-consuming tasks with the click of a single button on their computer desktop. They describe what they need on an online form, which is then sent to one of two Indian service-outsourcing firms. When a request is received, a team member in India calls the Pfizer employee to clarify what's needed and by when. The team member then e-mails back a cost specification for the requested work. If the Pfizer employee decides to proceed, the costs involved are charged to the employee's department. About this unique arrangement, Cain said that he relishes working with what he prefers to call his "personal consulting organization."

The number 66,500 illustrates just how beneficial PfizerWorks has been for the company. That's the number of work hours estimated to have been saved by employees who've used PfizerWorks. What about Joe Cain's experiences? When he gave the Indian team a complex project researching strategic actions that worked when consolidating company facilities, the team put the report together in a month, something that would have taken him six months to do alone. He says, "Pfizer pays me not to work tactically, but to work strategically."

DISCUSSION QUESTIONS ✪

1. Describe and evaluate what Pfizer is doing with its PfizerWorks.

2. What structural implications—good and bad—does this approach have? (Think in terms of the six organizational design elements.)

3. Do you think this arrangement would work for other types of organizations? Why or why not? What types of organizations might it also work for?

4. What role do you think organizational structure plays in an organization's efficiency and effectiveness? Explain.

ORGANISATION CULTURES AND CONTEXTS

Learning outcomes

When you have read this chapter you should be able to:

1 Compare systematically the cultures of two organisational units

2 Use the five forces model to analyse an organisation's competitive environment

3 Use the PESTEL framework to analyse the wider environment of an organisation

4 Explain the meaning and purposes of corporate governance

5 Use ideas from the chapter to comment on the management issues in the Nokia case study

Activity 3.1   What are 'organisational cultures and contexts'?

Before reading this chapter, write some notes on what you understand by the term 'organisational cultures and contexts'.

Choose the organisation or people you hope may be able to help you learn about the topic. You may find it helpful to discuss the topic with a manager you know, or reflect on an activity you have managed.

- Make brief notes on the main features of the organisation's culture and how people describe it.
- What are likely to be the main factors outside the organisation which affect it?
- How (if at all) have changes in those external factors altered what managers do?

Keep these notes as you will be able to use them later.

3.1   Introduction

Nokia's performance depends on the ability of its managers to understand what consumers expect from a mobile phone and to meet those requirements more effectively than competitors. It also depends on staff identifying scientific research that may lead to new features in its handsets – and assessing whether customers would value them in the next generation of products. The early success of the company was helped by recognising that many users see a mobile as a fashion accessory, and by using its design skills to meet that need. It also gained when the European Union established common standards for mobile telephony, which the Finnish government supported. In recent years, the company has found it hard to compete with devices such as the iPhone from Apple, and with lower cost producers of basic handsets. It has recently formed an alliance with Microsoft to try to recover its position in the industry.

All managers work within a context which both constrains and supports them. How well they understand, interpret and interact with that context affects their performance. Finkelstein (2003) (especially pp. 63–68) shows how Motorola, an early market leader in mobile communications, failed to take account of changes in consumer preferences (for digital rather than the older, analogue mobile phones). By the time managers understood this change, Nokia had a commanding lead in the market. Each business is unique, so the forces with which they interact differ: those who are able to identify and shape them (Nokia) will perform better than those who are not (Motorola). In 2009, Nokia in turn may have underestimated the effect which smartphones would have on the market, allowing Apple to take market share.

Figure 3.1 shows four environmental forces. The inner circle represents the organisation's **internal environment (or context)** – introduced in Chapter 1. That includes its culture, often a major influence on performance. Beyond that is the immediate **competitive environment (or context)**, sometimes known as the micro-environment. This is the industry-specific environment of customers, suppliers, competitors and potential substitute. The outer circle shows the **general environment (or context)**, sometimes known as the macro-environment – political, economic, social, technological, (natural) environmental and legal factors that affect all organisations. Forces in the internal and competitive environments usually have more impact on, and are more open to influence by, the organisation than those in the general environment.

The competitive and general environments make up an organisation's **external environment (or context)** – a constantly changing source of threats and opportunities: how well people cope with these affects performance.

Forces in the external environment become part of the 'management agenda' in an organisation only when internal or external stakeholders draw attention to them in some way. In

The **internal environment (or context)** consists of elements which make up the organisation – such as its structure, culture, people and technologies.

A **competitive environment (or context)** is the industry-specific environment comprising the organisation's customers, suppliers and competitors.

The **general environment (or context)** (sometimes known as the macro-environment) includes political, economic, social technological, (natural) environmental and legal factors that affect all organisations.

The **external environment (or context)** consists of elements beyond the organisation – it combines the competitive and general environments.

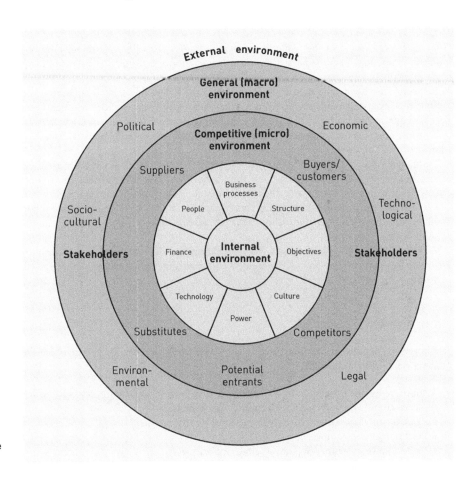

Figure 3.1
Environmental
influences on the
organisation

terms of Figure 3.1, they are a fourth force. Managers (who are themselves stakeholders) balance conflicting interpretations of their context. They work within an internal context, and look outside for actual and potential changes that may affect the centre of Figure 3.1. The figure implies a constant interaction between an organisation and its external environment.

Managers do not passively accept their environment, but try to shape it by actively persuading governments and other agencies to act in their favour (known as 'lobbying'). Car manufacturers and airlines regularly seek subsidies, cheap loans or favourable regulations, while most industry bodies (such as the European Automobile Manufacturers Association – **www.acea.be**) lobby international bodies such as the European Commission – often through professional lobbying companies.

The next section presents ideas on organisational culture. Beyond that, managers need to interact intelligently with their external environments, so the chapter also outlines stakeholder expectations and introduces ideas on governance and control.

> **Culture** is a pattern of shared basic assumptions that was learned by a group as it solved its problems of external adaptation and internal integration, that has worked well enough to be considered valid and transmitted to new members (Schein, 2004, p. 17).

3.2 Cultures and their components

Developing cultures

Interest in organisation **culture** has grown as academics and managers have come to believe that it influences behaviour. Several claim that a strong and distinct culture helps to integrate individuals into the team or organisation (Deal and Kennedy, 1982; Peters and Waterman,

1982). Deal and Kennedy (1982) refer to culture as 'the way we do things around here' and Hofstede (1991) sees it as the 'collective programming of the mind', distinguishing one group from another. They claim that having the right culture explains the success of high-performing organisations.

Someone entering a department or organisation for the first time can usually sense and observe the surface elements of the culture. Some buzz with life and activity, others seem asleep; some welcome and look after visitors, others seem inward looking; some work by the rules, while others are entrepreneurial and risk taking; some have regular social occasions while in others staff rarely meet except at work.

Distinctive cultures develop as people develop and share common values. They use these to establish beliefs and norms which guide their behaviour towards each other and to outsiders. Positive outcomes reinforce their belief in the values underlying their behaviour, which then become a stronger influence on how people should work and relate to each other: Should people have job titles? How should they dress? Should meetings be confrontational or supportive?

A shared culture provides members with guidelines about how they can best contribute. The more they work on these issues to develop a common understanding, the better they will perform.

Components of cultures

Schein (2004) identifies a culture's three levels, 'level' referring to the degree to which the observer can see its components.

- **Artifacts** represent the visible level – elements such as the language or etiquette which someone coming into contact with a culture can observe:
  - Architecture (open plan offices without doors or private space)
  - Technology and equipment
  - Style (clothing, manner of address, emotional displays)
  - Rituals and ceremonies (leaving events, awards ceremonies and away-days)
  - Courses (to induct employees in the culture as well as the content)

While it is easy to observe artifacts, it is difficult for outsiders to decipher what they mean to the group, or what underlying assumptions they reflect. That requires an analysis of beliefs and values.

- **Espoused beliefs and values** are the accumulated beliefs that members hold about their work. As a group develops, members refine their ideas about what works in this business: how people make decisions, how teams work together, how they solve problems. Practices that work become the accepted way to behave:
  - 'Quality pays'
  - 'We should stick to our core business'
  - 'Cultivate a sense of personal responsibility'
  - 'We depend on close team work'
  - 'Everyone is expected to challenge a proposal – whoever made it'

Some companies codify and publish their beliefs and values, to help induct new members and to reinforce them among existing staff. Such beliefs and values shape the visible artifacts, though companies vary in the degree to which employees internalise them. The extent to which they do so depends on how clearly they derive from shared basic underlying assumptions.

- **Basic underlying assumptions** are deeply held by members of the group as being the way to work together. As they act in accordance with their values and beliefs, those that work become embedded as basic underlying assumptions. When the group holds these strongly, members will act in accordance with them, and reject actions based on others:

- 'We need to satisfy customers to survive as a business'
- 'Our business is to help people with X problem live better with X problem'
- 'People can make mistakes, as long as they learn from them'
- 'We employ highly motivated and competent adults'
- 'Financial markets worry about the short-term: we are here for the long-term'

Difficulties arise when people with assumptions developed in one group work with people from another. Staff in companies that merge with another business sometimes find it difficult to work with their new colleagues because of historic cultural differences.

Management in practice   **A strong culture at Bosch**   **www.bosch.com**   **FT**

Franz Fehrenbach is chief executive of Bosch, Germany's largest privately owned engineering group, and the world's largest supplier of car parts. In 2009 he said:

The company culture, especially our high credibility, is one of our greatest assets. Our competitors cannot match us on that because it takes decades to build up.

The cultural traditions include a rigid control on costs, an emphasis on team thinking, employees being responsible for their errors, cautious financial policies and long-term thinking. For example, to cope with the recession in 2009 Mr Fehrenbach explained that:

We have to cut costs in all areas. We will reduce spending in the ongoing business, but we will not cut back on research and development for important future projects.

Source: Adapted from Space to breathe amid the crisis (Daniel Schaefer), *Financial Times*, 2 March 2009, p. 16.

3.3   Types of culture

This section outlines three ways of describing and comparing cultures.

Competing values framework

The competing values model developed by Quinn *et al.* (2003) reflects inherent tensions between flexibility or control and between an internal or an external focus: Figure 2.1 (p. 30) shows four cultural types.

Rational goal

Members see the organisation as a rational, efficiency-seeking unit. They define effectiveness in terms of production or economic goals that satisfy external requirements. Managers create structures to deal with the outside world. Leadership tends to be directive, goal-oriented and functional. Key motivating factors include competition and the achievement of goals. Examples are large, established businesses – mechanistic.

Internal process

Here members focus on internal matters. Their goal is to make the unit efficient, stable and controlled. Tasks are repetitive and methods stress specialisation, rules and procedures. Leaders tend to be cautious and spend time on technical issues. Motivating factors include security, stability and order. Examples include utilities and public authorities – suspicious of change.

Human relations

People emphasise the value of informal interpersonal relations rather than formal structures. They try to maintain the organisation and nurture its members, defining effectiveness in terms of their well-being and commitment. Leaders tend to be participative, considerate and supportive. Motivating factors include attachment, cohesiveness and membership. Examples include voluntary groups, professional service firms and some internal support functions.

Open systems

This represents an open systems view, in which people recognise that the external environment plays a significant role, and is a vital source of ideas, energy and resources. It also sees the environment as complex and turbulent, requiring entrepreneurial, visionary leadership and flexible, responsive behaviour. Key motivating factors are growth, stimulation, creativity and variety. Examples are start-up firms and new business units – organic, flexible operations.

Charles Handy's cultural types

Charles Handy (1993) distinguished four cultures – **power**, **role**, **task** and **person**.

Power

A dominant central figure holds power: others follow the centre's policy and interpret new situations in the way the leader would. Many entrepreneurial firms operate in this way, with few rules but with well-understood, implicit codes on how to behave and work. The firm relies on the individual rather than on seeking consensus through discussion.

Role

Typical characteristics of this culture are the job description or the procedure. Managers define what they expect in clear, detailed job descriptions. They select those who meet the specifications. Procedures guide how people and departments interact. If all follow the rules, co-ordination is straightforward. Someone's position in the hierarchy determines their formal power.

Task

People focus on completing the task or project rather than their formal role. They value each other for what they can contribute and expect everyone to help as needed. The emphasis is on getting the resources and people for the job and then relying on their commitment and enthusiasm. People often work in teams, combining diverse skills to meet a common purpose.

Person

The individual is at the centre and any structure or system is there to serve them. The form is unusual – small professional and artistic organisations are probably closest to it, and perhaps experiments in communal living. They exist to meet the needs of the professionals or the members, rather than some larger organisational goal.

A **power culture** is one in which people's activities are strongly influenced by a dominant central figure.

A **role culture** is one in which people's activities are strongly influenced by clear and detailed job descriptions and other formal signals as to what is expected of them.

A **task culture** is one in which the focus of activity is towards completing a task or project using whatever means are appropriate.

A **person culture** is one in which activity is strongly influenced by the wishes of the individuals who are part of the organisation.

Multiple cultures

Martin (2002) proposed that organisations have not one, but several cultures: observers take one of three perspectives towards a culture:

- **Integration** – a focus on identifying consistencies in the data, and using those common patterns to explain events.
- **Differentiation** – a focus on conflict, identifying different and possibly conflicting views of members towards events.
- **Fragmentation** – a focus on the fluid nature of organisations, and on the interplay and change of views about events.

Table 3.1 Hierarchical position and cultural perspectives

Position in hierarchy	Cultural perspective	Description	Example
Head office managers	Integration	Cultural values should be shared across the organisation. Unified culture both desirable and attainable	'If we can get every . . . part of the company doing what they should be doing, we'll beat everybody.'
Store managers	Differentiation	Reconciling conflicting views of head office and shop floor. See cultural pluralism as inevitable	'People up at head office are all pushing us in different directions. Jill in Marketing wants customer focus, June in Finance wants lower costs.'
Store employees	Fragmented	Confused by contradictory nature of the espoused values. See organisation as complex and unpredictable	'One minute it's this, the next it's that. You can't keep up with the flavour of the month.'

Source: Based on Ogbonna and Harris (1998).

Ogbonna and Harris (1998) provided empirical support for this view, based on interviews with staff in a retail company. They found that someone's position in the hierarchy determined their perspective on the culture (see Table 3.1). As consensus on culture was unlikely, they advised managers to recognise the range of sub-cultures within their oganisation, and only seek to reconcile those differences that were essential to policy. They also observed that culture remains a highly subjective idea, largely in the eye of the beholder:

and is radically different according to an individual's position in the hierarchy. (p. 45)

Culture and performance

Peters and Waterman (1982) believed that an organisation's culture affected performance, and implied that managers should try to change their culture towards a more productive one. Others are more sceptical about the effects on performance and question whether, even if a suitable culture has a positive effect, managers can consciously change it. Thompson and McHugh (2002), while also critical of much writing on the topic, observe the potential benefits that a suitable culture can bring to not-for-profit organisations:

Creating a culture resonant with the overall goals is relevant to any organisation, whether it be a trade union, voluntary group or producer co-operative. Indeed, it is more important in such consensual groupings. Co-operatives, for example, can degenerate organisationally because they fail to develop adequate mechanisms for transmitting the original ideals from founders to new members and sustaining them through shared experiences. (pp. 208–09)

As managers work within an organisational culture, they also work within an external context – whose participants have expectations of the organisation. They need tools with which to analyse that external world.

3.4   The competitive environment – Porter's five forces

Managers are most directly affected by forces in their immediate competitive environment. According to Porter (1980a, 1985) the ability of a firm to earn an acceptable return depends on five forces – the ability of new competitors to enter the industry, the threat of substitute products, the bargaining power of buyers, the bargaining power of suppliers and the rivalry among existing competitors. Figure 3.2 shows Porter's **five forces analysis**.

Porter believes that the *collective* strength of the five forces determines industry profitability, through their effects on prices, costs and investment requirements. Buyer power influences the prices a firm can charge, as does the threat of substitutes. The bargaining power of suppliers determines the cost of raw materials and other inputs. The greater the collective strength of the forces, the less profitable the industry: the weaker they are, the more profitable. Managers can use their knowledge of these forces to shape strategy.

Five forces analysis is a technique for identifying and listing those aspects of the five forces most relevant to the profitability of an organisation at that time.

Threat of new entrants

The extent of this threat depends on how easily new entrants can overcome barriers such as:

- the need for economies of scale (to compete on cost), which are difficult to achieve quickly;
- high capital investment is required;
- lack of distribution channels;
- subsidies which benefit existing firms at the expense of potential new entrants;
- cost advantages of existing firms, such as access to raw materials or know-how; and
- strong customer loyalty to incumbent companies.

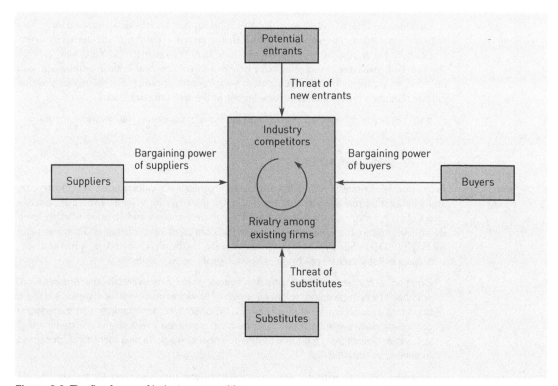

Figure 3.2 The five forces of industry competition
Source: Porter (1980a), p. 5.

Nokia faces competition from new entrants to the mobile phone industry, especially Apple and Research in Motion (BlackBerry), at the top end of the market. The Chinese ZTE Corporation is supplying cheap mobiles to consumers in emerging markets.

Intensity of rivalry amongst competitors

Strong competitive rivalry lowers profitability, and occurs when:

- there are many firms in an industry;
- there is slow market growth, so companies fight for market share;
- fixed costs are high, so firms use capacity fully and overproduce;
- exit costs are high; specialised assets (hard to sell) or management loyalty (in old family firms) deter firms from leaving the industry, which prolong excess capacity and low profitability; and
- products are similar, so customers can easily switch to other suppliers.

A highly competitive market will also be one in which the threat of new entrants is high. While Nokia was still the largest player in the mobile phone industry in 2011, it faced pressure from established competitors Motorola, Siemens and Ericsson, and from new entrants in Asia.

Power of buyers (customers)

Buyers (customers) seek lower prices or higher quality at constant prices, thus forcing down prices and profitability. Buyer power is high when:

- the buyer purchases a large part of a supplier's output;
- there are many substitute products, allowing easy switching;
- the product is a large part of the buyer's costs, encouraging them to seek lower prices; and
- buyers can plausibly threaten to supply their needs internally.

Management in practice   **Walmart's power as a buyer**   www.walmart.com

Walmart (which owns Asda in the UK) is the world's largest company, being three times the size of the second largest retailer, the French company Carrefour. Growth has enabled it to become the largest purchaser in America, controlling much of the business done by almost every major consumer-products company. It accounts for 30 per cent of hair-care products sold, 26 per cent of toothpaste, 20 per cent of pet food and 20 per cent of all sales of CDs, videos and DVDs. This gives it great power over companies in these industries, since their dependence on Walmart reduces their bargaining power.

Source: *Business Week*, 6 October 2003, pp. 48–53, and other sources.

Bargaining power of suppliers

Conditions that increase the bargaining power of suppliers are the opposite of those applying to buyers. The power of suppliers relative to customers is high when:

- there are few suppliers;
- the product is distinctive, so that customers are reluctant to switch;
- the cost of switching is high (e.g. if a company has invested in a supplier's software);
- the supplier can plausibly threaten to extend their business to compete with the customer; and
- the customer is a small or irregular purchaser.

Threat of substitutes

In Porter's model, substitutes refer to products in other industries that can perform the same function – using cans instead of bottles. Close substitutes constrain the ability of firms to raise prices, and the threat is high when buyers are able and willing to change their habits. Technological change and the risk of obsolescence pose a further threat: online news services (such as that freely available from the BBC) and recruitment sites threaten print newspapers.

Analysing the forces in the competitive environment enables managers to seize opportunities, counter threats and generally improve their position relative to competitors. They can consider how to alter the strength of the forces to improve their position by, for example, building barriers to entry or increasing their power over suppliers or buyers. Chapter 8 (Managing strategy) examines how managers can position their organisation within the competitive environment.

3.5 The general environment – PESTEL

Forces in the wider world also shape management policies, and a **PESTEL analysis** (short for political, economic, socio-cultural, technological, environmental and legal) helps to identify these – see Figure 3.3. GlaxoSmithKline (**www.gsk.com**), like other pharmaceutical companies, works in an environment which includes:

PESTEL analysis is a technique for identifying and listing the political, economic, social, technological, environmental and legal factors in the general environment most relevant to an organisation.

- governments trying to reduce the cost of drugs supplied to citizens;
- companies making cheap generic alternatives to patented drugs;

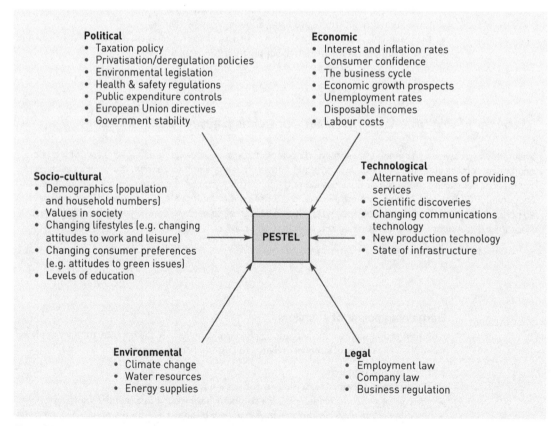

Political
- Taxation policy
- Privatisation/deregulation policies
- Environmental legislation
- Health & safety regulations
- Public expenditure controls
- European Union directives
- Government stability

Economic
- Interest and inflation rates
- Consumer confidence
- The business cycle
- Economic growth prospects
- Unemployment rates
- Disposable incomes
- Labour costs

Socio-cultural
- Demographics (population and household numbers)
- Values in society
- Changing lifestyles (e.g. changing attitudes to work and leisure)
- Changing consumer preferences (e.g. attitudes to green issues)
- Levels of education

Technological
- Alternative means of providing services
- Scientific discoveries
- Changing communications technology
- New production technology
- State of infrastructure

PESTEL

Environmental
- Climate change
- Water resources
- Energy supplies

Legal
- Employment law
- Company law
- Business regulation

Figure 3.3 Identifying environmental influences – PESTEL analysis

- slow transfer of scientific knowledge into commercial products; and
- regulators requiring longer and more costly trials of new drugs.

Political factors

Political systems vary between countries and often shape what managers can and cannot do. Governments often regulate industries such as power supply, telecommunications, postal services and transport by specifying, among other things, who can offer services, the conditions they must meet and what they can charge. Regulations differ between countries and are a major factor in managers' decisions.

When the UK and most European governments altered the law on financial services, non-financial companies like Virgin and Sainsbury's quickly began to offer banking services. Deregulating air transport stimulated the growth of low-cost airlines, especially in the US (e.g. Southwest Airlines), Europe (easyJet), Australia (Virgin Blue) and parts of Asia (Air Asia), though as the Ryanair case in Chapter 1 showed, these companies still work in a political environment. The European Union is developing regulations to try to manage the environmentally friendly disposal of the millions of personal computers and mobile phones that consumers scrap each year.

Managers aim to influence these political decisions by employing professional lobbyists, especially at international institutions. The European Commission relies on contributions from interested parties to inform its decisions and lobbying firms provide this. They focus on those people who have decision-making power, often members of the European parliament.

Economic factors

Economic factors such as wage levels, inflation and interest rates affect an organisation's costs. During the recession, Unilever (**www.unilever.com**) detected significant changes in shopping habits, with many customers doing without expensive bubble baths, body moisturisers and upmarket cleaning products in favour of less expensive purchases. The consumer goods company said that sales of stock cubes were growing very rapidly as more people 'cooked from scratch' instead of buying prepared meals.

Increasing competition and the search for cost advantages drive globalisation. Ford (**www.ford.com**) has invested in a plant to make small cars in India, where demand is growing rapidly as people become more prosperous. The same economic trend encouraged Tata (**www.tata.com**), the Indian conglomerate, to launch a low cost car, the Nano: Renault/Nissan (**www.renault.com**) expect to sell more cars in emerging markets than in developed ones by 2015.

The state of the economy is a major influence on consumer spending, which affects firms meeting those needs. Managers planning capital investments follow economic forecasts: if these suggest slower growth, they may postpone the project.

Socio-cultural factors

Demographic change affects most organisations, apart from those most clearly affected by the ageing population – healthcare and pharmaceuticals businesses. A growing number of single people affects the design of housing, holidays and life assurance. Demographic change affects an organisation's publicity to ensure, for example, that advertising acknowledges racial diversity. Leading banks develop investment and saving schemes that comply with *sharia* law, to attract devout Muslim investors. Rising expenditure on live music encouraged HMV Group (**www.hmv.com**) to buy companies already working in this market (Chapter 8 case study).

> ### Management in practice — Changing tastes challenge pubs
>
> Across Europe people are drinking more alcohol at home and less in pubs. The trend is particularly marked in Britain, where about 40 pubs close each week. They are gradually being usurped as the biggest sellers of beer in the UK, with supermarkets supplying most ale and lager. Many pub managers have adapted to this change by selling more food, some pubs have become gastro-pubs – offering high quality food in the simple 'public house' environment. A manager at a company with several gastro-pubs said:
>
> > Our pubs are doing really well and we want to raise our exposure to this market. The new pubs are in good areas such as west London where people are going to eat out two or three times a week, and want a relaxed place where they can meet their friends without [having to spend too much].
>
> Source: *Financial Times*, 26 August 2008, and other sources.

Consumer tastes and preferences change. Commenting on a decision to increase the number of healthier products, the chief executive of Nestlé said:

> I think this shows you where the future direction of the company is. This emphasis on [healthier products] is a strategic decision, reflecting changing economic and demographic conditions.

Technological factors

Companies pay close attention to the physical infrastructure – such as the adequacy of power supplies and transport systems. Even more, they monitor advances in information technology, which are dramatically changing the business environment of many companies. Advances in technology do not only affect data systems. Computers traditionally handled data, while other systems handled voice (telephones) and pictures (film and video). These components of the information revolution are familiar as separate devices, but their use of common digital technology greatly increases their ability to exchange information. Digitisation – presenting images and sounds in digital form – has profound implications for many industries as Table 3.2 illustrates.

Table 3.2 Examples of digital technologies affecting established businesses

Technology	Application	Businesses affected
Digital Versatile Discs (DVDs)	Store sound and visual images	Sales of stereophonic sound systems decline sharply
IPOD, MP3 and smartphones	Digital downloads of talking books	New markets created for talking books, with titles to suit new audience
Broadband services delivering online content	Enables advertisers to use online media rather than print or television	Media companies respond by building an online presence (NewsCorp acquired MySpace)
Voice over Internet Protocol (VoIP)	Enables telephone calls over the internet at very low cost	Threat to revenues of traditional phone companies
Digital photography	Enables people to store pictures electronically and order prints online	Photographic retailers such as Jessops lose significant part of business

Nokia is facing major challenges as the mobile phone and computing industries come together, allowing a company like Apple (originally a computer business) to offer the iPhone range of smartphones. Bernoff and Li (2008) show how social networking (Facebook) and user generated content sites (YouTube) change the technological context – to which established media companies need to work out a profitable response.

Political pressure is also mounting on Europe's leading telecoms companies to increase their spending on high-speed broadband networks. The European commissioner responsible for the EU's digital agenda has told them that their inadequate investment plans meant that targets to increase broadband speeds across Europe are unlikely to be met (*Financial Times*, 27 April 2011).

Environmental factors

The natural resources available in an economy – including minerals, agricultural land and the prevailing climate – affect the kind of businesses that managers create: the mills at New Lanark (Chapter 2 case study) were built beside a source of water power.

Many senior managers know that climate change will have major implications for their organisations, and are working out how best to respond. It will put most businesses at risk, with the probability of more droughts, floods, storms and heat waves – less rainfall in some places, more in others. For some it represents a threat – insurance companies, house builders and water companies are only the most visible examples of companies that are being affected. For others sustainability brings opportunities – alternative energy suppliers, emission control businesses and waste management companies are all seeing more interest in their products and services.

Legal factors

Governments create the legal framework within which companies operate, most obviously in areas like health and safety, employment, consumer protection and pollution control. They also create the legal basis for business – such as when the UK parliament passed the Joint Stock Companies Act in 1862. People had been reluctant to invest in new companies as they were personally liable for the whole of a company's debts if it failed. The Act of 1862 limited their liability to the value of their shares – they could lose their investment, but not the rest of their wealth. This stimulated company formation and other countries soon passed similar legislation, paving the way for the countless 'limited liability' companies that exist today.

The PESTEL analysis is just as relevant to public and voluntary sector organisations. Many public service organisations are in business to do things that the market does not, so a PESTEL analysis can identify emerging issues that need attention. An example is the age structure of the population: a country with growing numbers of elderly people has to finance changes in community care services, social services and hospitals. Public sector organisations are often unable to expand their operations where new problems or needs are identified, but the results can be used to lobby for increased funding or to target their existing budgets.

The PESTEL framework is a useful starting point for analysis if managers use it to identify factors that are relevant to their business, and how these are changing.

3.6 Stakeholders

All managers need to deal with stakeholders – individuals, groups or other organisations with an interest in, or who are affected by, what the enterprise does. Organisations depend on their micro and macro environments (Figure 3.1) for the resources they need. Stakeholders in these environments make resources available or withhold them, depending on their view of the organisation. Managers in any sector need to pay attention to stakeholder expectations, and meet these to an acceptable degree to ensure a positive view.

Stakeholders may be internal (employees, managers, different departments or professional groups, owners, shareholders) or external (customers, competitors, bankers, local communities, members of the public, pressure groups and government). The challenge is that:

> Different stakeholders do not generally share the same definition of an organization's 'problems', and hence, they do not in general share the same 'solutions'. As a result, the typical approaches to organizational problem solving, which generally presuppose prior consensus or agreement among parties, cannot be used; they break down. Instead a method is needed that builds off a starting point of disagreement . . . (Mitroff, 1983, p. 5)

Stakeholders have expectations of organisations and managers choose whether or not to take account of these. Nutt (2002) shows the dangers of ignoring them: he studied 400 strategic decisions, and found that half of them 'failed' – in the sense that they were not implemented or produced poor results – largely because managers failed to attend to stakeholders.

Faced with evidence of excessive risk-taking in banks, shareholders have begun to become more active in criticising directors over the pay and bonus systems through which they reward senior managers in their companies. This has led to changes in corporate governance arrangements.

3.7 Corporate governance

Why have governance systems?

Scandals and failures in prominent public and private organisations lead people to question the adequacy of their systems of **corporate governance**. They show that senior managers cannot always be trusted to act in the best interests of the citizens or shareholders. To reduce this risk, people develop 'governance systems' – rules and processes to control those managing public and private organisations. They aim to make them accountable to others for what they do, in the hope that this will achieve a closer balance between the interests involved.

> **Corporate governance** refers to the rules and processes intended to control those responsible for managing an organisation.

In capitalist economies, ownership typically becomes separated from control. The founder provides the initial capital but growth requires further finance – which investors provide in exchange for an income. They cannot supervise management decisions, but need to be confident that the business is secure before they provide further funds.

Berle and Means (1932) highlighted the dilemma facing owners who become separated from the managers they appoint to run the business:

> The corporation is a means by which the wealth of innumerable individuals has been concentrated into huge aggregates and whereby control over this wealth has been surrendered to a unified direction . . . The direction of industry other than by persons who have ventured their wealth has raised the question . . . of the distribution of the returns from business enterprise. (p. 4)

Their observations led others to develop what is now termed 'agency theory', which seeks to explain what happens when one party (the principal) delegates work to another party (the agent). In this case, the shareholders (principals) have financed, and own, the business, but delegate the work of running it to managers (agents). The principal faces the risk that managers may not act in their (the principal's) best interests: they may take excessive investment risks, or withhold information so that the state of the business appears better than it is. The agent can use this to personal advantage. Failures at major financial institutions, caused in part by staff lending money to risky borrowers in the hope of high bonuses, show that the separation of ownership from management, of principal from agent, is as relevant as ever.

Similar issues arise in the public sector, where elected members are nominally in charge of local authorities, health boards and other agencies – and who appoint professional managers to run the organisation on behalf of the citizens. Elected members face the risk that the people they have appointed act in their narrow professional or personal interests, rather than of those of the electorate. Hartley (2008) writes:

> a new awareness of the social, economic and cultural contribution of government, public organizations and public services has resulted in a significant period of reform and experimentation. At the heart of these initiatives is the idea that improvements to the way public services can be governed, managed and delivered will produce improved outcomes for citizens. (p. 3)

Stakeholder theory is also relevant, as it tries to explain the evolving relationship between an organisation and its stakeholders. Many believe that governance systems should take account of the interests of this wider group, as well as those of shareholders with only a financial interest.

The substance of corporate governance

Mallin (2007) suggests that governance systems should have:

- an adequate system of internal controls which safeguards assets;
- mechanisms to prevent any one person having too much influence;
- processes to manage relationships between managers, directors, shareholders and other stakeholders (such as the practice of separating the jobs of chairman and chief executive, to avoid a concentration of power in any one person);
- the aim of managing the company in the interests of shareholders and other stakeholders; and
- the aim of encouraging transparency and accountability, which investors and many external stakeholders expect.

Proposals to deal with these issues affect the context in which managers work, and the book will examine the topic as an integrating theme at the end of each chapter.

Activity 3.2   What are 'organisational cultures and contexts'?

Recall the organisation you used in Activity 3.1.

Having read the chapter, make brief notes summarising the main cultural and external factors affecting the company.

- What type of culture do you think is dominant within the company, and how does this affect the way it works? (Refer to Section 3.2 and 3.3.)
- What are the main competitive factors affecting it? (Refer to Section 3.4.)
- What are the main factors in the general environment affecting it? (Refer to Section 3.5.)
- What, if any, governance issues has it had to deal with? (Refer to Section 3.7.)

Compare what you have found with other students on your course.

Summary

1 **Identify the main elements of the environments in which organisations work**
   - They include the immediate competitive environment, the wider general (or macro) environment and the organisation's stakeholders.

2 **Compare the cultures of two organisational units, using Quinn's or Handy's typologies**
   - Quinn *et al*. (2003) – rational goal, internal process, human relations and open systems.
   - Handy (1993) – power, role, task and person.

3 **Use Porter's five forces model to analyse the competitive environment of an organisation**
   - This identifies the degree of competitive rivalry, customers, competitors, suppliers and potential substitute goods and services.

4 **Use the PESTEL framework to analyse the wider environment of an organisation**
   - The PESTEL model of the wider external environment identifies political, economic, social, technological, environmental and legal forces.

5 **Explain the meaning and purpose of corporate governance**
   - Corporate governance frameworks are intended to monitor and control the performance of managers to ensure they act in the interests of organisational stakeholders, and not just of the managers themselves.

Review questions

1 Describe an educational or commercial organisation that you know in terms of the competing values model of cultures.

2 What is the significance of the idea of 'fragmented cultures' for those who wish to change a culture to support performance?

3 Identify the relative influence of Porter's five forces on an organisation of your choice and compare your results with a colleague's. What can you learn from that comparison?

4 How should managers decide which of the many factors easily identified in a PESTEL analysis they should attend to? If they have to be selective, what is the value of the PESTEL method?

5 Since people interpret the nature of environmental forces from unique perspectives, what meaning can people attach to statements about external pressures?

6 Illustrate the stakeholder idea with an example of your own, showing their expectations of an organisation.

7 Explain at least two of the mechanisms which Mallin (2007) recommends should be part of a corporate governance system.

Further reading

Tapscott, E. and Williams, A. D. (2006), *Wikinomics: How mass collaboration changes everything*, Viking Penguin, New York.

   Best-selling account of the radical changes which convergent technologies bring to society, especially the relationship between producers and consumers.

Hawken, P., Lovins, A. B. and Lovins. L. H. (1999), *Natural Capitalism: The next industrial revolution*, Earthscan, London.

Generally positive account of the environmental challenges facing us all, and what organisations are doing about it.

Weblinks

These websites have appeared in, or are relevant to, the chapter:

www.acea.be.
www.bosch.com
www.walmart.com
www.gsk.com
www.unilever.com
www.ford.com
www.tata.com
www.Renault.com
www.hmv.com
www.nokia.com

Visit some of these, or any other companies which interest you, and navigate to the pages dealing with recent news, press or investor relations.

- What can you find about their culture?
- What are the main forces in the external environment which the organisation appears to be facing?
- Compare and contrast the issues you identify on the two sites.
- What challenges may they imply for those working in, and managing, these organisations?

Annotated weblinks, multiple choice questions and other useful resources can be found on **www.pearsoned.co.uk/boddy**

Case study   Nokia   www.nokia.com

Nokia is struggling to survive in the very competitive mobile phone business. In 2008 it had 40 per cent of the world handset market, but at the end of March 2011 that had fallen to 29 per cent. This was still well ahead of Motorola, and many times the number sold by rivals such as Samsung and Ericsson: but its position was being challenged by competitors. Managers were making big changes in the company to meet the expectations of customers and share-holders. In April 2011, it announced that 4000 jobs would be lost by the end of 2012, most of them in Denmark, Finland and the UK: in June it warned that profits for the year would be well below expectations. The value of shares in the company fell to their lowest level since 1998.

The Finnish company was founded in 1895 as a paper manufacturer, and then grew into a conglomerate with wide interests including electronics, cable manufacture, rubber, chemicals, electricity generation and, by the 1960s, telephone equipment. In the early 1990s senior managers decided to focus on the new mobile phone industry.

Two factors favoured this move. First, the Finnish government had taken a lead in telecoms deregulation and Nokia was already competing vigorously with other manufacturers supplying equipment to the national phone company. Second, the European Union (EU) adopted a single standard – the Global System for Mobile Telephony (GSM) – for Europe's second generation (digital) phones. Two-thirds of the world's mobile phone subscribers use this standard. Finland's links with its Nordic neighbours also helped, as people in these sparsely populated countries adopted mobile phones enthusiastically.

Nokia had strong design skills, but above all, managers were quick to recognise that mobile phones were now a fashion accessory. By offering smart designs, different ring tones and coloured covers, Nokia became the 'cool' mobile brand for fashion-conscious people. Nokia had also mastered the logistics of getting millions of phones to customers around the world.

While many competitors subcontract the manufacture of handsets, Nokia assembles most of its own, with factories in many countries across the world. Managers believe this gives them a better understanding of the market and the manufacturing process. Nokia buys about 80 billion components a

Courtesy of Nokia.

year, and has close relationships with its most important suppliers.

In March 2011 it reported sales of 108.5 million units in the previous quarter. It is continuing to add value to its devices by integrating them with innovative services providing music, maps, apps and email. It also believes that its wide range of handsets means it will be able to meet demand if customers begin to prefer cheaper handsets.

One factor in the company's sustained success was believed to have been a culture which encourages co-operation within teams, and across internal and external boundaries. Jorma Ollila, CEO until 2006, believed that Nokia's innovative capacity springs from multi-functional teams working together to bring new insights to products and services. Staff in the four divisions work in teams which may remain constant for many years – but sometimes combine with other teams to work on a common task.

Informal mentoring begins as soon as someone steps into a new job. Within a few days, the employee's manager lists the people in the organisation whom it would be useful for the employee to meet. They also review what topics the newcomer should discuss with the suggested contact, and why establishing a relationship with them is important. The gift of time – in the form of hours spent on coaching and building networks – is a crucial part of the collaborative culture.

Nokia also encourages a culture of communication by creating small groups to work on a strategic issue for four months. This helps them to build ties with many parts of the company – some of which continue during later work. The Induction process for new employees also encourages team-building and co-operation: the newcomer's manager must introduce them to at least 15 people within and outside the team.

It is struggling to compete at the top end of the market, where smartphones offer a range of multimedia services: these probably represent about 20 per cent of handset sales, and sell for much higher prices than basic models. The convergence of the technologies underlying the mobile and computing industries has enabled companies like Apple (originally a computer business) to launch the iPhone, which has gained a strong position in the smartphone market. Other companies have adopted Google's Android software to develop a further range of devices to compete with Nokia.

As profits declined, shareholders began to demand that Nokia's board act to improve its performance – especially when the company's market share declined from 36.4 per cent at the end of 2009 to 28.6 per cent in the last quarter of 2010. One consequence was to dismiss the then Chief Executive, and replace him with Steve Elop, who had worked for Microsoft.

In early 2011 the company announced it would collaborate with Microsoft to develop a new range of devices and software – which included using the Microsoft Windows Phone 7 operating system for next generation of smartphones. Microsoft has been keen to build presence in smartphones, but its own brands have not established a strong presence. It hoped that an alliance with Nokia would help it improve its position.

Sources: Grattan and Erickson (2007); Doz and Kosonen (2008); *Financial Times*, 17 July 2009, 22 January 2010, 8 April 2011, 28 April 2011, 1 June 2011; company website.

Questions

1 Which of the cultural types identified by Quinn *et al.* (2003) would you expect to find within Nokia's handset business? (Refer to Section 3.3.)

2 Use Porter's five forces model to outline Nokia's competitive (micro) environment. (Refer to Section 3.4.)

3 Which PESTEL factors are most affecting the macro environment of the industry? Are they likely to be positive or negative for Nokia? (Refer to Section 3.5.)

4 Who are the main stakeholders in Nokia, and what are their interests in the success of the company? (Refer to Section 3.6.)

5 Visit Nokia's website, and read their most recent trading statement (under investor relations). What have been the main developments in the last year?

MANAGING INNOVATION AND CHANGE

Learning outcomes

When you have read this chapter you should be able to:

1 Outline the links between creativity, innovation, change and strategy

2 Describe types of innovation, with examples

3 Explain the links between innovation and its context

4 Compare life-cycle, emergent, participative and political theories of change

5 Explain the forms and sources of innovation

6 Illustrate the organisational factors believed to support or hinder innovation and change

7 Use ideas from the chapter to comment on the management issues in the Google case study

Activity 11.1 **What does 'managing innovation and change' mean?**

Before reading the chapter, write some notes on what you think 'managing innovation and change' means in management. Choose the organisation or people who may be able to help you learn about the topic. You may find it helpful to discuss the topic with a manager you know, or reflect on an activity you have managed.

- Identify a significant change or innovation in which someone has been involved, and describe it briefly.
- Gather information on the process(es) through which people managed the change.
- Was there any evidence of resistance to change?
- Which organisational factors helped or hindered the innovation?

Keep these notes as you will be able to use them later.

11.1 Introduction

Google is an organisation founded on innovation and continual change (see chapter case study). The founders developed a search engine that works at astonishing speed to supply internet users with the information they need – and they continue to adjust the algorithm to improve the relevance of the search results to users. They regularly add new features, and are using the accumulating revenues from the search business to invest in new areas such as blogging, online payments, mobile phone operating systems (Android) and an online bookstore. Google managers are also innovative in the way they manage the business: as well as extending their services, they are refining the management processes and skills they need to deliver them. Consumer products companies like Unilever and Procter & Gamble also depend on a constant flow of innovation.

Others work in organisations which change very slowly, even when the evidence is clear that something is wrong. Senior managers at BP face the challenge of continuing to transform the company from a relatively small (for that industry), diversified business into the world's second-largest oil company, and to embed a strong safety culture. The scandal at Mid Staffordshire NHS Trust (Chapter 17 case study) clearly showed the need for radical change in control systems and ways of working – but these will be hard to introduce into such an established organisation. Anecdotal evidence suggests that while most managers accept the need for innovation and change, many are critical of their organisation's ability to introduce it. They experience great difficulty in implementing major changes – often underestimating how long it takes people to accept the need for change, how uncomfortable it can be for those on the receiving end, and the organisational complexity of making apparently small changes.

This chapter presents theories about the nature of innovation and change in organisations. It shows how the external environment is the main source of pressure for change, and how this may prompt people to change one or more elements of the (internal) organisation: there is a continuing interaction between internal and external contexts. It presents four complementary perspectives on how people manage that interaction, and suggests the sources of innovation. It concludes with ideas on the organisational factors that can help or hinder innovation and change. Figure 11.1 shows the themes of the chapter.

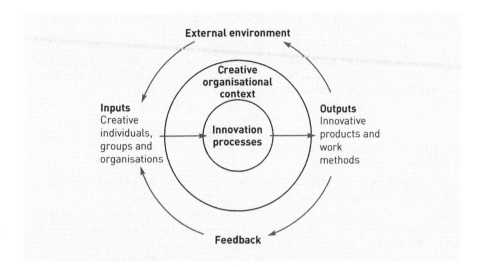

Figure 11.1
A systems view
of innovation
and change

11.2 | Initiating innovation and change

Chapter 1 introduced the idea that managers interact with their contexts (external and internal environments) in the sense that the contexts shape what they do, and managers in turn shape their contexts. People begin to innovate and change when they see an actual or potential gap between current outputs and those they desire – products do not perform well enough, new ideas show they can re-design what they do and how they do it, or present working methods are too costly to sustain in a competitive market. They see a gap between desired and actual performance – usually because the internal context of the organisation is unable to meet external opportunities and threats. They try to generate innovative ideas from individuals, groups or other organisations, and implement them – in the hope that this will close (or prevent) the performance gap. Practical issues of design and implementation affect the outcomes – which in turn shape external and internal contexts – the starting point for future innovation and change.

The external context

Chapter 3 described the external environment (or context) of business and successive chapters have illustrated the changes taking place, such as internationalisation and the radical effects of the internet. Together with deregulation and the privatisation of former state businesses, these transformed the competitive landscape of established businesses. Managers at British Airways and KLM had to respond to competition from low-cost airlines. Established banks faced competition from new entrants such as retailers (Sainsbury's) or conglomerates (Virgin) offering financial services. The internet enables online news organisations to compete with print newspapers – some of which now offer online editions. Apple and Facebook were created as innovative businesses, but continually strive to increase the pace and quality of successive innovations.

These forces have collectively meant a shift of economic power from producers to consumers, many of whom now enjoy greater quality, choice and value. Managers wishing to retain customers continually seek new ways to add value and retain their market position. Unless they do so they will experience a widening performance gap.

Perceived performance gap

A **perceived performance gap** arises when people believe that the performance of a unit or business is out of line with the level they desire. If staff do not meet a customer's expectations, there is an immediate performance gap. Cumulatively this will lead to other performance

A **perceived perform-
ance gap** arises when
people believe that the
actual performance of a
unit or business is out of
line with the level they
desire.

gaps – such as revenue from sales being below the level needed to secure further resources. If uncorrected, this will, sooner or later, cause the business to fail.

In the current business climate, two aspects of performance dominate discussion – what Prastacos *et al.* (2002) call '**performance imperatives**': the need for flexibility and the need for innovation. In a very uncertain business world, the scope for long-term planning is limited. Successful businesses are those which are both flexible and efficient. This paradox reflects the fact that while companies need to respond rapidly they also need to respond efficiently. This usually depends on having developed a degree of stability in the way they transform resources into outputs. Apple is very flexible in the way it brings out new products, but has very stable and robust systems to produce and deliver them.

Performance imperatives are aspects of performance that are especially important for an organisation to do well, such as flexibility and innovation.

The other imperative identified by Prastacos *et al.* (2002) is innovation:

> to generate a variety of successful new products or services (embedding technological innovation), and to continuously innovate in all aspects of the business. (p. 58)

In many areas of business, customers expect a constant flow of new products, embodying the latest scientific and technological developments: companies that fail to meet these expectations will experience a performance gap. Nokia selling an advanced mobile phone profitably depends not only on the quality of the applied research which goes into producing a better screen display, but also on turning that research into a desirable product *and* delivering it at a price which customers will pay. This depends on organisation – the internal context.

The internal context

Chapter 1 introduced the internal context (Figure 1.3) as the elements within an organisation that shape behaviour. Change begins to happen when sufficient influential people believe, say, that outdated technology or a confusing structure is causing a performance gap, by inhibiting flexibility or innovation. They notice external or internal events and interpret them as threatening the performance that influential stakeholders expect. This interpretation, and their (implicit) theory of change, encourages them to propose changing one or more aspects of the internal context organisation (see Table 11.1).

Table 11.1 Examples of change in each element of the organisation

Element	Example of change to this element
Objectives	Developing a new product or service Changing the overall mission or direction
Technology	Creating an online community Building Terminal 5 at Heathrow
Business processes	Improving the way maintenance and repair services are delivered Redesigning systems to handle the flow of cash and funds
Financial resources	A set of changes, such as closing a facility, to reduce costs New financial reporting requirements to ensure consistency
Structure	Reallocating functions and responsibilities between departments Redesigning work to give staff more responsibility
People	Designing a training programme to enhance skills Changing the tasks of staff to offer a new service
Culture	Unifying the culture between two or more merged businesses Encouraging greater emphasis on quality and reliability
Power	An empowerment programme giving greater authority to junior staff Centralising decisions to increase the control of HQ over subsidiaries

They then have to persuade enough other people that the matter is sufficiently serious to place on the management agenda. People in some organisations are open to proposals for change, others tend to ignore them – BP faced new competitive pressures throughout the 1980s, but it was only around 1990 that sufficient senior people took the threats seriously enough to initiate rapid change.

People initiate change for reasons other than a conscious awareness of a performance gap – fashion, empire building or personal whim can all play a part. Employees or trade unions can propose changes in the way things are done to improve working conditions. The need for innovation and change is subjective – what some see as urgent others will leave till later. People affect that process by managing external information – magnifying customer complaints to support change, minimising them to avoid it.

11.3 Forms of innovation and change

Creativity and innovation

Creativity refers to the ability to combine ideas in a new way, or to make unusual associations between ideas. This helps people and organisations to generate imaginative ideas or ways of working: but that in itself does not bring value. Figure 11.1 shows that achieving more valuable outputs (more innovative products or work methods) depends on both the inputs AND the transformation of those inputs.

Inputs include having creative people and groups who are able to generate novel ideas and methods, but they only flourish in a favourable context. Managers need to create a context which encourages both creative people *and* the application of their ideas into goods and services that people buy. In the business context, it is useful to see **innovation** as the process through which new ideas, objects, behaviours and practices are created, developed and implemented into a product or service.

Innovation is the process through which new ideas, objects, behaviours and practices are created, developed and implemented into a product or service that can be sold for profit.

The 4 Ps of innovation

Innovations become manifest in one or more of four areas – the product itself, the process of delivery or manufacture, its position in the market and the overall paradigm of the business.

Product innovations

This refers to a new function or feature of a product such as incorporating a music player into a mobile phone or offering an online banking facility. They are intended to enhance the utility of the product to increase sales – such as the Nike+ (developed with Apple), which contains a sensor that transmits data from one of the shoes to the runner's iPod or iPhone.

Process innovations

An example is adding a self-service checkout at a supermarket so that customers can scan and pay for their purchases using a barcode reader. An example in manufacturing would be using robots to assemble higher quality products more efficiently, while another (very radical) would be when managers try to change their underlying philosophy and approach to managing the business.

Position innovations

These are changes in the target market for a product or service. Lucozade is a familiar example – once aimed at people recovering from illness, it is now for healthy people engaged in sport. Another example is the four-wheel drive vehicle: originally intended for off-road work, now sold as fashionable family cars.

Paradigm innovations

These are changes in how companies frame what they do; for example reframing a supermarket such as Tesco from a food retailer to one which provides many more of a family's needs such as petrol, clothing and financial products. This also brings further synergies, since shoppers can buy food, petrol and clothes – and pay for it all with their Tesco credit card.

Degrees of innovation – radical and incremental

Some innovations – such as the aerofoil that allows heavier than air flight and the transistor that is the basis of all modern electronics – have fundamentally changed society. Others such as Velcro or the ball-point pen are useful, but have more modest effects on our lives.

The effects of an innovation depend on what people use them for, what they replace and who is evaluating them. Using hydrogen-fuelled engines instead of fossil-fuelled ones will have little effect on how people drive cars, so from the driver's perspective it is an **incremental** innovation. It will have a large environmental benefit – so from the point of view of those who care about the environment it will be a **radical** innovation.

Incremental innovations are small changes in a current product or process which brings a minor improvement.

Radical innovations are large game-changing developments that alter the competitive landscape.

Organisational change

Turning innovative ideas or products into something that adds value depends on **organisational change** – an attempt to change one or more of the elements shown in Figure 1.3. Table 11.1 illustrates this with examples of changes that people initiate under each element. Most change combines several of these – when Paul Polman (chief executive of Unilever, the food and consumer products company) began to make substantial changes to the way it worked, he acknowledging it would be a long process, because:

> we need to change the strategy and structure as well as the culture. (*Financial Times*, 5 April 2010)

Change in any of these areas will have implications for others – and these interconnections make change difficult. When Tesco introduced its online shopping service, managers evidently needed to create a website (technology). They also needed to decide issues of structure and people (would it be part of the existing stores, or a separate unit with its own premises and staff?) and about business processes (how would an order on the website be transformed into a box of groceries delivered to the customer's door?). They had to manage these ripples initiated by the main decision. Managers who ignore, or are unable to manage, these consequential changes achieve less than they expect.

Organisational change is a deliberate attempt to improve organisational performance by changing one or more aspects of the organisation, such as its technology, structure or business processes.

11.4 The interaction of context and change

How managers implement change depends on their theory about its nature. This section presents an **interaction model**, a theory of how change and context interact, and the next section outlines four complementary perspectives on managing that interaction.

The **interaction model** is a theory of change that stresses the continuing interaction between the internal and external contexts of an organisation, making the outcomes of change hard to predict.

People introduce change to alter the context

Management attempts to change elements of its context to encourage behaviours that close the performance gap. If Google's online bookstore is to be a success, the company will need (at least) to change technology, structure, people and business processes to enable staff to deliver the new service. When people plan and implement a change they are creating a new context, which they hope will guide the behaviour of people involved in the activity.

People do not necessarily accept the new arrangements, or without adapting them in some way: in doing so they make further changes to the context. As people begin to work in new circumstances – with a new IS or a new job description – they make small adjustments to the original plan, deciding which aspects to ignore, use or adapt. In time, some of these changes in behaviour become routine and taken for granted – and so become part of the context that staff have created informally. These add to, or replace, the context that those formally responsible for planning the change created, and may or may not support the original intentions of the project. People and context continue to interact.

The context affects the ability to change

While people managing a project aim to change the context, the context within which they work will itself help or hinder them. All of the elements of Table 11.1 will be present as the project begins, and some of these will influence how people react. Managers who occupy influential positions will review a proposal from their personal career perspective, as well as that of the organisation. At Tesco the existing technology (stores, distribution systems, information systems) and business processes would influence managers' decisions about how to implement the internet shopping strategy.

The prevailing culture (Chapter 3) – shared values, ideals and beliefs – influences how people view change. Some will welcome a project they believe fits their culture, and resist one that threatens it. Culture is a powerful influence on the success or failure of innovation. Some cultures, like those at Asos or Facebook, encourage people to welcome and support change – they provide a **receptive context**. A manager in a leading electronics company commented on his fast-moving business:

> A very dynamic organisation, it's incredibly fast and the change thing is just a constant that you live with. They really promote flexibility and adaptability in their employees. Change is just a constant, there's change happening all of the time and people have become very acclimatised to that, it's part of the job. The attitude to change, certainly within the organisation, is very positive at the moment.

In others, the culture discourages change and encourages caution – especially if the change proposed would challenge ways of thinking that have worked well for many years. Music publishers like EMI found it hard to respond to competition from digital downloading, in part because they have a **non-receptive context**. Book publishers think of their business from the perspective of printed books, and some find it hard to see how they can work with digital methods of delivering content, such as Kindle. Cultural beliefs shape how people respond, and are hard to change, yet:

> Managers learn to be guided by these beliefs because they have worked successfully in the past. (Lorsch, 1986, p. 97)

The distribution of power also affects receptiveness to change. Change threatens established practice, and those who benefit from present arrangements will resist it. Innovation depends on those promoting it being able to use, or develop, sufficient power and expertise to overcome entrenched interests – who will, of course, resist changes in the distribution of power.

Receptive contexts are those where features of the organisation (such as culture or technology) appear likely to help change.

Non-receptive contexts are those where the combined effects of features of the organisation (such as culture or technology) appear likely to hinder change.

The context has a history and several levels

The present context is the result of past decisions and events, so managers implement change against that background. The promoter of a project in a multinational firm noted his colleagues' attitudes:

> They were a little sceptical and wary of whether it was actually going to enhance our processes. Major pan-European redesign work had been attempted in the past and had failed miserably. The solutions had not been appropriate and had not been accepted by the divisions. Europe-wide programmes therefore had a bad name. (Boddy, 2002, p. 38)

Beliefs about the future also affect how people react. Optimists are more open to change than those who feel threatened and vulnerable.

The context represented by Table 11.1 occurs at corporate, divisional and operating levels. People at any of these will be acting to change their context – which may help or hinder those managing change elsewhere. A project at one level may depend on decisions at another about resources, as this manager leading an oil refinery project discovered:

> One of the main drawbacks was that commissioning staff could have been supplemented by skilled professionals from within the company, but this was denied to me as project manager. This threw a heavy strain and responsibility on myself and my assistant. It put me in a position of high stress, as I knew that the future of the company rested upon the successful outcome of this project. One disappointment (and, I believe, a significant factor in the project) was that just before commissioning, the manager of the pilot plant development team was transferred to another job. He had been promised to me at the project inception, and I had designed him into the working operation. (Boddy, 2002, pp. 38–39)

The manager's job is to create a coherent context that encourages creativity and innovation, by using their preferred model of change.

11.5 Four models of change

There are four complementary models of change, each with different implications for managers – life-cycle, emergent, participative and political.

Life-cycle

Much advice given to those responsible for managing projects uses the idea of the project **life-cycle**. Projects go through successive stages, and results depend on managing each one in an orderly and controlled way. The labels vary, but common themes are:

- define objectives;
- allocate responsibilities;
- fix deadlines and milestones;
- set budgets; and
- monitor and control.

Life-cycle models of change are those that view change as an activity which follows a logical, orderly sequence of activities that can be planned in advance.

This approach (sometimes called a 'rational – linear' approach) reflects the idea that people can identify smaller tasks within a change and plan the (overlapping) order in which to do them. It predicts that people can make reasonably accurate estimates of the time required to complete each task and when it will be feasible to start work on later ones. People can use tools such as bar charts (sometimes called Gantt charts after the American industrial engineer Henry Gantt, who worked with Frederick Taylor), to show all the tasks required for a project and their likely duration. These help to visualise the work required and to plan the likely sequence of events – illustrated in Figure 11.2.

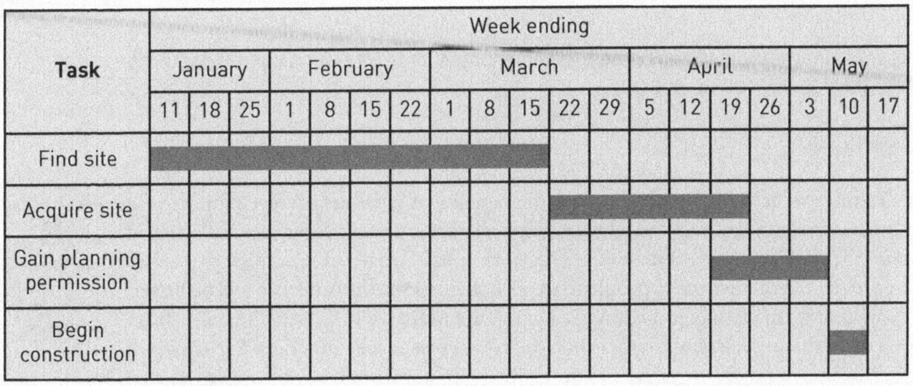

Task	Week ending																		
	January			February				March					April				May		
	11	18	25	1	8	15	22	1	8	15	22	29	5	12	19	26	3	10	17
Find site	▓	▓	▓	▓	▓	▓	▓	▓											
Acquire site										▓	▓	▓	▓						
Gain planning permission															▓	▓			
Begin construction																		▓	

Figure 11.2 A simple bar chart

The life-cycle model implies that managing change depends on specifying these elements at the start and monitoring them to ensure the project stays on target. Large industrial research laboratories tend to work in this way.

Many books on project management, such as Lock (2007), present advice on tools for each stage of the life cycle. Those advising on IS changes may recommend 'system development life cycle' approaches (Chaffey, 2003). These give valuable guidance, but may not be sufficient, since people may be unable at the start to specify the end point – or the tasks which will lead to it. In uncertain conditions, it makes little sense to plan the outcomes in detail. It may be wiser to set the general direction, and adapt the target to suit new conditions that develop during the change. Those managing such change need an additional theory to cope with emergent change.

Emergent

Chapter 8 (Section 8.3) mentions the strategy process at IKEA, showing how many of its major business ideas emerged from chance events or external conditions. Evidence of similar processes in other firms led scholars to see companies' strategies as an *emergent* or adaptive process. These ideas apply to innovation and change projects as much as they do to broad strategy. People with different interests and priorities influence the direction of a project and how they want to achieve it. The planning techniques associated with the life-cycle approach can help, but their value will be limited if the change is closer to the **emergent model**.

Emergent models of change emphasise that in uncertain conditions a project will be affected by unknown factors, and that planning has little effect on the outcome.

Boddy *et al.* (2000) show how this emergent process occurred when Sun Microsystems began working with a new supplier of the bulky plastic enclosures that contain their products, while the supplier wished to widen their customer base. There were few discussions about a long-term plan. As Sun became more confident in the supplier's ability it gave them more complex work. Both gained from this emerging relationship. A sales co-ordinator:

> It's something we've learnt by being with Sun – we didn't imagine that at the time. Also at the time we wouldn't have imagined we would be dealing with America the way we do now – it was far beyond our thoughts. (Boddy *et al.*, 2000, p. 1010)

Mintzberg believes that managers should not expect rigid adherence to a plan. Chance and 'eureka moments' (see Section 11.6) are valuable sources of innovation. Some departure from plan is inevitable as circumstances change, so a wise approach to change recognises that

> the real world inevitably involves some thinking ahead of time as well as some adaptation en route. (Mintzberg, 1994a, p. 24)

Participative

Those advocating **participative models** stress the benefits of personal involvement in, and contribution to, events and outcomes. The underlying belief is that if people can say 'I helped to build this', they will be more willing to live and work with it, whatever it is. It is also *possible* that since participation allows more people to express their views, the outcome will be better. Employees who participate fully in planning a change are more likely to view the issues from the perspective of the organisation, rather than their own position or function. Participation can be good for the organisation, as well as the individual. Many innovative firms invite customers to participate in product and service design.

While participation is consistent with democratic values, it takes time and effort and may raise unrealistic expectations. It may be inappropriate when:

- the scope for change is limited, because of decisions made elsewhere;
- participants know little about the topic;
- decisions must be made quickly;
- management has decided what to do and will do so whatever views people express;
- there are fundamental disagreements and/or inflexible opposition to the proposed change.

Participative approaches assume that a sensitive approach by reasonable people will result in the willing acceptance and implementation of change. Some situations contain conflicts that participation alone cannot solve.

The **participative model** is the belief that if people are able to take part in planning a change they will be more willing to accept and implement the change.

Political models

Change often involves people from several levels and functions pulling in different directions:

> Strategic processes of change are . . . widely accepted as multi-level activities and not just as the province of a . . . single general manager. Outcomes of decisions are no longer assumed to be a product of rational . . . debates but are also shaped by the interests and commitments of individuals and groups, forces of bureaucratic momentum, and the manipulation of the structural context around decisions and changes. (Whipp *et al.*, 1988, p. 51)

Several analysts propose using a **political model of change**. Pettigrew (1985) was an early advocate of the view that change requires political as well as rational (life-cycle) skills. Successful change managers encourage others to accept the change as necessary – often by manipulating apparently rational information to build support for their ideas and enhance their power.

Power is essential to get things done, since decisions in themselves change nothing – people only see a difference when someone implements a visible change. Change frequently threatens the *status quo*: people who have done well are likely to resist it. Innovators need to ensure the project is put onto the senior management agenda, and that influential people support and resource it. Innovators need to develop a political will, and to build and use their power. Buchanan and Badham (1999) conclude that the roots of political behaviour

Political models of change reflect the view that organisations are made up of groups with separate interests, goals and values, and that these affect how they respond to change.

> lie in personal ambition, in organisation structures that create roles and departments which compete with each other, and in major decisions that cannot be resolved by reason and logic alone but which rely on the values and preferences of the key actors. Power politics and change are inextricably linked. Change creates uncertainty and ambiguity. People wonder how their jobs will change, how their work will be affected, how their relationships with colleagues will be damaged or enhanced. (p. 11)

Reasonable people may disagree about means and ends, and fight for the action they prefer. This implies that successful project managers understand that their job requires more than technical competence, and are able and willing to engage in political actions.

The political perspective recognises the messy realities of organisational life. Major product and service innovations will be technically complex and challenge established interests. These will pull in different directions and pursue personal as well as organisational goals. To manage these tensions, managers need political skills as well as those implied by life-cycle, emergent and participative perspectives.

Management in practice   **Political action in hospital re-engineering**

Managers in a hospital responded to a persistent performance gap (especially unacceptably long waiting times) by 're-engineering' the way patients moved through and between clinical areas. This included creating multi-functional teams responsible for all aspects of the flow of the patient through a clinic, rather than dealing with narrow functional tasks. The programme was successful, but was also controversial. One of those leading the change recalled:

> I don't like to use the word manipulate, but . . . you do need to manipulate people. It's about playing the game. I remember being accosted by a very cross consultant who had heard something about one of the changes and he really wasn't very happy with it. And it was about how am I going to deal with this now? And it is about being able to think quickly. So I put it over to him in a way that he then accepted, and he was quite happy with. And it wasn't a lie and it wasn't totally the truth. But he was happy with it and it has gone on.

Source: Buchanan (2001), p. 13.

These perspectives (life-cycle, emergent, participative, political) are complementary in that successful large change is likely to require elements of each. Table 11.2 illustrates how each perspective links to management practice.

Table 11.2 Perspectives on change and examples of management practice

Perspective	Themes	Example of management practices
Life cycle	Rational, linear, single agreed aim, technical focus	Measurable objectives; planning and control devices such as Gantt charts and critical path analysis
Emergent	Objectives change as learning occurs during the project, and new possibilities appear	Open to new ideas about scope and direction, and willing to add new resources if needed
Participative	Ownership, commitment, shared goals, people focus	Inviting ideas and comments on proposals, ensuring agreement before action, seeking consensus
Political	Oppositional, influence, conflicting goals, power focus	Building allies and coalitions, securing support from powerful players, managing information

11.6 Sources of innovation

Innovative ideas can come from any or all of the elements shown in Figure 11.1, if managers create a suitable context.

Eureka moments – capturing the unexpected

The word 'eureka' is associated with the experience of having an idea. A common example is when Art Fry used a recently invented 'sticky but not too sticky' adhesive to keep his bookmark in place. This gave him the idea for the Post-It note which, after more design and development, became the familiar product range. The Management in Practice feature describes a recent example.

Management in practice   Plugging a 'mole' in the market   www.magnamole.co.uk

Sharon Wright had her eureka moment while having a phone-line installed in her home. Under pressure for time she offered to help the engineer thread the cable through the wall of her house. To Sharon's surprise the engineer produced a makeshift tool made out of a wire coat-hanger. As well as being difficult to use Sharon's experience in health and safety management told her this device was unsuitable and hazardous. Market research showed there were no alternatives tools available for cable threading.

Within hours she had sketched the design of the Magnamole tool, a plastic rod with a magnet at one end and an accompanying metallic cap for attaching to the wire to be threaded through the wall. She soon had a prototype, and orders followed from large customers around the world.

What is remarkable about Sharon is that she had little knowledge or experience of this area of business, but that did not stop her from taking advantage of an obvious gap in the market.

Source: Company website.

Knowledge push

Most innovation now comes from the research and development laboratories of large companies. GlaxoSmithKline (pharmaceuticals) spends large sums to develop new drugs in its laboratories. It depends on innovation, and this is reflected in the systematic organisation of scientific staff, equipment and facilities to find potentially profitable solutions to known medical conditions. It also draws on the expertise of other companies through many joint-venture arrangements – as does Procter & Gamble, the world's largest consumer products company. It is an acknowledged leader in product innovation, and its chief executive, Bob McDonald, believes that they should increasingly embrace other people's good ideas. The company embraces the idea of 'open innovation', by working with outside partners to increase the speed at which it brings new products to market – Tide Total Care was developed with external research from the University of Lund in Sweden, and from two smaller chemical companies.

Need pull

No matter how innovative a new product, it will not make money (add value) unless it has a market, so before investing in development, managers assess the likely demand. This is difficult, as it is hard to assess human needs in isolation. Before the technology arrived, sportsmen and women trained without equipment to combat boredom, and, if asked, would have been unable to express a need for a product. Yet lightweight digital music players and headphones are now an essential part of a runner's or cyclist's training kit. Many products, especially in the area of consumer electronics, were inconceivable a few years ago. While it is logical that the typewriter could pave the way for a product such as Microsoft Word, it is less conceivable that it would lead to Powerpoint. While the link between the home phone and the mobile phone is clear, the jump from the basic mobile to the functionality embodied in the iPhone would have been difficult to envisage.

Regulation changes

Changes to the external context – new laws and regulations – are another source of innovation. Measures to limit climate change and environmental pollution are current examples, which encourage entrepreneurs to search for commercially viable solutions in solar, wind, wave or biomass technologies. Regulations to improve road safety led to the development of speed cameras and air bags. Potential innovators seek opportunities in relevant regulations.

Staff as innovators

Staff (part of the internal context) are a valuable source of innovation, even if it is not expected as a major part of their job. Employee participation became fashionable when people publicised the 'Quality Miracle' of Japanese manufacturers, enabled by the system of 'Kaizen' or 'continuous improvement' (Imai, 1986). Under this method, employees were encouraged to question work processes and look for incremental improvements in all that they did, leading to a better production process, better product quality and organisational efficiency.

While suggestion schemes are not new, the more systematic and proactive approach of the Japanese encouraged 'continuous improvement'. This is now joined by other systems such as 'total quality management' and 'lean manufacturing'. While differing in emphasis, all aim to involve employees in thinking behind the product and process, and encouraging them to generate ideas that lead to value-adding innovations.

Users as innovators

Users are sometimes the source of ideas for innovation, three categories being particularly important:

- **Lead users** – people who not only use the product but also help in its development. Ivor Tiefenbrun, the founder of hi-fi maker Linn Products (Chapter 16, p. 324), developed his model when he became dissatisfied with products then available.
- **User communities** – are groups of users who congregate around a product or product platform, such as early personal computer users, and find new and innovative ways to use the systems.
- **Extreme users** – push products to their limit creating a need for improved performance. The bicycle is an example, with the relentless drive for more durable and higher performing machines.

11.7 Organisational factors in innovation

The process of innovation

Organisations which depend on innovation implement deliberate systems to ensure an adequate flow. Figure 11.3 shows the innovation process as a filter through which ideas are gathered, channelled and focused before selecting those believed to have most potential. The model appears to be a linear process, but in reality there is continual 're-cycling' back to

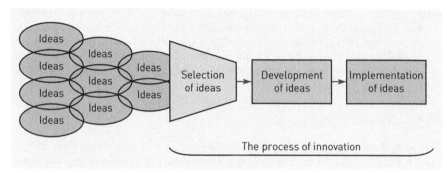

Figure 11.3
A model of the innovation process
Source: Based on Tidd and Bessant (2009).

earlier stages for revisions and to incorporate new ideas. Generating the initial idea is necessarily random – but thereafter firms try to create order as quickly as possible. They apply resources to develop promising ideas into something they can use. The steps are sequential but their duration and complexity will vary – some requiring significant research and development, others merely a change in the focus of the sales effort.

Organisational factors in managing innovation

Organisations who depend on innovation (like Asos – Chapter 10 case study) encourage all staff to help create and implement a strong flow of successful new things. Smith *et al.* (2008) developed a prescriptive model of the organisational features shaping the effectiveness of innovation – 'the four Ss' of innovation.

- **Strategy** – the organisational strategy must communicate a shared vision and goals, indicating that innovation is central to its competitive advantage.
- **Style** – the strategy must be enacted by the management style of the senior team to reinforce the strategic intention. A 'facilitate and empower' style is more likely to foster innovation than a 'command and control' style. For this to work, staff will need resources and time for ideas to emerge.
- **Structure** – a highly specialised division of tasks is detrimental to innovation, while enriched jobs (Chapter 13) and easy horizontal communication will support it. While lone employees can be innovative, teams of employees working together are more likely to succeed.
- **Support** – technology can facilitate the transfer of knowledge by creating a knowledge repository, enabling staff to access information easily.

Pixar – with a unique record of technological and artistic innovation – illustrates some of these points: see the Management in Practice feature below.

Management in practice   Behind Pixar's magic   www.pixar.com

Ed Catmull (co-founder of Pixar, and president of Pixar and Disney Animation Studios) has written about the 'collective creativity' at the company: many of its methods are relevant to other organisations. He emphasises the uncertainty of the innovative process – the idea which starts the process may not work – by definition it is new, and the innovator cannot know at the start if it will lead to a worthwhile result:

> at the start of making [*Ratatouille*] we simply didn't know if [it] would work. However, since we're supposed to offer something that isn't obvious, we bought into somebody's initial vision and took a chance. (2008, p. 66)

'Taking chances' that consistently succeed is not due to luck, but to the principles and practices that Pixar uses to support the people who turn the idea into a useful product. These include:

Getting talented people to work effectively with each other... [by constructing] an environment that nurtures trusting relationships and unleashes everyone's creativity. If we get that right, the result is a vibrant community where talented people are loyal to one another and their collective work. (p. 66)

Everyone must be free to communicate with anyone ...the most efficient way to deal with numerous problems is to trust people to work out the difficulties directly with each other without having to check for permission. (p. 71)

We must **stay close to innovations happening in the academic community.** We strongly encourage our technical artists to publish their research and participate in industry conferences. Publication may give away ideas ... but the connection is worth far more than any ideas we may have revealed: it helps us attract exceptional talent and reinforces the belief throughout the company that people are more important than ideas. (p. 71)

[Measure progress]. Because we're a creative organization, people [think that what we do can't be measured]. That's wrong. Most of our processes involve activities and deliverables that can be quantified. We keep track of the rates at which things happen, how often something had to be reworked, whether a piece of work was completely finished or not when it was sent to another department ... Data can show things in a neutral way, which can stimulate discussion. (Catmull, 2008, p. 72)

Source: Catmull (2008).

Activity 11.2   What does 'managing change and innovation' mean?

Having read the chapter, make brief notes summarising the change and innovation issues evident in the organisation you chose for this activity.

- Compare the type of change or innovation you have studied with the frameworks outlined in the chapter. (See Section 11.2, especially Table 11.1.)
- How closely did the way people managed the change correspond to one or more of the four models of change in Section 11.5. If it did not, what model (theory) guided practice?
- What was the main sources of the innovation? (Refer to Section 11.6.)
- Which organisational factors helped or hindered the innovation? (Refer to Section 11.7.)

Compare what you have found with other students on your course.

Summary

1 Outline the links between creativity, innovation, change and strategy
- Many organisations increasingly depend on creativity and innovation as they respond to external demands. If innovation is at the centre of their strategy, they need to create an organisation that supports innovation.

2 Describe types of innovation, with examples
- Product – what the organisation offers for sale.
- Process – how it creates the product.

- Position – changes in target market.
- Paradigm – how a company frames what it does.

3 **Explain the links between innovation and context**

- A change programme is an attempt to change one or more aspects of the internal context, which then provides the context of future actions. The prevailing context can itself help or hinder change efforts.

4 **Compare life-cycle, emergent, participative and political theories of change**

- Life-cycle: change projects can be planned, monitored and controlled towards achieving their objectives.
- Emergent: reflecting the uncertainties of the environment, change is hard to plan in detail, but emerges incrementally from events and actions.
- Participative: successful change depends on human commitment, which is best obtained by involving participants in planning and implementation.
- Political: change threatens some of those affected, who will use their power to block progress, or to direct the change in ways that suit local objectives.

5 **Illustrate the sources of innovation**

- Eureka moments – capturing the unexpected.
- Knowledge push.
- Need pull.
- External changes – such as regulations.
- Staff.
- Users.

6 **Illustrate the organisational factors believed to support innovation**

- Strategy – innovation is explicitly called for in the corporate strategy.
- Structure – roles and jobs are defined to aid in innovative behaviour.
- Style – management empowers the workforce to behave innovatively.
- Support – IT systems are available to support innovative behaviour.

Review questions

1 What does the term 'performance gap' mean, and what is its significance for change?
2 What are the implications for management of the systemic nature of innovation?
3 Give examples of three types of innovation mentioned in the chapter.
4 How could a manager alter the receptiveness of an organisation to change?
5 Outline the life-cycle perspective on innovation and explain when it is most likely to be useful.
6 How does it differ from the 'emergent' perspective?
7 Describe three sources of innovation, preferably with a new example.

Further reading

Tidd, J. and Bessant, J. (2009), *Managing Innovation: Integrating technological, market and organisational change*, Wiley, Chichester.

An easy to read text combining a comprehensive account of innovation theories with many contemporary examples.

Weblinks

These websites have appeared in, or are relevant to, the chapter:

www.magnamole.co.uk
www.pixar.com
www.google.com
www.apple.com
www.nokia.com
www.inamo-restaurant.com
www.pret.com
www.co-operative.coop
www.asos.com

Visit two of the business sites in the list, or others that interest you, and navigate to the pages dealing with corporate news, investor relations or 'our company'.

- What signs of major innovations can you find?
- Does the site give you a sense of an organisation that is receptive or non-receptive to change?
- What factors appear designed to encourage innovation in the company?

 Annotated weblinks, multiple choice questions and other useful resources can be found on **www.pearsoned.co.uk/boddy**

Case study   Google   www.google.com

Sergey Brin and Larry Page founded Google in 1999 and by 2011 it was the world's largest search engine, with the mission: 'to organise the world's information and make it universally accessible and useful'. The need for search services arose as the World Wide Web expanded, making it progressively more difficult for users to find relevant information. The company's initial success was built on the founders' new approach to online searching: their PageRank algorithm (with 500 million variables and 3 billion terms) identifies material relevant to a search by favouring pages that have been linked to other pages. These links were called 'votes', because they signalled that another page's webmaster had decided that the focal page deserved attention. The importance of the focal page is determined by counting the number of votes it has received.

Photo courtesy Google UK.

As a business Google generates revenue by providing advertisers with the opportunity to deliver online advertising that is relevant to the search results on a page. The advertisements are displayed as sponsored links, with the message appearing alongside search results for appropriate keywords. They are priced on a cost-per-impression basis, whereby advertisers pay a fixed amount each time their ad is viewed. The charge depends on what the advertiser has bid for the keywords, and the more they bid the nearer the top of the page their advertisement will be.

A feature of Google is the speed with which it returns search results – usually within a second. From the start its focus has been on developing 'the perfect search engine', defined by Page as something that 'understands what you mean and gives you back what you want'. Rather than use a small number of large servers that tend to run slowly at peak times, Google invested in thousands of linked PCs that quickly find the answer to each query.

Beyond its core search and advertising capabilities, the company has embarked on many new ventures. It's Android mobile phone operating system is capturing a large share of the market, outselling Apple by the end of 2010. It is also involved in blogging, radio and television advertising, online payments and social networks: in 2010 it opened an online book store, known as eBookstore. It often acquires technology from other companies such as Picasa for photo management; YouTube for online videos; DoubleClick for web ads and Keyhole for satellite photos (now Google Earth).

Google simultaneously tests and markets new applications to the user community – testing and marketing are virtually indistinguishable from one another. This creates a unique relationship with consumers, who become an essential part of the development team – moving seamlessly from testing to using products as they would any other commercial offering.

The company allows independent developers to share access and create new applications that incorporate elements of the Google system. They can easily test and launch applications and have them hosted in the Google world, where there is a large target audience – and a practically unlimited capacity for customer interactions.

Google has a distinctive technocratic culture, in that individuals prosper based on the quality of their ideas and their technological acumen. Engineers are expected to spend 20 per cent of their time working on their own creative projects. The company provides plenty of intellectual stimulation which, for a company founded on technology, can be the opportunity to learn from the best and brightest technologists.

There are regular talks by distinguished researchers from around the world. Google's founders and executives have thought through many aspects of the knowledge work environment, including the design and occupancy of offices (jam-packed for better communication); the frequency of all-hands meetings (every Friday); and the approach to interviewing and hiring new employees (rigorous, with many interviews). None of these principles is particularly novel, but in combination they suggest an unusually high level of recognition for the human dimensions of innovation. Brin, Page and Schmidt (the company's CEO) have taken ideas from other organisations – such as the software firm SAS Institute – that are celebrated for how they treat their knowledge workers.

The company has rapidly extended the range of services it offers, while remaining rigorously focused on search. Although the headquarters is in California, their mission is to facilitate access to information across the world – more than half of their searches are delivered to users living outside the US, in more than 35 languages. The company offers volunteers the opportunity to help in translating the site into additional languages.

The company acquired YouTube, the video-sharing site, in 2006, as a further extension of its services. Such acquisitions can be seen as a way of growing the business in a way that stays focused on Google's distinctive competence (developing superior search solutions) and earning revenue from these through targeted advertising. In 2011, it was hiring many more staff, and was also changing the recruitment process to encourage more entrepreneurial people to join the company.

Sources: Based on Harvard Business School case 9-806-105, *Google Inc.*, prepared by Thomas R. Eisenmann and Kerry Herman; Iyer and Davenport (2008); company website; *Financial Times*, 25 February 2010, 7 December 2010, 7 February 2011; *Independent*, 23 October 2010.

Questions

1 The chapter mentions the 4Ps of innovation (refer to Section 11.3). What examples of these can you find in the case?

2 What examples are there in the case of the sources of innovation mentioned in the chapter? (Refer to Section 11.6.)

3 List specific examples from the case of the organisational factors encouraging innovation. (Refer to Section 11.7.)

Index

180